Gabriele Fahr-Becker

Ryokan
A Japanese tradition

Photographs by Narimi Hatano and Klaus Frahm

KÖNEMANN

Notes

Unless otherwise indicated the dimensions of objects are given as height x width
or height x width x depth.

When the location of the objects in the illustrations is not given, these are either
privately owned or in unidentified collections.

In most cases the Hepburn system, also called Hebon-shiki, was used for the transcription of Japanese concepts, titles of works and proper names.
An alternative transcription system was selected where necessary in quotations, for
specialized terms, and for proper names.
Depending on the transcription system used, length marks indicate lengthened
vowels and an apostrophe is used for spaces between words.
For the period before the Meiji reform of 1868 names are written in the traditional
way with the surname first. For all later periods, the first name is followed by the
principal name.

Illustrations

Jacket: **Hakkei-tei**
The Hōshō-dai guest house (1677/1679) of the lords of Hikone, constructed in the
sukiya style, which is the Hakkei-tei ryokan of today. The pavilions are reflected in
the pond of the *chisen-kaiyu* landscape garden, Genkyu-en, laid out in 1677 in the
grounds of the Hikone-jo fortified castle (1603).

Front end paper: **Nagasaki**
Photograph by Wilhelm Burger, 1870, Ethnology Museum, Vienna

Back end paper: **Village near Fujiyama**
Photograph by Wilhelm Burger, 1870, Ethnology Museum, Vienna

Frontispiece Maruyama Okyo (1733-1795)
Byōbu "Wisteria"
Screen, painting on gold leaf background,
Pair of screens, each with six panels 62 x 142 in.s (detail),
Nezu Institute of Fine Arts, Tokyo

Page 6: ***Ensō* circle**
Artist unknown,
Photo: Asahi Tazaki

© 2000 Könemann Verlagsgesellschaft mbH
126 Bonner Straße, D-50968 Cologne

Publishing and Artistic direction: Peter Feierabend
Layout: Hans Wolfgang Leeb
Translation of Japanese original texts: Nabuko Machida
Project organisation in Japan: Atsuko Oikawa
Production: Mark Voges
Reproduction: Typografik, Cologne

Original title: *Ryokan – Zu Gast im traditionellen Japan*

© 2001 for the English edition:
Könemann Verlagsgesellschaft mbH

Translation from the German: Jane Brown, Neale Cunningham
Editing: Barbara Baylis, Neale Cunningham
Typesetting: Linkup Mitaka, Leamington Spa
Printing and Binding: Mladinska knjiga tiskarna d.d., Ljubljana

Printed in Slovenia
ISBN: 3-8290-4829-7

10 9 8 7 6 5 4 3 2 1

Contents

* Inserts

Preface

The idea of depicting Japan's traditional architecture, art and way of life in the form of ryokan – traditional Japanese inns – is the perfect framework for illustrating the theme vividly and not solely as an academic historical review.

The enthusiasm the Japanese have for travel is legendary. In 1728, the naturalist Engelbert Kämpfer wrote about his visit to Japan: "Every day, the major highways of this country are crowded by an unbelievable number of travelers, and at certain times I found more people here than in the capital cities of Europe."

At the height of the Edo period, circa 1750, each year about 1.5 million people traveled the Tōkaidō, the chief route to and from Yedo (Tokyo) and Kyōto, and this already impressive figure rose notably in subsequent years. Thus, an extraordinary number of inns were required along the highway to provide travelers with lodging. Consequently, over the centuries, a distinct 'inn culture' developed necessarily, which, to this day, reflects Japanese architecture and living styles since the Heian period (794–1185).

It is a stroke of luck that many of the ryokan are situated in the countryside, and so were spared the destruction of war and conflagrations. Moreover, the majority remained untouched by the wave of modernisation that swept the country post 1950, and, unlike many parts of old Japan, they were not bulldozed into the ground. New ryokan, built in the traditional style, are being opened and old buildings worthy of conservation are being converted into ryokan. The popularity of the inns stems from the fact that they allow Japanese tradition to be experienced, a tradition which continues to be venerated, although, all too frequently, is lost in the "modern" living conditions of everyday life.

What could be a better place to experience old Japan than in a ryokan?

This book aims, as a "synthesis," to be mediator of traditional arts and culture, still largely unknown in the West, and therefore attempts to make the subject matter accessible to a wider audience. The ready interpretations and even hubris of Western experts, as well as enthusiasts, frequently leaves little of the original art remaining, which, in view of its creative and spiritual character, should be approached with respect and a certain humility, and not with the desire to evaluate, pigeon hole and categorise.

Witness to this respect is also the decision to explain traditional customs and objects with 'Japanese words.' The publication "We Japanese" describes in a loving and always humorous manner the native tradition, without any trace of Western presumption. Many thanks to the translator for the sensitive and careful choice of words.

In this volume, the acknowledgements belong on the first page since a successful outcome of this project would not have been possible without the help of numerous Japanese friends. I owe them a great debt. The hospitality shown in all ryokan toward the foreigner was beyond all expectations, also in those not mentioned here for space reasons, and laid the foundation proper for a privileged insight into a different, wonderful world. I wish many readers the same incomparable and impressive experience.

Gabriele Fahr-Becker

Ryokan – A Japanese tradition

Here I found what I had hoped to find in Japan – human equilibrium, calm and elegant proportions.

Saul Bellow[1] [freely translated by Neale Cunningham]

Travelers lodging at a ryokan – a Japanese inn – can experience at first hand and in depth Japan's handed down customs and traditions. They are privy to the perfection of a way of life that combines buildings and nature harmoniously. The design of a ryokan contains everything that the "city dweller" – a prisoner in an inhuman industrial society – could dream of. The Westerner crosses the threshold of the genuine ryokan, which is almost ascetic in its simplicity, and is swallowed up in a past, almost overrefined culture, uniquely luxurious, with exquisite rooms, gardens, baths and a sophisticated cuisine. The utmost attention is paid to every detail, no matter how minute. Chores reflect behavioral etiquette while beauty may be found in even the most mundane objects.

The living "area" – not rooms in the Western sense – comprises an ingenious modular system of sliding doors and walls which can be opened or even removed, thereby creating a flexible division of space, whether for seclusion or to accommodate social functions, taking advantage of cooling breezes and views of the greenery outside. As a result of these underlying design principles, the Japanese have always lived close to nature, and have become acutely sensitive to all its subtle signs and moods: the sounds of birds and autumn insects, the breeze whispering in the pine needles, and the smell of the earth after a summer shower.

Aside from the "luxury" of a near-to-nature harmony, guests experience and are spoiled by the comfort of an unobtrusive, caring service, provided by numerous "hosts," whose sole desire is the guests' well-being. Guests take meals in their private quarters on floor cushions, which are replaced at night by the *futon*. The evening meal is a *kaiseki* dinner, the traditional courtly meal consisting of more than twenty courses, each a culinary delight. The room suites have an *o-furo*, a hot bath made of cedar wood, in which the guest may relax. The ryokan also has a community bath, either a natural pool in the garden or an indoor pool with a view of nature outside. In suitably comfortable, loose garments – the kimono and the *yūkata*, a luxurious cotton kimono for men – one can leave behind everyday life and immerse oneself in an atmosphere characterised by calm and equilibrium. The textures of the wood and the plasterwork, in fact of all the materials used, retain their original beauty as complementary elements to nature. And the guest should not be surprised if the beautifully proportioned rectangles and contrasts of white and dark grey appear modern to our 20th-century eyes, because these buildings provided the inspiration and model for the Bauhaus and a whole generation of Western architects, designers and artists – from Charles Rennie Mackintosh to Piet Mondrian, and particularly Frank Lloyd Wright, who understood better than anyone else that the site and the building are equally important components in architecture.

In Japanese, inns are called *yadoya, hatagoya* or "ryokan"

"You will be greeted, at the porch of a Japanese inn, by a number of maids, who, sitting in the Japanese way, on the floor, either of matting or of wood, bow so politely with their hands nicely put side by side on the floor. Your shoes have to be taken off, for the Japanese wear no shoes inside a dwelling-house, and pair of slippers will be given you

Opposite
Futami-kan Hinjitsu-kan
Shimenawa, he sacred rope of twisted rice straw, on the crossbeam above the entrance to the ryokan.

Right
Two *jochū-san* or inn maids greet the guest in the traditional way upon his or her arrival at the ryokan.
Line drawing from: *We Japanese*, Fujiya Hotel Ltd. (publisher), Miyanoshita, Hakone 1949, p. 525

Above
Shouro-tei
An open *shōji* window allows a view of
the inner garden from a corridor.
The corridor connects the parts of the
building and originates from the *watadon*,
the covered corridors of the *shinden*
architectural style.

Opposite
Futami-kan Hinjitsu-kan
A guest room leading to the *engawa*,
the attached wooden veranda, often
furnished with a Western suite in 1920s
or 1930s style. In the foreground, on the
low table, tea is always available and
there is the voluminous *suigara-oke*,
the ashtray.

instead. A maid will take you into a nice Japanese room, almost devoid of furniture, in the foreign sense of the term; no table, no chair, no bed-stead, no wash-stand; there being in the room a low Japanese desk and a *hibachi* (fire-brazier), which is the only heater in the room, containing a fire made of charcoals and an iron-kettle on it for boiling water for tea. The room is simple but artistically decorated in the Japanese way with a few pieces of art. A Japanese kimono is soon brought in, because a Japanese feels more comfortable and at home in it than in foreign clothing.

The proprietor of the hotel or a chief clerk comes in with a register-book, in which you have to write your name, address, age, where from and where-to, etc.

Japanese tea is served by a maid in a small tea-cup, with no sugar or milk in it because the Japanese take their tea plain. There being no fixed time for tea in Japan, you will be served with a cup of tea no matter at what time of the day you visit a Japanese inn.

No guest-room, in a Japanese inn, for so it is called in Japan, has a bath-tub attached to it, but all its guests take a bath in a common bath-room one after another, or sometimes several persons together in the same bath-tub, instead of throwing the water out every time when one takes a bath. Hence the bath-tub of an inn is large enough to accommodate several persons at one time. Soap is never used in a bath-tub, but you must soap yourself outside the bath-tub, which you enter after rinsing all soap off your body. Nor is a towel properly used in it.

Every Japanese inn is operated on the Japanese plan, and two meals, evening and morning, are included in the hotel rate. But while a foreign hotel has a menu, leaving the choice of food to its guest, a Japanese inn serves its guest with food of its selection, and he has to eat whatever is served him for the hotel rate he has accepted. And instead of being served with food dish after dish in a course, as in a foreign hotel, all food is brought in at once, in a Japanese inn, on what is called *o-zen* (lit. honorable meal-tray), which will be placed before the cushion on which you sit. Unless you order for bread, you will have to eat *gohan* (boiled rice), which is served in a bowl on the same meal-tray. Nor is a knife or fork brought in, but instead you will have to manipulate a pair of chopsticks, 5 inches or so long. A maid will sit before you while you eat, so that she might serve you with more bowlfuls of rice, if you require, and you can have as many bowlfuls of rice as you please, though usually we do not ask for a second help [*sic*] of any other food. And it is considered to be ill-behaved in Japan to leave any grains of rice in a rice-bowl; though any other kinds of food may be left over with little impropriety. When you finish eating, the maid will give you a cup of what is called *bancha* (inferior tea) to wash your throat down [*sic*].

You will see no bedding in your room when you get in, for it is kept in a closet, usually attached to your guest-room, and it will be spread out when you go to bed. Our bedding consists generally of two wadded beds with two or three wadded covers, which an average foreigner finds rather too heavy. Bedding is folded up and put into a closet again when you get up on the following morning.

In the morning you go to the same wash-place as do the other guests. A maid will make tea for you before she brings breakfast, also on a meal-tray, consisting generally of rice and vegetable soup, with two or three other light kinds of food." [2]

Visiting a ryokan is often an excursion into Japanese history. Many ryokan are either located at historical sites or themselves have an illustrious past, rich in history. Therefore, every ryokan has, as it were, its own themes and lodgings may be chosen in line with one's own interest in particular aspects of Japanese art, architecture, history, tradition or society. However, the guest should always keep in mind that lodging at a ryokan is not a plain overnight stay in the typical Western sense, where the guest possibly arrives late in the evening, exhausted by the day's sightseeing, only to depart hastily early the next morning. Ryokans do not permit arrival before three o'clock in the afternoon as the time before is required for the exacting preparation of all the comforts available to the guest, on the other hand, the guest is expected by five p.m. A later arrival would disrupt the "rituals." The visitor uses the *o-furo*, the Japanese bath, to relax and wind down before supper, which is served between six and seven p.m., and never later, and arriving later would mean the procedure would be far too rushed. Departure from the ryokan is always before eleven a.m. This apparently strict timetable is not just a matter of etiquette but also serves to enhance the well-being of visitors as they are not disturbed by latecomers in their privacy and during the

amusement offered after supper. This schedule is upheld at all ryokan, be it in the highly elegant Kyoto inns or in the old *minka* in the countryside. This timetable alone, which clashes with Western habits and practices, partly explains the reservations some ryokan have against accepting Western visitors, while also implying deeply seated misconceptions. Frequently, a rather distressed Western visitor to Japan, a Japan-enthusiast no less, narrates a lamentable tale about having being turned away from a certain ryokan. This experience is then often used to articulate the conclusion that the Japanese are cold toward foreigners, which would be incorrect. The foreign guest is not rejected per se, rather the refusal expresses the concern at having to encumber him or her with Japanese customs and the inability to offer the guest the usual comforts and daily routines of a Western hotel. It is the many seemingly trivial things, such as wearing the kimono correctly, conduct at mealtimes and the use of the community bath, all essential elements of the Japanese way of life, which one does not want to impose upon and lecture the visitor about. On the other hand, disregarding such living traditions may bring misfortune upon the establishment because deeply rooted beliefs and superstitions are part of everyday life in Japan and thus integral to staying at a ryokan. If the guest shows that he or she is versed in the traditions and customs, and these conventions are respected, the guest will experience a degree of hospitality, attention and cordiality that will surpass the wildest expectations the *gaijin* or foreigner might have had.

The ryokan in this book were chosen carefully in order to introduce and impart the widest range of Japanese art and aspects of the Japanese lifestyle. Staying in a ryokan offers the guest a unique opportunity to experience history "at first hand." The tradition, cultural heritage and aesthetic sensitivity of a foreign people do not have to be consumed academically, that is, in dusty museums or in literature, but can be experienced and "lived."

A life in harmony with nature is reflected by a close relationship to the seasons in an especially vivid and gloriously colourful way. Spring, summer, autumn and winter have different ambassadors, from the evergreen pine, the blossoming plum and cherry trees, through the azalea and the iris, down to the summer grasses, the bamboo and the chrysanthemum, not forgetting the glowing colors of the autumn leaves and finally the white of the snow. Shades and motifs of the individual seasons can be seen as exquisite round dances on dinner services, picture scrolls, architectural details and textiles, as well as on the menu. Seasonal moods are also not forgotten, the radiant clear blue sky, the overcast rainy day, the pale grey of the mist and the frosty atmosphere of a winter's day. Indeed, the scenic and the climatic contrasts of the Japanese islands, from an almost Siberian north, to a subtropical south, are also reflected in its architecture, the elaborate gardens and in the way of life. The rugged mountain regions and the open spaces of the Sea of Japan have also left their mark on the construction designs and styles since the earliest days of Japanese history. In fact the different categories of ryokan allow aristocratic feudal styles of architecture and archaic rural characteristics to be traced effectively.

Opposite
Fuji-san
Fuji-san on an early January morning, seen from the Daruma Mountains on Izu. Japan's sacred mountain, *Fuji-san*, is here a synonym for the clarity and the spirituality of Japanese design.

Below
Ise, "stepping stones"
Sacred "stepping stones," upon which no mortal may tread, in the grounds of the Shinto Ise Shrine, the principal Japanese sacred site, whose beginnings extend into the 3rd century. The shrine was constructed in the classic Japanese style before China's influence reached the island kingdom in the 6th century.

Above left
Inro
Inro, small portable cases for holding small items and medicine, of wood, metal or lacquer, worn on the *obi* (girdle) and secured by a *netsuke*, an ornamental toggle-like piece at the end of the cords (carved wood or ivory miniatures). The small, movable beads on the *netsuke-inro* cords are called *ojime*.

Above right
Odori
Three dancers performing the classic Japanese *odori*. The *odori* is a posture dance, with slow movements of the body, feet, arms and hands.
Line drawing from: *We Japanese*, Fujiya Hotel Ltd. (publisher), Miyanoshita, Hakone 1949, p. 74.

The "way" *dō* in the ryokan

"The journey is the destination", this creed of Zen wisdom is likely to become apparent to the visitor to a ryokan or minshuku (a simple Japanese lodging place). The description of the "sequences" of a ryokan sojourn should not be seen as a set of instructions or even as a user guide along the lines of: how do I hold chopsticks or how low do I have to bow? Rather it is intended to reduce the possibly unsettling novelty which could lessen the cultural experience – it is more or less a visual familiarisation with the circumstances and the objects whose meanings and use, once explained, result automatically in the "correct conduct." Nothing could be more lamentable than a stay in a ryokan with the "user guide" clutched in one hand. Uninhibited enjoyment would be lost and immersion in a world of calm composure and subtly diversified perception would be impossible.

As has often been correctly noted, Japan is not a country of contradictions but a contradiction per se. This also applies to traditional Japanese lodgings. The locations are infinite in variety and frequently a massive jolt for Western guests. Rural or elegant inns in appropriate surroundings do not raise an eyebrow. However, there are numerous inns which constitute an island in a foreign world. For example, in a provincial city with its multitude of eyesores, between concrete tower blocks, highway bridges and pachinko parlors, and behind an inconspicuous fence, the surprised visitor may stumble across a highly elegant *sukiya* form of ryokan, or in Osaka, dwarfed by futuristic glass-fronted high-rise buildings, the visitor may suddenly stand before a weather-beaten *minka* inn. Or the

"Genre-specific" are also the room partitions and furnishings, the everyday and the feudal utensils. Thus, visiting a ryokan is an expedition into Japanese tradition and history, for instance, the life of the samurai or the Heian-period aristocrats. Like an opened treasure chest, a rich fund of centuries-old accessories, products of artistic craftsmanship and artworks, are offered the treasure hunter. Occasionally known and yet still exotic, or entirely unknown terms are filled with life: *futon*, *tokonoma*, folding screens, hanging scrolls, fans, picture books, *ukiyo-e*, *wandansu*, *hibachi*, *andon*, *kago*, lacquer ware, ceramics, *ike-bana* and much more.

The tea aesthetic, in conjunction with the tea ceremony and its specific objects, such as the *raku* bowl, is experienced with all its peculiarities. It is closely linked to a specific code of dress and behavior and special "behavioral aesthetics," expressed on the one hand in the "regeneration" in the ryokan, which includes the observation of nature, calligraphy, meditation, the art of poetry, literature and Zen; on the other, in the art of clothing oneself, *iki*, which includes the kimono, the *kosode*-kimono, the *yūkata*, the *obi*, the *sagemono*, the *inro* and the *netsuke*.

Traditional entertainment is offered by geishas, by *maiko*, in the form of dances, singing and musical instruments, and by the subtle erotic overtones of the "spring pictures." This goes hand-in-hand with the customs and traditions, the religious holidays, the festivals, the special days in the calendar, the myths and legends, belief in the supernatural, mysticism and the daily rituals.

Opposite
Shouro-tei
An *agesudo*, a trellised bamboo gate, separates the inner and the outer garden, which borders the bay. The stepping stones, which display different contours and qualities, are a striking example of the asymmetry found in Japanese art.

visitor's gaze may be refreshed by an aesthetically perfect Hortus Conclusus nestled between the beehive structures rampaging like wild weeds up and down the mountain slopes near a hot spring. And faceless hotel boxes may contain whole floors with traditional rooms of unsurpassable taste. The opposite also applies: besides the *tatami* braid trimmings, the courtly *shinden* type of inn offers Internet access.

Despite all the contrasts, the basic principle of every ryokan and the sojourn there is the same. Without exception, all ryokan adapt to their environment and reflect the surrounding environs and nature in their construction and lifestyles. The aforementioned island-like "relics" have without reservation kept their former essence within changed environmental conditions. The world outside is irrelevant, one crosses the demarcation line, leaves everyday life behind and enters a different world.

The border to the here and now takes on different forms: an unadorned enclosing castle wall, *tsujibei*, a trellised bamboo fence, a green meadow, a completely normal pavement, a carpeted hotel floor. If the ryokan is situated in one of Japan's three traditional gardens, *tsukiyama*, the landscape garden, *chaniwa*, the tea garden, or *karesansui*, the dry garden, the guest experiences an initial impression of the old Japanese construction principles before entering the building. Common to all gardens is that they always adhere to the *shakkei* rule, literally, "borrowed scenery." Japanese architects and gardeners have learned to design and align walls and hedges with the purpose of obscuring less attractive sights and of including the more pleasing ones, such as neighbouring treetops or mountains – a skilful means to hold at arm's length a disturbing exterior world. Frequently in the garden, the guest might spot a hidden teahouse or a pond teaming with well-fed and valuable *kingyo*, goldfish.

The entrance façade of a ryokan has many designs. If the ryokan is on a street in a city, one may pass without recognising the inn hidden behind. Closed off by a *fusuma*, a wooden sliding door, or an *andon*, a wooden shutter, solely the coat of arms on the *noren*, the entrance door hanging, or a Chinese character give away the real purpose of the building. Ryokan with drives are easier to recognize but basically it holds that the Westerner cannot reckon with the Latin alphabet on the sign. Decoration is provided in the form of twisted rice-straw rope, folded paper or flowers and plant bouquets above the entrance, which are never just window-dressing, but rather religious symbols to protect the person entering and the house itself.

As if the guest's arrival had been anticipated, male service staff, *banto*, wait to receive the luggage. By the way, Japanese travel lightly with small bags, which can easily be stowed away. Huge suitcases trigger a certain disquiet, particularly in view of the fact that in a ryokan one literally does not need a thing: footwear, clothing, washing and bathing utensils are all provided.

Opposite, left
Dan-bayashi
The architecture and decoration of the Dan-bayashi ryokan reveal the spirit and the lifestyle of the samurai. Gloriously appointed interior rooms are in sharp contrast to the dark *amado*, the exterior wooden sliding doors, and the bare *shōji* screen windows.

Opposite, right
Chikutei Yagyu-no-sho
A green maple in early summer in front of a *renjimado*, a window with narrow horizontal wooden battens, a feudal characteristic of the *shinden* style. The blind allowed the nobility to see ordinary folk, while they remain invisible from outside.

Right
Hakkei-tei
View of the veranda of the Hōshō-dai- inn (1677/1679) of the Lords of Hikone, built in the *sukiya* style. In a nearly unchanged form, the former summer pavilion sited above the pond now houses the Hakkei-tei ryokan.

At the threshold, shoes are shed and thus the dust from the street, the mundane and everyday burdens per se. Outdoor shoes are immediately gathered up and stored away but always remain close at hand when one wishes to leave the ryokan. The guest slips into the prepared slippers – in special sizes for the Western visitor – the first entity of the various items of footwear that will follow: not especially attractive and somewhat aesthetically disappointing, in brown leather or even plastic, though they are followed by more respectable models.

Once the guest leaves the ground level, *dōma* in *minka* ryokan, and enters the wooden-floored reception room, he or she is welcomed by the lady of the house, the *okami-san*. The reception area, the *genkan*, has meanwhile acquired a Western flavour in many ryokan and reminds one of a hotel lobby. Depending on the custom of the house, the first tea is now served, the guest is handed a hot terry towel, *o-shibori* – the first of numerous – for freshening up and the guest is registered. In a *sukiya* or *shinden* style inn, the traditional

frothy green tea, *matcha*, is offered ceremonially, *koi-cha*, in a *raku* bowl; the more simple alternative is the clear green tea, *ocha* or *usu-cha*. At all events, the tea is supplemented by the traditional Japanese red-bean sweet, *yōkan*, whose sticky sweetness is intended to lessen the bitter nature of the tea. The described procedure is often delayed until the guest reaches the allocated guest room, after being guided there by a personal maid, the *jochu-san*, who attends to guest for the duration of the stay at the inn.

These private rooms are of various designs and depend on the class of ryokan, the reservation and the price category. Possible are: a simple *tatami* room with or without anteroom, without private bath, with or without shared washbasin. The luxury class inns have more rooms (up to three) with private *o-furo*, cypress-wood baths, bath anteroom, separate toilet, private kitchenette and an open veranda, *nure-en*. The non plus ultra is one's own cottage, *hanare*, also with several rooms and a personal thermal bath outside, *rotemburo*. No matter how small the premises are, the guest always has a private

Opposite
Wano-sato
Guest room in a *hanare*, a cottage, at Wano-sato. The *tokonoma* has a *menkawabashira* supporting pillar with rough, unfinished and non-bevelled edges, two *kakemono*, hanging picture scrolls, an *ike-bana* flower arrangement of the *rikka* style and a *kobako*, an incense holder.

Above
Ike-bana, the art of flower arranging in the *tokonoma*.
Line drawing from: *We Japanese*, Fujiya Hotel Ltd. (publisher), Miyanoshita, Hakone 1949, p. 24.

Right
Chikutei Yagyu-no-sho
Tokonoma decorated with a *kakemono*, a hanging picture scroll and a *kobako*, the incense holder.

peripheral veranda, *engawa*, and a small garden – also in multi-storey buildings and in urban ryokan! – or at least a view of nature in the *tsubo-niwa*, the inner courtyard garden, or of the borrowed scenery. A private garden, sometimes only the size of a towel, always contains as a basic element a water basin, *tsukubai* or *chozubashi*, with wooden ladles for cleaning one's mouth and hands, a stone lantern, *ishi-doro*, and stepping stones. The ability to create the atmosphere of a Zen garden in even the most limited space is a miracle in itself.

The *tatami*-covered room (entered without slippers, in socks, never barefoot), independent of the size, always has the following furnishings, which differ solely in design from inn to inn: room partitions such as the *fusuma*, wall sliding doors of wood with metal fittings for the door-pulls, *hikite*; *shōji*, sliding screens and windows of wooden latticework and covered with rice paper (the "window" to be opened, *yukimi-shōji*, close to the floor, where one sits); *byōbu*, folding, standing screens, *tsuitate*, standing room partitions, *amado*, veranda shutters; decorative nail covers of metal, *kugikakushi*.

Built-in furniture such as the *jōdan*, the base of the ornamental alcove, the *tokonoma*, with multilevel or graduated shelves, *chigaidana*, and the integrated writing desk which functions as a table, *tsukeshoin*, the opened up supporting beam for the supply of light and air, *ramma*, and ceilings of wood planking, secured by a wood or bamboo weave, with bamboo straps, *saobuchi*.

The embellishment of the *tokonoma*, the traditional picture alcove, is nowadays diverse. The guest may find the following objects in the alcove: a hanging picture scroll, *kakemono*, (the motif for the picture depends on the season, the holiday and the calendar); flower arrangements *ike-bana*, (created according to the season, holiday and the calendar); the incense burner, *koro*, and the incense holder, *kobako*; the sutra (Buddhist doctrinal work) case, *kyobako*; precious ceramics and porcelain; very seldom and rather contentious are modern elements such as sculptures.

"At this aesthetic pastime the guests, as rare incenses are burned, try to guess the name of the incense. Sometimes participants form two groups, the group making the greatest number of correct guesses winning the prizes. In olden days, when nobles formed the parties, swords, armour, and many other treasures were given away as prizes.

The burning of incense has always been associated with Buddhism, but as a cult it was developed by the luxurious 8th Ashikaga Shogun, Yoshimasa (shogun from 1443–73), a patron of the fine arts, landscape gardening, tea ceremony, etc. A pastime of the aristocracy, it was later largely dropped by them but still has its votaries among the upper classes of Japan.[…] The refined sense of smell developed by incense burning is believed to cultivate mental composure in the same way that the tea-ceremony (*cha-no-yu*) and flower arrangement (*ike-bana*) cultivate mental and physical poise. The basis of the incense of the present day is *awase-ko* ("combined incense"), introduced from China in the 10th century.

In the 15th century, as previously noted, in addition to the cult of the burning incense practiced by Japanese dilettanti, the use of incense was started for secular and recreation purposes – a use which has prevailed up to the present time. In the secular sense burning incense serves to scent the air of a room, and it is used as well to impart an agreeable perfume to clothing, toilet accessories, etc. In its recreational aspect, it tests the accuracy of the sense of smell. When the olfactory nerves become somewhat numbed by much smelling, their sensitivity is partially restored by rinsing the mouth at intervals with vinegar.

There are nearly a hundred distinct kinds of incense that are recognized and distinguished by names derived from literary allusions." [3]

The sparser the furnishings in a traditional Japanese living-room, the more opulent the countless utensils, which differ in artistic form depending on the category of ryokan. However, some of the following objects of Japanese lacquer, wood or metal are always found: *suzuri-bako* (boxes for writing equipment), *fubako* (letter caskets), *bondai* (a lectern), *hon* (books), and *han* (seals), all of which are accessories for dedicating oneself to poetry and calligraphy. Picture books serve to stimulate the imagination. Further "treasures" are the *chabako* (tea boxes), and the *zeni-bako*, (yellow money boxes). A playful requisite are the puppets, *ningyo*, which are considered lucky charms.

"Further inspection" of the room serves the furniture, sparsely distributed and hardly required; it also differs from ryokan to ryokan. In the middle of the room, opposite the *tokonoma*, is a low table with the seating cushions, *zabuton*, sometimes with a seat pan and armrests, *soku* or *kyosoku*. The place of honour is with one's back to the hanging picture scroll. Frequently, the table is a *kotatsu*, the traditional Japanese multipurpose piece of furniture, source of heat, dining table, and footwarmer at night-time. Further sources of warmth are the *hibachi*, filled with charcoal, portable "chests" of wood or lacquered work, which are also available in "handwarmer" format; *anka* are also charcoal-filled

Opposite, left
Sage-ju
Sage-ju, a kind of picnic utensil, a portable, stacking bowl set, *jubako.* *Kin-maki-e,* lacquer work decorated in gold.

Opposite, right
Reigi, Japanese etiquette
A *jochū-san,* a maid, "on her knees," opens the *shōji* to serve the meal. Line drawing from: *We Japanese,* Fujiya Hotel Ltd. (publisher), Miyanoshita, Hakone 1949, p. 403

Above left
Ryugon
Impressions formed by winter light and shadows through the *shōji* in a guest room of the Ryugon inn.

Above right
Ryugon
Paper-covered and painted *fusuma,* wooden sliding doors, in the *keisetsu-no-ma,* one of the oldest guest rooms of the Ryugon inn.

receptacles which are used in the same way as hot-water bottles. A guest cottage sometimes has an *irori,* an open fireplace with the *jizai-kagi,* the adjustable hearth hook, assembled from wood, metal and bamboo, and on its hook the *cha-gama* or *tetsubin,* the tea kettle.

Further possible furniture items are the *tansu,* storage chests; *wadansu,* a chest of drawers for storing small objects; *haribako,* sewing packets; the dressing table with veiled mirror, *kyōdai,* on which is placed the "cosmetics" box, *keshobako;* the hat or kimono stands *iko* and the smaller embodiment *tenugui-kake* for clothing accessories or towels. The *yūkata* or the kimono is laid out ready in a "kimono tray," *midaré-bako,* with the potpourri cushion, *ebiko,* the sash or belt, *obi,* the *tabi* sock with a divided big toe, and in cooler regions the *tanzen,* a kind of greatcoat, and the *haori,* a jacket-like coat. Less for practical use but more nostalgic memory, the kimono accessory *netsuke,* the belt toggle and *inro,* a small portable case worn on the girdle. Both objects are fine works of miniature art of lacquer, ivory, wood, metal or porcelain.

Every room has a tray with a tea box, a tea-set and the hot water container, *yūto,* today often a thermos flask as well. The guest should be able to prepare fresh tea at any time, stale tea being taboo.

No longer taboo are modern requisites such as the minibar, the television and the telephone, usually modestly hidden by a brocade cloth.

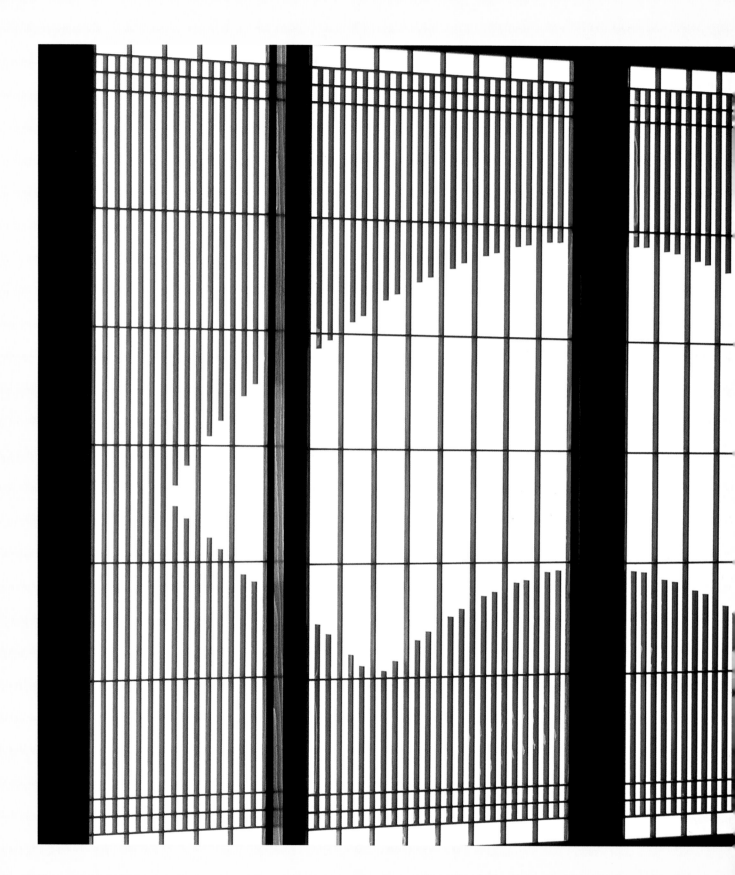

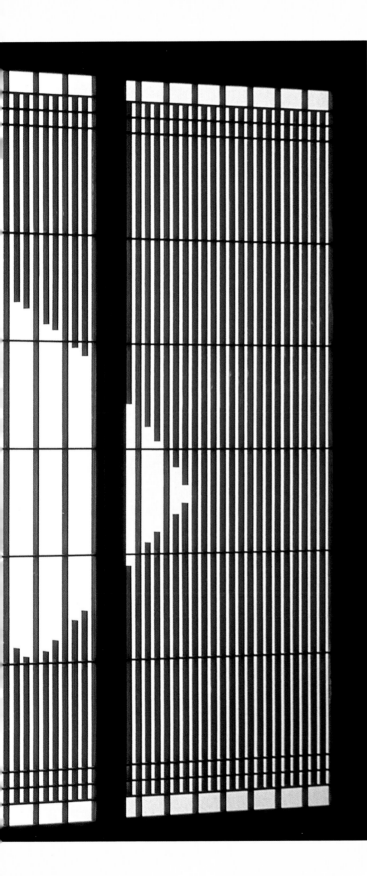

Cottages have a further small room in which the maid prepares the food and which is used to store meal utensils.

Free of everyday garments, the guest inspects the "sanitary facilities." Rooms without these comforts will point out the common wash-room and the toilet there. The private bath usually has an anteroom with the washbasin, tooth brushes, towels and cosmetic accessories. The old-fashioned category of ryokan is equipped with a standing washbowl and towel rack, *haisen* and *tenugui-kake*. If there is no anteroom to the bath, all the utensils are provided within reach of the washbasin in the room. The toilet is always separate from the bathroom and, because bathing is tantamount to a ritual, the mixed variety of bathroom found in the West is frowned upon. For hygienic reasons, a separate pair of slippers is provided for the toilet (usually identified as such to avoid embarrassment) and one also never enters the toilet barefoot. When the toilet is flushed, water also flows into a small basin on top of the cistern, which is used for washing one's hands, before touching the door handle. Frequently, the smallest room is a technical miracle, with heated toilet seat, integrated bidet, warm air and a self-cleaning mechanism. The display looks like a television remote control, though only in Japanese characters – there are hundreds of curious anecdotes concerning this point!

A private *o-furo* means pure luxury, a hot bath in a cedar wood or sumptuous stone tub, heated from below and already filled with water for relaxation. First one washes oneself thoroughly using the shower attachment in front of the tub, sitting on a wooden or a plastic stool. A souvenir of olden times is a wooden or a plastic pail for dousing oneself with hot water. The entire bathroom is clad in wood or tiled due to the intensive cleaning procedure.

Even if the guest can enjoy the comfort of a private bathroom, he or she should at all events visit the community bath, if only for the thermal water, the social experience and the aesthetic enjoyment of the bath which is frequently located in the open. On the way there, wearing the *yūkata* (*yū*, hot water, *kata*, robe) and slippers (note: not the toilet slippers, but the slippers one receives at the entrance), the guest can explore the premises of the ryokan. He or she can stroll through the long corridors, *rō*, in the building or through the covered passages outdoors. Possible common rooms are a library, the traditional *soin* study and meeting rooms, separate dining rooms, kendo or other Japanese sports halls, for example, for archery, as well as

Left
Ryogon
Shitajimado, decorative *shōji* window in a guest room of the ryokan. The fragile wooden slats and rice paper covering create irregular patterns. The window allows the gaze outwards but otherwise provides intimacy. The window is a decorative masterpiece.

exhibition rooms with tableware collections or color woodblock prints, *ukiyo-e*. There are also souvenir shops with the regional culinary and hand-crafted art specialities; one can also find Western rooms such as the lobby or conference rooms.

The way to the *onsen*, the common thermal bath, is marked, either with separate signs to a men-only 男性, a women-only 女性, or to a "mixed" bath 家族風呂. The *o-furo* may be an *onsen* in a natural pool in the garden or an indoor bath with a view of the greenery outside.

Before entering the bathroom itself, one undresses in an anteroom and deposits the kimono in a basket provided for each guest. After one has washed oneself thoroughly with soap sitting on a small wooden stool, and carefully washed off the soap, one douses oneself with warm water which is filled into a special wooden pail. Completely "clean," one surrenders oneself, wearing solely the small towel, *tenugui*, which was laid out in the room, to the unforgettable experience that is the *onsen*. The actual procedure involved in taking a bath has been ritualised in Japan and, due to a virtually religious character, the bath has become a devout act. In his book *Common-sense Architecture*, John Taylor defined the act of bathing as one of the exemplary art forms of Japanese culture.

Some ryokan also offer the possibility of reserving a small family bath, the *kazuko-buro*. Here one can share a pleasurable soak with family or friends, even if the common baths are separated by sex. Prompt reservation is recommended. The common baths may even be open for up to 24 hours a day.

The second milestone in the visit to a ryokan approaches, the *kaiseki* dinner in the *riyori* Kyoto style, or the hearty rural form. The host always prepares the meal with the greatest deference, reflecting the season and the region. The food is served after the bath either in the guest's private room or in one of the ryokan's dining rooms; and after the guest is led there by the maid. The individual courses are brought on meal trays, *bon* or *zen*. The trays are flat or have short legs. *Sanbo* are tray-like mats for sake and snacks.

"*O-zen*, the meal-tray: The Japanese take three meals a day; at 7 or 8 a.m., at noon and at 6 or 7 p.m. ... though they are not so particular or punctual as most foreigners are, about the time of eating. Most urban people use a small table around which a whole family sit at meal, after the manner of the Western people. But, properly speaking, as one still sees in the country or at a regular Japanese restaurant, a meal is served on an *o-zen* (meal-tray), about a foot square (formerly a stand 2 or 3 inches high), on which all food is served in small bowls or dishes at once at the beginning of the meal, instead of being brought in dish after dish in a course.

Left
Ryugon
The "corridor" leading to the *o-furo*. Like many ryokan, Ryugon has a bath for men *otokoburo* or *otokoyu*, a bath for women *onnaburo*, *onnayu* or *fujin yokushitsu*, and an open air bath *rotemburo*. There is also the exceptional "cascade bath", the *takiyu* or *utase-yu*.

Below
A men's bath *otokoburo* or *otokoyu* with a view of *fuji-san*.

Line drawing from: *We Japanese*, Fujiya Hotel Ltd. (publisher), Miyanoshita, Hakone 1949, p. 33

Opposite
Ishidaya
In the spacious garden of the ryokan, the covered passage connects the individual buildings and allows the guest to reach all areas of ryokan without getting wet. In the background the is a stone lantern, *ishi-doro*.

Boiled-rice is [the] main food for the Japanese. It is served in a porcelain bowl, placed in the nearer corner on the left-hand side of [the] *o-zen*, side by side with a wooden bowl, on the right, in which a vegetable soup is served. One may take three bowlfuls or a third help [*sic*] of boiled-rice without violating good manners, or, on the contrary, a polite Japanese will ask for a second help at least. But it is a sign of ill-behavior to leave a single grain of boiled-rice over [*sic*] in a bowl. If you leave any grains over in it, you must eat them when you drink tea or hot water at the end of the meal. We never had cold water at meal, though modern people seem to prefer cold water to hot. All dishes are served at once, artistically arranged on *o-zen*.

Japanese food consists of a greater proportion of vegetables than of meat, of which beef, pork, chicken, milk included, are of recent introduction. The *toguyu-boku* or the first-butchered-cow-tree [...] marks the place where the first cow was butchered with the object of meeting the desire of Townsend Harris, the first U.S. Minister to Japan. But the Japanese are great eaters of fish, perhaps the greatest in the world, because Japan, surrounded by clean seas on all sides, has many good fishing-places where fish can be caught all the year round.

The Japanese do not use a knife, or a fork or a spoon at table, [*sic*] but they use a pair of chopsticks, 5 or 6 inches long, of wood, bamboo, metal, glass, or ivory, either painted, lacquered or plain. It is against good manners to touch any food with fingers, and the Japanese are very clever at the manipulation of chopsticks, which are as useful to them as a knife, a fork and a spoon combined, or even more." [4]

Occasionally, the meal is also served in a portable, stacking bowl set, *jubako*. The serviette is again a hot terry towel. The bamboo, straw, cloth, paper or lacquered placemats display considerable artistic creativity. No part of the dinner service – dishes, dishes with lids, plates, small bowls, goblets, noodle cups – is like the other. The dinner service comprises ceramics, porcelain, glass, wood, bamboo and *nurimon*, exquisite lacquered work. A set of chopsticks is used for eating, *o-hashi*, of wood or bamboo, sometimes lacquered. Chopsticks that are not "disposed of" after the meal are deposited in the chopstick box, *hashibako*. During the meal, the chopsticks are placed in a rectangular chopstick holder, *hashitate*, or are rested on a small "bench." Beer, sake or tea is served for refreshment. Sake, the Japanese rice wine, is proffered in small cups or bowls, *sakazuki* or *choko*, made of a wide range of materials. The

massage, which, of course, the guest enjoys in his or her own room.

Many ryokan have classic Japanese games such as the sea-shell matching game *kai-awase* and the card games *uta-karuta*, *uta-kai* and *hana-awase*. Certainly the most exclusive forms of entertainment are music and dance, which are offered by a geisha or a *maiko*, an apprentice geisha.

"Geisha (*gei*, art, and *sha*, person [...]): Geisha are highly specialized types of Japanese women entertainers – mistresses of song and dance. A foreign writer describes them as 'the perfect arrangement for the tired Japanese businessman.' Fascinating and mysterious, geisha are like brilliant butterflies floating from flower to flower. Few ask what becomes of the joyous creatures when the winter winds blow. The geisha's glossy, jet-black hair, wonderfully arranged, her gay kimono and gorgeously-brocaded *obi*, her airs and graces, make her unlike any woman in the world. She forms a conspicuous feature of the life of Japan's chief cities. She sings, dances, and plays Japanese melodies on the *samisen*. When banquets or gatherings of merrymakers are held, she is hired to drive dull care away. She is a mistress of etiquette, and in her profession is usually an accomplished artist – and an expensive one. Also she is most trustworthy and loyal to her patrons. In the past, and even today, many important conferences of politicians and big businessmen are held in the *machiai*, or head geisha-houses – but whatever the geisha overhears seldom leaks out.

A budding geisha, called *hangyoku* or *maiko*, embarks early on her career. From her 10th year to 16 or 18 years of age she is trained in singing, dancing, music, etiquette, deportment, writing, flower arrangement, the tea ceremony and other accomplishments. When proficient she takes on the duties of her profession in earnest. In her mature years she may become the mistress of a geisha establishment, or be fortunate enough to be chosen as a wife and preside over a house and family. Many are not so fortunate, and the butterfly wings are broken and soiled in the mire of a great city. Some of the geisha find wealthy patrons who buy them out of bondage. The majority are not so lucky, and the butterfly existence of the geisha does not always end happily.

A geisha is engaged for a period of from five to ten years, a certain sum of money being paid for her to parents or relatives, the highest prices being paid for the most beautiful. Her earnings go to her mistress, to whom she is always in debt for her training and resplendent clothing. There are thousands of these professional women in Tokyo, Kyoto, and

guest may choose a receptacle, each a work of art. The delicate cups often rest in a *hai-dai*, a sake cup stand. Sake is served in special vessels and small sake bottles, *tokkuri*, or from the *choshi*, a special sake pourer, of wood or lacquer. For a cherry-blossom viewing picnic, for example, there are also special *jubako* for sake cups and bottles. Indeed, all in all, there are a large number of "small containers" for sake vessels.

A Japanese dinner is not only an occasion for hearty drinking, tobacco is also heavily consumed. The ashtrays are therefore accordingly large, usually filled with water and lavishly designed. Smokers' sets, *tabako-bon*, with the traditional pipe, *kisen*, are provided in the rooms.

Satisfied by the choice culinary experience, the guest can now enjoy the traditional entertainment in a ryokan; the selection is large. It is almost imperative before further evening activities to sample an extremely agreeable Japanese

sprays of blossoms, baskets of flowers, flags and other accessories according to the story the dancers endeavor to interpret. They are accompanied by one or more *samisen* players, and frequently by players on Japanese drums. At banquets and parties, geisha are often hired to perform for the entertainment of guests. They are well trained in the *odori*. Neither expression nor emotion is shown on the faces of *odori* dancers. In society, *odori* dancing by young maidens is frequently engaged in as part of the entertainment of the evening.

The *odori* of today is the same as that of the Tokugawa period. Many *odori* are adopted from the *nō*-plays, and the dancers strive to keep their faces as expressionless as the masks of the *nō*. No *odori* represents the present life of the Japanese. Each *odori* depicts a story, one of the *samisen* players singing the story – but the music is only supplemental to the dance itself, it is not paramount as in the Western dance.

Opposite
Masu-no-ya
Jizai-kagi, the adjustable hearth hook above the *iroro*, a wood, metal and bamboo construction in the traditional family room of the ryokan.
On the hook is the *tetsubin* or *cha-gama*, the kettle. Close to the kettle on the hook is a large horizontal balance of worked wood, frequently a beautiful sculpture. Especially popular motifs were colossal hooks, propeller blades or fish – lucky symbols. The *jizai-kagi* is raised or lowered depending on the heat, and whether food or tea water is to be kept warm, boiled or cooked.

Above
Shouro-tei
A delicacy in a ryokan close to the sea and part of the always fresh and elaborate *kaiseki* cuisine – very much alive fish in a special herb drink.

Right
Wanto-sato
On a lacquered *o-zen*, meal tray, numerous delicacies of the winter rural *kaiseki* cuisine, color compatible and prepared to reflect the local region.

Osaka, while every provincial town has its quota, as well as all resorts.

The most noted geisha school in Japan is in Kyoto, in the Gion amusement quarter. […] In Tokyo the geisha houses are grouped together in certain districts.

The vogue of Western dancing and entertainment means the eventual doom of the geisha, and to meet this competition many geisha are taking up the western style of dancing – but like other old-established customs in Japan the end of the geisha system is far in the future.

[…] *Odori* dance: The Japanese *odori* is a dance very different from the Western dance; not the least difference is that women are not held in men's arms. In fact, apart from men who make it a profession, the *odori* is seldom danced by men. The *odori* is a posture dance, with slow movements of the body, feet, arms and hands. The dancers employ fans,

Above
Maiko dancer
A young *maiko* dancer in summer in Gion, Kyoto's entertainment quarter, with a subtly made-up neck – symbol of a hidden eroticism – and an ingeniously tied *obi*, of lavish design, itself a minor work of art.

Opposite
Puppet from the "Awa no Nouson Butai," Awa Farm Theater
Awa is the old name for the Japanese prefecture of Tokushima on Shikoku Island. The *awa* puppet show is similar to the classical Japanese puppet theater called *bunraku* from the Edo period (1615–1868), where large, elaborately

costumed dolls are used, over three feet tall (around one meter). The puppets are turned by up to three puppeteers, who can be seen on the stage behind the doll. The plays are mostly borrowed from *kabuki*. The *awa* puppet theater uses dolls with heads usually larger than for *bunraku* and the accompanying chanted narrative is easier to understand. For centuries, the *awa* puppet show has been a popular form of entertainment in the rural communities of Tokushima. (From: Awa no Machinami Kenkyu-kai, Awa City Study Group)

18 years old, specially chosen and trained for this dance. They are assisted by a chorus of six singers, called *jikata*, and six *samisen* players on one side of the approach to the stage, and an orchestra of eleven girls on the opposite side who beat the *taiko* with drum-sticks, and *tsuzumi*, or 'long snare drum beaten with the hand,' both being drums of different shapes. Each season several different themes are portrayed: 'The music of the Fifty Bells,' 'The Morning Sun on the Waves,' etc. The dance is always divided into nine scenes or acts, eight of them being shown with a graceful posture dance and one with music only. All are in beautiful settings and the costumes of the dancers are gorgeous creations.

In the spring-time in Tokyo, at the Shimbashi Embujo, geisha perform the Cherry and other dances.

[...] Japanese musical instruments: The *koto*, or Japanese horizontal harp, is somewhat like a zither. It has a wooden frame and curved sounding-board made of paulownia wood, with 13 strings of silk mounted on ivory bridges. When played, the *koto* is laid flat and its strings are plucked by the thumb and the two first fingers of the right hand, to each of which is fastened a small ivory plectrum. In length the *koto* is slightly less than 8 feet.

The *samisen*, 3-stringed, is the most popular of Japanese musical instruments. In skilful hands it is capable of rendering a great variety of tones. The frame of the body, almost square in shape, is made of quince or oak wood, and both faces are covered like a drum with cat's skin. Its neck and fingerboard [*sic*], about 3 ft. long, is made of oak or red sandalwood. The bridge is made of buffalo-horn and the plectrum of ivory, buffalo-horn, or tortoise-shell. When playing, the performer holds the plectrum, quite large, in the right hand. The strings are graded in thickness. It may be called the Japanese banjo.

The *biwa*, a kind of lute, or mandolin, picked with the fingers, has a body semi-oval in shape, the extreme end of the neck being curved backward. It is a little over 4 ft. in length. Most *biwa* are 4-stringed. *Biwa* compositions are largely martial narratives, with a strong tinge of Buddhist fatalism.

[...] The *tsuzumi* [is a] 'long snare-drum beaten with the hand.' *Shakuhachi* (lit., 1 ft. 8 in. – the length of the flute) are bamboo flutes, played like a clarionet. In the streets, especially during the New Year holidays, *shakuhachi* players are sometimes seen, wearing a rush hat, like an inverted waste-basket, over their heads to conceal their faces while soliciting contributions. These players are known as *komuso* (lit., *komo*, a coarse straw matting; *so*, a

The most elaborate and spectacular of the *odori* dances is the *miyako-odori*, which is performed at Kyoto five times daily during the month of April. It is one of the greatest stage spectacles in Japan. The 32 uniformly and richly-clad participants are all young and attractive geisha, from 15 to

A female and a male *nō*-mask
Paper, wood and ivory,
Nogakushiryokan, Museum of Nō

The male mask, called "Kantan Otoko,"
was made by Mitsushige Deme, the 5th
master from the Deme family in Echizen
(Fukui prefecture) during the early Edo
period (1615–1868). "Kantan Otoko"
has melancholy features and the dignity
of a man who might one day become
emperor. Originally, this mask was only
used in the *nō*-play "Kantan" but is
nowadays also used in other dramas.
H ca. 9 in.; W 5¹/₂ in.; D 3¹/₃ in. (22.2 x
14.1 x 8.5 cm)

The female mask of the type "Zo Onna"
was made in 1723 by Mitsunori Deme.
"Zo Onna" is a based on a creative idea
from the artist Zoami in the early
Muromachi period (1392–1573).
The mask represents a not so young lady
and shows a divine facial expression.
It is used in *nō*-plays such as
"Hagoromo" and "Nonomiya." The mask
shown is one of the artist's
masterpieces.
H 8¹/₂ in.; W 5¹/₃ in.; D 3 in.
(21.3 x 13.6 x 7 cm)

While the immovable masks stand as
representative of the rather subdued
presentation of *nō*-theater, the
elaborate costumes express the dramatic
themes.

Left
Hatago Oohashi-ya
A storage container, tied together by
twisted rice-straw rope, leans against
the closed exterior sliding door. Because
rice cultivation is wide-spread
throughout Japan, very many examples
of rice straw used as a packaging
material exist. The aesthetic of packing
using natural materials represents an
individual form of the appreciation of
beauty. The Japanese usually prefer the
condition of equilibrium to be left to
nature and as little as possible is done
to artificially change this state.

 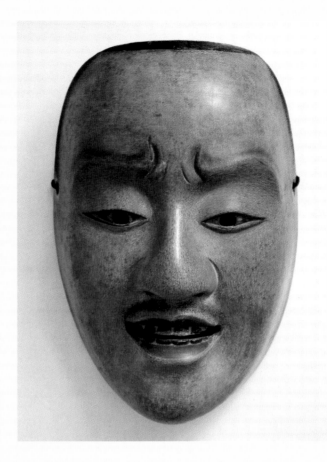

priest) for the reason that originally priests of a branch of the Zen sect played the *shakuhachi* while sitting on a coarse straw mat. This eventually evolved into the basket-shaped hat – which was used by spies disguised as *komuso* while endeavoring to discover military and political secrets, and by criminals as a means of concealment. *Sho* [...] consists of graduated bamboo reeds or pipes which are used in Shinto shrines while the address is being read, and at Shinto ceremonies. [...] This instrument is played in unison with other instruments, never alone. Its notes are soft and melodious." [5]

Anyone interested in experiencing classical Japanese entertainment outside of the ryokan in a theater is sure to be directed by the host to a suitable program in the vicinity. Because the traditional plays and forms of theater are still very popular today, these are not folkloric presentations but living theater such as *kabuki*, *kyogen*, *bunraku* and *nō*.

"The Japanese classic *nō*-plays: The word *nō*, used to designate a certain kind of theatrical performance, is obscure in its origin, and Japanese scholars and Buddhist priests have various theories. One of the most plausible is that *nō* was a term in Buddhism and that it referred to the unity of mind between the audience and the actors, chorus, and musicians. The *nō* is not a dance, since it is a creative movement, a unity of the arts rather than a mere dance.

The *nō* has a history of over 1,000 years. However, it was in 1368, under the patronage of Shogun Yoshimitsu, that it was elevated and became the aristocratic entertainment of the court and nobility which it continues to be today.

There are similarities in the *nō* to the ancient Greek drama in its principle of unity and use of pure sound in the place of music. The *shite*, or leading actor, is the pivot upon which the whole performance turns. The chorus and the musicians are like his two arms – they aid and support him. The music is not music in the western sense; it is pure sound only. Three drums and a flute are the instruments employed, while the chorus, kneeling at the right of the stage, comments on the characters and describes the changing scenes. The principal actors speak, but present all the emotions of the play by their actions and the type of mask

Left
Suzuki Harunobu
(1725–1770, active: 1760–1770)
8 views: Migration of the Wild Geese
1766,
Nishiki-e, color woodblock print, *Chūban*-format 11.25 in. x 8.27 in. (28.6 x 21.0 cm), Hiraki-Ukiyo-e Museum, Yokohama. The bridges of the *koto*, the Japanese horizontal harp, upon which the strings are mounted, remind one of a formation of wild geese. The young girl is fastening the plectrum to her finger.

Opposite, top
Wano-sato
The *futon*, the head directed towards the *tokonoma*, is ready for the night. The "snowy light" of the winter moon, which causes the *shōji* to glow, is brighter than the light spent by the artificial lamps.

Opposite, centre
"The Japanese sleep on the floor!"
Line drawing from: *We Japanese*, Fujiya Hotel Ltd. (publisher), Miyanoshita, Hakone 1949, p. 47

Opposite, bottom
Hakkei-tei
In his or her room, each guest will find the *midaré-bako*, a traylike, open case, which is used to store the *yūkata*, a rural Japanese kimono worn in the summer, made of cotton and decorated with white and blue stencil-dyed patterns.

they wear for various interpretations – the masks succeeding in concentrating attention upon the theme of the play. Among the most interesting things about the *nō* are the imaginative, wonderfully suggestive properties, the houses, castles, shrines, boats, bell towers, etc., being made of pieces of bamboo.

There are six different types of plays: the divine *nō* in which the gods appear, the fighting *nō* where the character describes war, involving much acrobatic performance, the *Katsura Hagaoromo*, featuring the life of women, the *Dojoji*, or the devils – which always are in the form of women, though acted by men, the *nō* dealing with human affairs, presenting some of the cardinal virtues of fidelity, justice, charity, etc.; and the Congratulation pieces, which form a lively ending." [6]

Whether one plans a visit to the theater, a walk to explore the city or the neighboring village, or simply a stroll around the garden of the ryokan, there is absolutely no need to change into everyday wear, one remains dressed in the *yūkata* or kimono, with the *tanzen* or *haori* pulled over. The *tabi* fit into the *geta* or *zōri*, the rice straw shoes. If it rains, a

kasa, a paper Japanese umbrella, is available, and in the summer when the humidity is high, there are various Japanese fans to use: *uchiwa*, a round fan which cannot be closed, or the folding fans *ogi* and *sensu*.

Underway in the dark in the city or in the countryside, the guest will come across a variety of Japanese lanterns: *chochin*, the portable lantern; *odawara-chochin*, a cylindrical, foldable lantern; *yumi-hari-chochin*, a lantern carried on a stick; *takahari-chochin*, a usually oval-shaped lantern used for festivals; *hako-chochin*, a cylindrical housed lantern; *gifu-chochin*, a lantern made of silk with fabulous motifs; *hozuki-chochin*, the "dwarf cherry lantern;" *kago-chochin*, the "basket lantern;" and *fugu-chochin*, the "blowfish lantern."

If one chooses to enjoy one's own four walls to perhaps meditate or observe the moon, one retires to the *engawa*, which is often furnished with a Western suite in 1920s or 1930s style, or to the *nure-en*, because the time to make the beds is approaching and the room has to be free. The table is removed, the *futon* is retrieved from the wall cupboard with sliding doors, *oshiire*, or a small adjoining room, and the bed is made directly on the *tatami*. This requires the mattress, *shikibuton*, a quilt-like top cover, *kakebuton*, and a *makura*, pillow. Nowadays the pillow is usually stuffed with rice husks and is not, as in earlier times, simply a wooden block or straw. Placed at the top end of the *futon* is a night lamp, *andon*, covered with rice paper; in addition there is often a torch and always a jug with water. The other lighting in the room, a basket lamp or a paper-covered lamp and candle holders, is extinguished for the night. Pretty, bamboo-weave baskets,

kago, are used to store personal belongings and they replace the bedside table.

The translucent *shōji* are darkened using the fitted wooden shutters, *amado*, or even curtains.

After a peaceful night, breakfast is served no later than 8 a.m. in the room and comprises green tea, fish, tofu, vegetables, bean paste and rice with miso soup. While one again takes a hot bath before breakfast, the *futon* is replaced by the table and the seating cushions. If one was satisfied with the attention received, one may hand one's personal maid "tea money" in an envelope.

The farewell is warm-hearted and after the bill is settled, usually in cash, the guest receives a small gift from the house. The staff stand and wave to the departing guest until he or she disappears over the horizon and is released back into the grip of "cold reality."

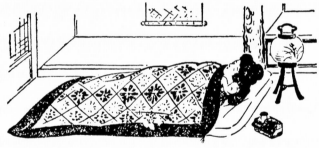

竹林院群芳園

Chikurin-in Gunpou-en, Yoshino

Sakura – Cherry blossom

Although the historical significance of the town of Yoshino has faded in the memories of the people, the town still has a special meaning to every native of Japan. The reason for this, however, is not its revered monuments or its turbulent past, but something completely different: for a short time in spring, usually at the beginning of April, a pale pink cloud of thousands upon thousands of cherry trees in blossom covers the mountain slopes around the small town.

Nowhere in Japan is the cherry blossom as spectacular as in Yoshino. Vast crowds of people make the pilgrimage to see the sacred cherry trees in this remote mountain region – there are around 1000 of them – and to experience and enjoy the "wonder of cherry blossom time in Japan," synonymous both with perfect

form and transitoriness, a symbol of life itself. The finest places for blossom viewing are *shimo-, naka-, kami-,* and *okusenbon.*

The matchless, fleeting beauty of the cherry blossom with its branches tinged with pink sets the minds of the Japanese into a sort of whirl, giving them "cherry blossom fever." The devotion of the entire nation to the color, the perfume and the powerful symbolic force of the cherry blossom is as old as the land itself.

Above
Chikurin-in Gunpou-en
View of the portico, *yashiro,* of the Shinto shrine linked to the ryokan. The so-called "sabre line" of the curved gutter is a feature of the early Tokugawa period, around 1700. On the right is the entrance to the ryokan, the former guesthouse belonging to the temple. Tradition has it that the ryokan once (circa 1300/1350) served as the seat of government of a tenno.

Opposite
Chikurin-in Gunpou-en
"Cascade of cherry blossom" on one of the lavishly blossoming cherry trees in the garden of the ryokan.

The cherry blossom is after all the national flower of Nippon, once used by poets as a simile for the noble yet short life of the young Samurai in battle.

"We live only for the moment when we can admire the splendor of the moonlight, the snow, the cherry blossoms and the colors of the maple leaves. Our spirits animated by the wine, we can enjoy the day without allowing ourselves to be disillusioned by the poverty that stares us in the face. We do not permit ourselves to become disheartened as we are carried along like a gourd swept downriver by the current. That is what is called the flowing, transitory world." [7]

Every newspaper headline lacks interest compared with news of the "current progress" of the opening blossom, and television and radio stations compete with one another to give the most accurate forecast. Picnic spots under cherry trees are occupied days in advance, cherry blossom festivals, *o-hana-mi* are planned down to the minutest detail, the numerous special "cherry blossom dishes" are prepared and in Yoshino tons of "cherry blossom ice-cream" are made. Sake, Japanese rice wine, flows freely – this too is a tradition and has allegorical significance. Cherry trees were a favorite abode of the spirits of the paddy fields. According to legend, they took up their position in the branches as soon as the buds appeared. As the cherry blossom season coincides with the first rice planting, rice farmers showed their respect by drinking sake under a cherry tree in order to ensure a good harvest; the more they drank, the more impassioned was their homage.

Opposite
Chikurin - in Gunpou - en
Gable decoration "à la baroque" on the roof of the shrine seen through the branches of a cherry tree in blossom.

Above left and right
Chikurin - in Gunpou - en
Bark on the trunk of a cherry tree and cherry blossom petals on the mossy surface of the garden.

There comes
a wood-gatherer,
Wending his way
down the tortuous
mountain path:
"Tell me, dear friend,
There on the mountain top,
Is that cherry blossom
Or clouds?"

Minamoto no Yorimasa (1104–1180)

[freely translated by Jane Brown]

Right
Chikurin-in Gunpou-en
View of the watchtower and thatched
main roof of the ryokan with a partial
view of the shingle-covered roofs of
the shrine.
Japanese houses originally had thatches
of straw or reeds. However, a perfect
balance of all sorts of roof shapes and
coverings such as straw, tiles, shingle
and stone can be found on just one
house. In the background can be seen
the mountainous countryside around
Yoshino.

Today's cherry blossom parties too are a mixture of an exuberant love of life and a still melancholy – thoughts of mortality and the fleeting nature of all existence mingled with a celebration of fertility and the life that is perpetually renewing itself.

The *hana – mi*, or blossom festivals, are a clear testimony to the attitude and philosophy of the Japanese people to life. "Another visual metaphor for things which come into being and then pass away again leaving scarcely any noticeable trace of their existence is the cherry blossom, one of the most influential (and most hackneyed) images of Japanese culture. Every spring the cherry trees are in bloom for a week at most. But a sudden shower of rain or gust of wind can cause the delicate, pale pink petals to fall at any moment. So people all over Japan spread out mats and blankets under the cherry trees. In this way a place – rather than a formal structure – and an occasion are created at one and the same time. The lasting, intense *wabi - sabi* power [*wabi* literally: wilted, *sabi* literally: a spiritual path, contemporary definition: an aesthetic ideal, a certain type of beauty] of this image of the cherry blossom is founded on the fact that we are always mindful of the fleeting quality of all existence: just now there was as yet no blossom; and in a short while hence the blossom will be no more..." [8]

"The cherry, the pride of Japan, the coronation of spring, breaks out into pink clouds of blossoms that gradually spread over the Empire in early April. They transform the country into a fairyland of loveliness that has given Japan its floral name of 'The Land of the Cherry Blossoms.' All through the month of April, the railway cars and all other conveyances are crowded with old and young, rich and poor, on their way to some noted place for cherry viewing (*hana-mi*).

Some of the young people are dressed in fantastic costumes as an incentive to merry-making – for it is a festive time, and for the brief life-time of the blossoms, a period usually not more than two weeks, the nation is practically on holiday and the cherry blossoms are the topic of the hour.

The *Sakura-no-hana*, the cherry blossom of Japan, is glorified and worshiped as no other flower in the entire world. It symbolizes perfection to the Japanese and satisfies their aesthetic sense. It has been the inspiration and theme of thousands of poems by the rulers, by the '100 poets,' and by the mass of the people.

Among many varieties of cherry trees there are sixteen principal species of blossoming trees. Almost all varieties bear their blossoms on leafless branches. The first trees to flower are the single white and pink varieties. After these arrive the double blossoms which last about two weeks. The trees do not bear fruit; only a few varieties bear tiny red pellets. The single mission of the tree is to be beautiful." [9]

Yoshino – refuge of spirits and of emperors

Shrouded in mystery, the Kii Mountains around Yoshino were looked upon in the dim and distant past as the seat of the *kami* – the gods and spirits of nature. For centuries afterwards they remained an important religious place. Shugendō, an alternative school of Buddhism that united old shaman rites with Shinto and with ascetic Buddhist traditions, had its centre here. The enlightenment of the *kami*, as a result of which they were transformed into *gongen*, or manifestations of Buddha, is attributed to the founder, En no Gyoja, an exorcist and necromancer. Until Shinto was made the state religion in the Meiji era, numerous *yamabushi*, or mountain priests dwelt in the mountains, enjoying great popularity with the local people because of their magical powers and their ability to cast out devils. The *yamabushi* trained their minds and bodies by living a life full of privation in the seclusion and solitude of the mountains, and in many mountain

ranges, including the area around Yoshino, Shugendō has survived the Restoration. In addition, the sect intervened on several occasions in the fortunes of Japan. Minamoto no Yoritomo (1192–1199), the first Kamakura shogun (Kamakura period, 1192–1333), who set up a military government in Kamakura in opposition to the decadent court in Kyoto, was the victim of a conspiracy instigated by his own brother. After being exposed, the latter fled to the Shugendō in Yoshino, where he found refuge.

Over a period of centuries the Kimpusen-ji in the heart of the small town of Yoshino was the main temple of the Shugendō School. The streets are lined with further shrines, pagodas and temples, and the equally historical site of Nanchō is nearby. The Chikurin-in Gunpou-en ryokan is part of one of the old temples situated in the middle of a charming landscape garden with a sumptuous historical shrine. The famous garden was created by Senno Rikyū (1522–1591), the outstanding aesthete and pioneer of the *cha-no-yū* (tea ceremony). The contemporary visitors' rooms are in the former temple guesthouse, which, as tradition would have it, once served as the seat of government of a tenno. Yoshino achieved real fame due to the fact that an entire period of Japanese history is termed the Yoshino Period (1336–1392).

The last *hojo*, or major-domos of the Minamoto shoguns, who had become weak in the latter stages of their rule, made themselves generally hated through their cruelty and extravagance. So the Emperor Go-Daigo (1288–1339) decided that the time had come to do away with the rival government in Kamakura and win back power. Initially the attempt failed, but after a ten-year struggle the Contra-shoguns were defeated and Kamakura was destroyed. However, the emperor was only able to enjoy his newly won power for just three years. He had omitted to reward the generals who had supported him in an appropriate manner and so their leader, the victorious commander Ashikaga no Takauji, seized power for himself (1338–1358). The emperor fled to Yoshino Mountain where he set up a rival court. The empire split into two dynasties, the legitimate southern one in Yoshino and the northern one in Kyoto with an usurper at its head; Ashikaga had himself appointed shogun by the latter in 1336. The rivalry between the two courts, *nanbokucho*, lasted almost sixty years (1288–1333). Ashikaga's promise that the two royal houses would alternate on the throne was never fulfilled. It was not until his grandson Yoshimitsu (1368–1395) brought the legitimate emperor back to Kyoto, thus bringing about reconciliation, that an end was put to the unrest. Yoshimitsu established his royal seat in Muromachi, a district of Kyoto, and there followed the so-called Muromachi Period (1392–1573).

Opposite
Chikurin-in Gunpou-en
View at evening through the glazed lattice sliding door into the reception hall of the ryokan.

Below
Chikurin-in Gunpou-en
Rear wall of the entrance hall with a "natural" (right) and an "artistically created" (left) flower arrangement.

Following double page
Byōbu **Screen, "Spring by the Tatsuta River in Yoshino," detail**
Part of the pair of screens "Spring and autumn by the Tatsuta River in Yoshino" (see also p. 224).

Edo period (1615–1868), Painting on gold paper, 6 panels, 177.3 x 418.5 cm or Ca. 70 x 165 in. (detail), Nezu Institute of Fine Arts, Tokyo

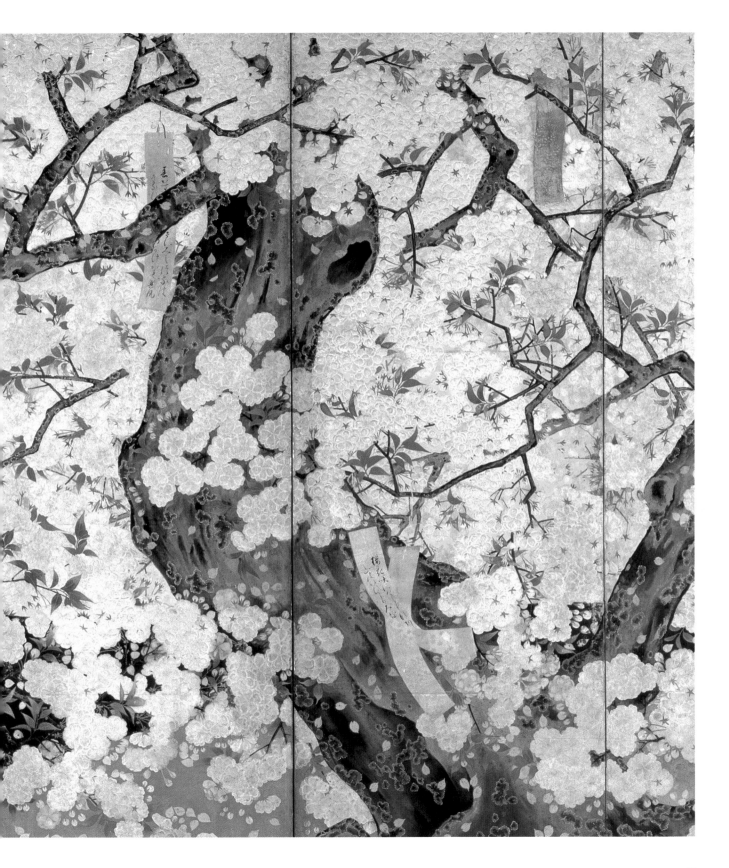

Chikurin-in Gunpou-en – Shrine and inn

A hotel or guesthouse that is "open to the general public" and yet is part of a temple with a shrine in the enclosure may seem unusual to the "Westerner." However, to the Japanese way of thinking it is a familiar and conventional combination. The architecture of a temple does not in any case differ in its external appearance from that of a middle-class home or a palace. Temples were originally residential buildings and they were only fitted out with sacred objects later on. In Western culture on the other hand the idea of living in a cathedral or a chapel would indeed be unusual.

Temple architecture underwent the same development as residential buildings. Alongside an ever refreshing and uplifting simplicity there was an increasing tendency to fashion the roof with consoles and various overhangs. The curves of the gutter became more sophisticated and the roof itself was provided with decorative features. Before the effect could descend into the over-ornate, the prevalent spiritual trend of Zen tamed everything into a quieter form; herein lies the architectural primacy of Japan over to the West.

An emperor takes lodgings in a temple guesthouse, setting up his court and palace in the mountains among the cherry trees. The Western interpretation of the concept of a palace is linked to the display of status. In Japan too the nobility wanted to set an example with high levels of culture, but this was never celebrated with grandeur and pomp, but rather with sophisticated taste. The desired effect was not one of distance, but perfection, with everything remaining modest. The predominant idea was "human equilibrium, calm and elegant proportions" (Saul Bellow, freely translated by N.C.).

The paintings of the Chikurin-in Gunpou-en

Some of the exquisite paintings that once completely covered the sliding doors and the alcoves of the guest rooms and dining room of the Chikurin-in Gunpou-en have been preserved. They date from the Genroku period (1688–1703), which is part of the Tokugawa or Edo period (1615–1868), when the development of the activities of craftsmen and merchants was at its zenith. The new middle-class culture loved the open display of a fundamental zest for life.

The victorious Tokugawa warlords had already built palaces with large reception rooms and audience chambers, and the leading artists of the land were commissioned to decorate them with wall paintings and screens. The underlying intention was to engender respect. The impressive, large-scale structure of the pictures, with their elaborate decorations in gold leaf, was intended to illustrate authority, prestige and lifestyle.

Tea dish with cherry blossom decoration
Kyō-yaki pottery, early Edo period
(1615–1868)
Kyō-yaki pottery is light-colored, painted
stoneware. Gold is used frequently and
the decorations are mostly pictorial –
preferably of blossoms and plants. A
distinction is made between *awata-yaki*,
pottery left in its natural state, *kiyo-mizu-
yaki* porcelain and *raku-yaki*, which are
produced without a potter's wheel. *Kyō-
yaki* pottery items were used for the tea
ceremony, for *ike-bana*, as incense
burners and as household containers.
The porcelains are made of stoneware
with a coating of enamel glazing and
come from the kiln near the Kiyomizu
Temple close to Kyoto, hence *kiyo-
mizuyaki*, which is today often used as
a generic term for porcelain of the Edo
period (1615–1868). With 1200 years
of development in technique and
decoration behind them, the *Kyō-yaki*
potters were able to evolve free artistic
designs and their pottery items were the
first to bear the "artist's signature."

Opposite, bottom
Makio Araki
Ohineri, traditionally a type of wrapping
for the money that was thrown to actors
on the stage as evidence of approval;
today also used as paper wrappings for
sweets, Kobe 1990.
Traditionally the wrapping process is
sacrosanct and must take place according
to strict rules. The way in which an item is
wrapped can signify happiness or sorrow.
Wrapping with paper has been customary
since the Kamakura Period (1185–1333)
and is a permanent, integral part of the
culture of both the samurai and the tea
ceremony.

Left
Chikurin-in Gunpou-en
Detail of the offertory box, the *saisen-
bako*, at the foot of the *haiden*, with
cherry blossom emblem, made of wood
with metal fittings and painted
decoration.
Visitors to the temple throw an offering
of few coins into the *saisen-bako*, clap
their hands two or three times and bow.
The offering *o-saisen* means "money in
return" for a good harvest or a favor
received. The standard quotation has
been handed down: *Jigoku no sata mo
kane shidai*, which, freely translated,
means: the judgement of hell is founded
on the amount of money contributed.
Nowadays the donation is above all a way
of showing respect for God.

The background to the pictures consists mostly of pure gold leaf and it is easy to imagine the effect of such a screen in the dark rooms of a temple lodging, whether it be lit by candle light or the diffuse daylight falling through a *shōji* sliding wall.

"Screen paintings are essentially movable, folding walls, and were used to delineate space and create a special atmosphere for some household activity. For example, a pair of screens with paintings on a seasonal theme might be brought out to create a more intimate area in a large room, and to provide a dramatic background for entertaining and impressing visitors. They were made of paper pasted on a lattice-like wooden frame, with the painted front usually bordered with brocade, and the whole arrangement framed with a thin wooden strip that was finished with red or black lacquer.

Usually screens were constructed with two or six panels (although occasional examples are seen with four or eight),

which are hinged so that the screen can stand in a zigzag shape and also be folded flat for storage. Six-panel screens are almost always made in pairs with some contiguity in the design or painting. A pair of screens with paintings of landscapes for example, will usually depict different seasons, but in viewing from right to left the composition moves from foreground to distance on one screen, and back from distance to foreground on the other. [...]

[G]old leaf was often applied for decorative effect – especially in screen paintings, where it was valued for the remarkable quality it has of picking up light from the weakest of sources, and of gleaming magically in the deep shadows of rooms lit by candle or lamp." [10]

The paintings of the Chikurin-in Gunpou-en are close to the dynamism and boldness of the Unkoku School, founded during the Momoyama period (1573–1615) by Unkoku Togan (1547–1618), and characterised by its impressionistic, almost abstract style in which no outlines are used to establish shapes. Togan and his pupils lived and worked principally in the west of Japan. With the exception of the first three generations, this school remains to date largely unresearched.

The free composition of the paintings is sensational in the way it simultaneously combines the precise observation of plants and flower blossoms together with graphic discipline and sensibility.

Opposite
Chikurin-in Gunpou-en
View from the "Kusan" (chrysanthemum) guest room across the *nure-en* (veranda) of the ryokan towards a cherry tree.

Below
Chikurin-in Gunpou-en
"Kusan" guest room with *zabuton* (floor cushions) with backrests, *tokonoma* alcoves, *shō* scroll and *ike-bana* (flower arrangement). This room has magnificent paintings on the *fusuma* (sliding doors). These date from the Genroku period (1688–1703) and have been attributed to the Unkoku School.

Above left and right / Opposite
Chikurin-in Gunpou-en
Detail views of the *fusuma* paintings in the guest room shown on p. 53, attributed to the Unkoku School, Genroku Period (1688–1703).

Outlines of flowers and chrysanthemums are portrayed amidst clouds of gold dust on a background of gold leaf and there is a mountain landscape that has been built up in the *suiboku* style (water color painting). The chrysanthemum is the

emblem of the tenno. The Emperor Go-Daigo dwelt in these rooms during the so-called Yoshino period (1336–1392), hence the use of the Imperial flower in the decorations.

This is particularly striking for anyone who is accustomed to European pictures, which show plants and flowers in their realistic context – with the ground below and the sky above. The omission of roots and stems and leaves lends vitality to the way in which the details of the flowers are portrayed.

Many paintings of the late 17th and early 18th centuries show this desire to cast off the shackles of dusty academia and return to the radiance of the works from the Momoyama period (1573–1615) by using glowing colors and gold.

Cherry blossom as a synthesis of the arts

The availability of seasonal foods is the decisive factor in traditional Japanese food, virtually taking over the role of the "chef de cuisine." The Japanese automatically associate a particular menu sequence or a typical dish with the appropriate season. Aside from the essential stimulus, the inherent aesthetic appeal, which goes to make up an exquisite meal, "closeness to nature" is a deciding factor in Japanese cuisine. Aesthetic appeal does not amount merely to perfecting the "taste" in the Western sense of giving a dish visual appeal, but also tradition,

custom, even mysticism and popular belief play a considerable role. Likewise, the presence of nature does not relate merely to fresh biological ingredients, but rather to the seasons, phases of the moon, religious and secular rituals, spirits of nature, landscapes and much more. A *kaiseki* meal is an almanac of the Japanese year and its key events. Japanese cuisine consists of delights for the taste buds and "feasts for the eyes" dictated by the seasons, and it also mirrors the cultural heritage. Even with all the refinement and elaborate details of the individual dishes and their decorations, everything still remains "natural," as the garnish is, with a few exceptions, part of the dish and is consumed with it – perfect equilibrium is maintained.

The cherry blossom is the herald of the awakening spring and is therefore a high spot of Japan's culinary calendar, both as natural produce and for garnish and ornamentation. A few delicate petals float in cherry blossom tea, and the *wagashi*, traditional Japanese sweets used to sweeten the tangy flavor of the tea, glow with all shades of pink, taking on the shapes of the numerous different cherry blossoms. The delicate perfume of *sakura* lingers over confectioners' shops. One of the favorites is *sakura-mochi*, small, soft balls of rice, the color of cherry blossom wrapped in a leaf from a cherry tree.

But there are also savory cherry blossom dumplings, which are first steamed in the easily digestible leaf of the cherry tree and then served in a clear soup with a small dot of pink in the top of each dumpling. Cherry blossom dumplings are on offer everywhere, but even the basics of Japanese cuisine such as miso soup, pickled vegetables, fish and rice are given a "touch of cherry blossom" through cherry blossom flavoring, leaves or buds, faint reddish nuances of color and leaves from the cherry tree. A twig with a few fragile buds is used for decoration. The balanced color tones used throughout in setting the table and decorating the room harmonize with one another and with the great cherry blossom event.

Almost every Japanese family and every ryokan has four different sets of eating utensils, one for each season. The style, material, color and design harmonize with the seasonal products. Among the treasured items in a dinner service are lacquered bowls, pieces of pottery and glass receptacles all bearing cherry blossom motifs. Packaging, too, for foodstuffs and various other items, even for amounts of money to be handed over discreetly,

whether it be of paper, material or straw, is covered in a shower of pink-colored blossom – *hana-mi* as a synthesis of the arts.

The princess and the cherry blossom

In the Japanese publication *We Japanese* of 1934 there are numerous "romances" and fables. The legend concerning the origin of the word *sakura*, which at the same time describes the character of Princess Kono-hana-no-Sakuya-Hime, who gave her name to the *sakura* or cherry, is also told in a touching manner, mindful of tradition.

Prince Nigini-no-Mikoto, was well known by his nickname "grandson of heaven," as he was the grandson of the Goddess Amaterasu, ancestress of the Imperial family. When he was sent down to rule the earth he landed on Mount Takachiho. At the foot of the mountain he met a charming princess who was walking along the beach. "And who might you be?" asked the prince. The young girl replied, "I am the daughter of

Left
Ogi, folding fan
Gold leaf with cherry blossom painting.

Above
"Cherry blossom princess,"
wearing the *juuni-hitoe*, the traditional ceremonial kimono, a *kosode* kimono, which consists of twelve layers of clothing, weighs about 20 kg (44 pounds) and was worn by Heian ladies in waiting. Painting on *washi*, hand-made Japanese paper.

Opposite
Maiko dancer
preparing herself for the *miyako-odori*, the spectacular "cherry blossom dance," which during April is performed five times a day in Kyoto. The 32 actresses dressed identically in luxurious costumes are all young, attractive geishas aged between 15 and 18, who have been specially selected and trained for this dance.

Oyamatsumi. My name is Kono-hana-no-Sakuya-Hime, and I have an older sister who is called Princess Iwanaga." When the Prince asked for her hand in marriage she told him to call on her father, Prince Oyamatsumi, to ask his permission. Oyamatsumi was so delighted at Prince Nigini-no-Mikoto's request to marry one of his daughters that he sent both of them the generous gift of one hundred carrying trestles of food, so that upon accepting the present the prince might live for as long as a rock, the name of the elder sister being a synonym for long life (*iwa* = rock; *naga* = long life). The name of the younger daughter stood for blossom-time and flowers in bloom, verbatim "tree-blossom-flowering-princess." Anyhow, Prince Nigini-no-Mikoto decided on the younger sister and sent the elder one back to her father. But when it turned out that Kono-hana-no-Sakuya-Hime was expecting a happy event the prince became mistrustful and disowned the unborn child. In answer to his suspicions the princess said to him, "I will go through fire, and if I come out of it unharmed, then the child is yours." The princess had an *uzumuro* built, (a room with no other means of access), and after locking herself inside, she set fire to it with her own hands. She remained safe and sound and the prince's doubts were allayed. The princess became the mother of Princes Ho-no-Teru-no-

Above
Chikurin-in Gunpou-en
The "closed" entrance façade of the
ryokan to the right of the shrine. There is
no visible sign to indicate the presence of
a hotel.

Opposite
Chikurin-in Gunpou-en
The landscape garden, *chisen-kaiyu* of the
ryokan with view across the pond to the
guesthouse and shrine and to the cherry

trees in full bloom, some of which are
more than several hundred years old; just
two days later the blossom will be "gone
with the wind," symbolizing the "fleeting,
transitory world."

Mikoto, Ho-no-Suseri-no-Mikoto and Ho-no-Ori-no-Mikoto,
the latter being the grandfather of the Emperor Jimmu, the first
ruler of the Japanese Imperial dynasty.

It is generally assumed that the "Sakuya" from the name
Kono-hana-no-Sakuya-Hime has changed into *sakura*, the
Japanese word for cherry, and as the cherry blossom is the most
popular of all flowers, the generic term for blossom trees and
blossoms was chosen as the term for the cherry.

The tale about the "blossom princess" exists in other versions
that are rich in imagery. Kono-hana-no-Sakuya-Hime is buried
on the mountaintop of the *fuji-san*, in order to be particularly close
to Mount Olympus, from whence she first fell to earth. Her "fall
from heaven" landed her right on top of a cherry tree in blossom,
in a cloud of pink, and that is how she came by her name.

The first reference to the cherry is in the *kojiki*, Japan's
oldest chronicle (712), in connection with the goddess
Amaterasu, who hid herself from the repeated attacks of her
brother Susanoo in the Celestial Cave. A *hahaka* twig, said to
have come from a cherry tree, served as a divining rod.

The first occurrence of the word *sakura* in Japanese
literature is in the name of the Wakasakura Palace, which was
built by the Empress Jingo (around 170 B.C.), in Iware, Yamato
Province. Shortly after that the Emperor Inkyo (the 19th tenno,
around 150 B.C.) wrote the first poem to be handed down
about the cherry trees of the Fujiwara Palace. The
contemplation of cherry blossom was no less popular in old
Japan than it is today. Japanese lyric poetry is full of verses
written by emperors and empresses, courtiers and ladies-in-
waiting, illustrating the delight felt at the spectacle of the
cherry blossom. A gathering of people who Lord Taigo invited
to Yoshino on the 24th of the second month in 1594 for the
"contemplation of the blossom" comprised at least 5000 guests.
There are numerous famous places in Japan where one can
abandon oneself to the delights of viewing the cherry blossom,
but without question there is none more popular than the small
mountain town of Yoshino, about which someone wrote: as far
as the eye can see nothing is visible but cherry blossom,
regardless of what is concealed, which remains invisible.

二見館

二見館

賓日館

賓日館

Opposite
Futami-kan Hinjitsu-kan
Detail of the entrance.
The crossbeam shows a particularly
artistic example of the sacred rice-straw
rope, *shimenawa*, one of Japan's many
allegorical images.

Futami-kan Hinjitsu-kan, Futamigaura

The way of the gods – Ise

The Futami-kan Hinjitsu-kan ryokan is situated on Futamigaura beach, facing the often stormy waters of the Ise-wan (Ise Bay), just a few yards from the stony seashore upon which the high waves break. After a hot bath, it is a special pleasure, before the delicious meal and already dressed in the kimono, to undertake a wind-buffeted stroll to enjoy the sea. However, the Futami-kan Hinjitsu-kan inn not only offers scenic edification, but also a unique culinary experience. This ryokan is located on the Ise Peninsula, not far from the legendary Ise Shinto Shrine.

Shinto, "the way of the gods," is the indigenous Japanese religion. In essence animistic, Shinto not only pays homage to anthropomorphous deities but also the spirit and manifestations of a deeply revered nature, above all mountains, trees, lakes, rivers, boulders and animals. Early Shinto complexes having nothing of the monumentality of later shrines, not even a central prayer hall; frequently a mountain in the background is the actual focal point of the site or even a rock or a tree. Today's Shinto shrines were given their typical form after Buddhism arrived in Japan in the 6th century and with the integration of Buddhist architectural elements into the Shinto style. However, the shrines are distinctive in design and easily distinguished from Buddhist temples because the divine is not represented by a holy image, such as a Buddha statute, for instance, but in a physical symbol, that is, in material objects, *goshintai*. These objects are not fetishes and are not themselves worshipped as divine, being solely symbols of a divine existence.

The Sacred Mirror of Ise symbolises the divine presence of the Goddess Amaterasu Ōmikami, who embodies the natural phenomenon of the sun and is the traditional progenitor of the Japanese Imperial family.

Opposite
Ise Shrine, Mie Prefecture, Japan
The Toyouke Shrine, the principal
sanctuary of the Outer Shrine, *gekū*.
The *gekū* is dedicated to Toyouke, the
god of fertility, a deity of agriculture and
the cultivation of silk. *naikū*, the Inner
Shrine, is dedicated to Amaterasu
Ōmikami, the sun goddess. Originally
erected under Emperor Temmu (673–686),
since 673 B.C., the shrine buildings at Ise
have been renewed every 20 years, with
the exception of a 100-year period during
the medieval civil wars. In all, 65
structures are replaced each time.

Right
The Futami Shrine at Ise
The Futami Shrine at Ise (circa 690), not
far from the Futamikan ryokan. Photo:
Bruno Taut, 1935.
From: Bruno Taut, *Das Japanische Haus
und sein Leben*, [Houses and People of
Japan], publisher Manfred Speidel,
Berlin 1997, p. 144.

The Ise Shrine, Japan's most sacred shrine, originates from the 3rd century and was erected architecturally in the classical Japanese style before China extended its cultural influence to the Japanese archipelago in the 6th century. The three classical Shinto styles are: *shimmei, taisha* and *sumiyoshi*. The Ise Shrine represents the pinnacle of the *shimmei* style and may be considered the incunabulum of genuine Japanese architecture.

The roots of this architecture extend back to the beginnings of Japanese civilisation. For example, the design of the Grand Shrine of Ise stands representative of the old raised granaries of prehistoric times, built on timber piles with high woodplank floors, a rigid triangle for the gable roof secured by means of interlocking joints, and distinctive free-standing columns, *munemochi-bashira*, that support the ridge. The inspired simplicity of the shrine awakens the same admiration as the crowning examples of the Buddhist tradition. "The art of omission is pushed to the extreme, and the open halls for waiting or for the priest's ceremonies manifest this in an architectural purity achieved by simplicity that cannot be surpassed and does not exist anywhere else in the world, not even in Japan." [11] The main hall is built with plain, unfinished cedar wood and is ringed by a raised veranda. The gently curved roof comprises several layers of cypress bark and has two x-shaped end-beam arrangements. The unpainted and unsculptured hall is located in a courtyard strewn with granite pebbles.

As a whole, Ise comprises two complexes: the Outer Shrine, *gekū*, and the Inner Shrine, *naikū*. Both areas are just under 4 miles (6 km) apart. The *gekū* is dedicated to Toyouke, a fertility goddess, *naikū* to Amaterasu Ōmikami, the sun goddess, who is represented by the octagonal mirror, which was originally kept in the Emperor's palace as the Imperial insignia. In earlier times, a princess who was a medium consulted the mirror as an oracle and influenced the government's decisions. This is probably the reason why the mirror and the princess were banished to Ise in order to reduce their political influence.

Since 673 B.C., the shrine buildings at Ise have been razed and rebuilt every twenty years, with the exception of a 100-year period during the medieval civil war. In total, each time 65 buildings are renewed. For about 8 years, 200,000 workers are employed as carpenters, roofers, goldsmiths, weavers, etc. 13,600 cypress trees, as much as 800 years old, 25,000 bundles of straw, and 12,000 bamboo canes are used. The enormous expense, about 45 million US dollars, is covered by private donations. The only building to remain standing is a small wooden hut in which there is a post, the *shin-no-mi-hashira*, the august column of the heart. The new shrine is erected over and around this post and its housing. The holiest and most mysterious object at Ise remains hidden to humans at all times.

Shimenawa – The sacred rope

On Futamigaura Bay, a mile or two from Ise, two rocks rise out of the sea. These rocks are known as the "Wedded Rocks," *meoto-iwa* (rock marriage), the personification of the central deities of the Japanese creation myth, Izanami and Izanagi, and the parents of Amaterasu Omikami, the sun goddess. From the sexual union of these two gods, the Japanese archipelago was created. The rock marriage – the ideal of a marriage between two gods – is symbolised by the straw rope tying together the two rocks and which is renewed every year on the 5th of January. The rocks are one of Japan's most important places of pilgrimage and at the same time a symbol for man and woman, the steadfastness of the union of both and an allegory for fidelity.

The sacred rice-straw rope, *shimenawa*, is one of Japan's many allegoric images. A particularly artistic example is found above the entrance to the Futami-kan inn.

"The *shimenawa*" or sacred rope is hung before a Shinto shrine, over the entrance gate to a dwelling-house or else round a place which is considered sacred or has to be kept sacred. According to the Shinto belief, no evil can pass beyond the line of the *shimenawa*.

The *shimenawa* consists of two strands of rice-straw plaited together, in a left-handed or positive way, representing positivity and negativity, to which nature owes its existence. In the proper arrangement of the *shimenawa*, its beginning or larger end should be on the left-hand side of the shrine

Above
***Shimenawa*, the sacred rice-straw rope**
Line drawing from: *We Japanese*, Fujiya Hotel Ltd. (publisher), Miyanoshita, Hakone 1949, p. 197

or the god, though this rule seems to be little observed today. The rope has along it a few rice-stalks hanging at intervals. Formerly, as the original name of the rope indicates, the root-ends of the straws were plaited into the rope, with the head hung partly down.

Though the straw is shorn of its ears and hung with the root-ends down, the ears were left on the stalks in former days, as they were the most significant part of the rope. Lastly, the *shimenawa* has stripes of white paper or cloth, called *nigite* or *nusa,* hanging between the clusters of the straws. According to a certain interpretation, these little pieces represent the hands of the Emperor reaching out for a good crop in the country.

When the Goddess Amaterasu, first ancestress of the Imperial family, was forced by Tajikarao, or Prince Mighty-power, out of the Celestial Cave in which she had hidden

herself because of the repeated offences of her brother, Prince Susanoo, a rope was put across the entrance of the cave by Prince Futodama to prevent the Sun Goddess from going back into the cave again. The rope was called *shiri-kume-na-nawa,* meaning "Don't-retreat-rope," which name was shortened to the present *shimenawa.* Like the *torii,* which cleanses the heart of the Shinto devotee, the *shimenawa* sanctifies the place or thing around which it is put." [12]

Above
Futamigaura Bay
On Futamigaura Bay, just a few yards from the Futamikan ryokan, two rocks rise out of the sea, tied together by a sacred rice-straw rope. These are the "Wedded Rocks," *meoto-iwa* (rock marriage), which symbolise fidelity among married couples.

Opposite, bottom
The *Shimenawa* above the entrance to the *haiden*, the worship hall, of the main temple of the Izuma Taisha Shrine on Shimane.
The Izuma Taisha Shrine is Japan's oldest Shinto shrine and second in importance only to Ise. Today's main shrine, however, only dates back to 1744.

Above
Futami-kan Hinjistu-kan
Entrance area with the curved *shoin* gable,
kara-hafu, above the "coach drive."
The "bible" of the *shoin* style is the *shomei*
manual, which appeared in 1608 and
which specifies the necessary proportions
exactly, *kiwari-jutsu*.

The ryokan was erected in
Meiji (1868–1912) and Taishō style
(1912–1926). Originally, Futami-kan and
Hinjitsu-kan were two separate buildings.
In 1911, they were combined following a
purchase of the properties and in 1930
remodelled by the
well-known Taishō architect Shitarō Ōe.

green color of the ocean. The delicate combination of natural surroundings and structures – the hallmark of Japanese buildings – comes to entirely unaffected fruition at Futami-kan. The guest can thus relax secluded in his or her room, absorbed in the "literature" on the buildings at Ise or simply enjoy the changing moods as the day passes and the bracing sea climate.

Meiji and Taishō – East and West

Futami-kan is built in the Meiji (1868–1912) and Taisho (1912–1926) style and is a notable example of these art forms. The young Crown Prince Mutsuhito ascended to the throne as Emperor Meiji and immediately launched a programme of modernisation. The first steps toward the Restoration were taken in an atmosphere pregnant with domestic strife. The shogun's fall was followed by the capitulation of the *daimyō*, whose estates were divided up into today's prefectures. Edo was declared the new capital and renamed Tokyo (the eastern capital). In just one generation this medieval feudal state caught up with European science, established modern heavy industries and created a strong navy along British and a powerful army along Prussian lines. In a dramatically short

Anyone lucky enough to have seen the two shrines, the "old" and the "new one" next to each other, shortly before the old one was torn down, will never forget the metaphysical impression. Such a procedure produces a type of cultural shock for our Western mentality. In the West, we meticulously protect, restore and conserve that which is old and we may be overpowered by this so diametrically opposed idea of preservation. Only a constant and orally transmitted tradition of reconstruction guarantees preservation, being the ultimate preservative measure. This way alone ensures that the smallest stylistic detail is retained. The aim is not to guard over the antiquarianisation of objects, what is important is the form and a spiritual approach.

Providing a delightful contrast to the surrounding ocean scenery and the somewhat rigorously designed landscape garden at Futami-kan are the blossoming cherry trees, which in spring spread a pale pink glow over the green of the pines and the blue-

time, Japan was able to revise the unequal foreign treaties and adopted a constitution (1889). Within ten years the country became a major power, within 30 years it had an efficient industrial base and within 60 years a world empire.

When Emperor Meiji died in 1912, his son Yoshihito was raised to the throne and ruled under the name Taisho.

The art and architecture of the Meiji period has different faces. On the one hand Western influences were eagerly absorbed, on the other traditional styles were cultivated. Moreover a "hybrid" style of Eastern and Western elements arose. However, the continuation of traditional building styles, for example, cannot be termed "historicism" as in the West because here styles are not adapted but continued within a strict canon of forms thousands of years old. The Imperial Palace built in 1869 in the centre of Tokyo is located on a site comprising 110 ha or some 272 acres, with woods, quiet gardens, small ponds, and is maintained to a scrupulous *shinden* and *shoin* style.

One of Japan's landmarks is the Meiji Jingū Shrine erected in 1920. It is dedicated to Emperor Meiji and Emperoress Dowager Shōken and is a prime example of Shinto architecture. The main hall is the work of famous Japanese architects committed to traditional styles.

1868 brought radical change to Japan which assumed proportions that the country had not seen since the adoption of culture and religion from the mainland in the 6th century.

After a long period of isolation, the closer contacts that Japan now forged with Europe and America after the Meiji Restoration resulted in significant changes in all areas of life, including painting and other arts. Not only the themes treated by painters expanded dramatically – including fields that until

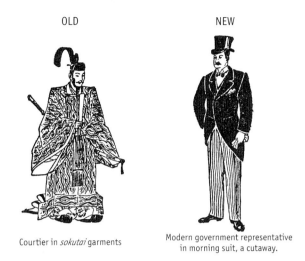

OLD   NEW

Courtier in *sokutai* garments   Modern government representative in morning suit, a cutaway.

that date had not received aesthetic recognition, such as still lifes and nude painting – but also the materials used by artists grew in variety.

The Futami-kan Hinjitsu-kan ryokan is an example of the Meiji period, its architecture and its variety of decorations. Originally, Futami-kan and Hinjitsu-kan were separate buildings, but came under common ownership in 1911. The two establishments were redesigned in 1930 by the well-known Taishō architect Shitarō Ōe. As a result, the rooms of Futami-kan display a harmonious blend of "classical" Japanese architectural forms and Western stylistic elements. Objects from the Meiji and Taisho period have meanwhile become eagerly sought-after collectors' items. Unique in stylistic design, they combine the unsurpassed skills of Japanese craftsmen and artists, that is, traditional techniques, and

Above
The old and the new in Japan
Line drawing from: *We Japanese*, Fujiya Hotel Ltd. (publisher), Miyanoshita, Hakone 1949, p. 295

Right
The *shoin* system
Drawing from: Nishi and Kazuo Hozumi, *What is Japanese Architecture? A survey of traditional Japanese Architecture*, Tokyo 1985, p. 76

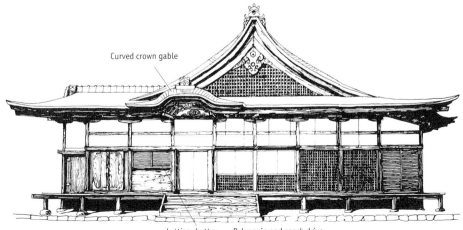

Curved crown gable

Lattice shutter   Palanquin and coach drive

Opposite
Futami-kan Hinjitsu-kan
Ishi-doro, a stone lantern in the garden of
the ryokan.

Above
Futami-kan Hinjitsu-kan
View beyond the interior veranda,
engawa, into the garden. The early 1930s

style rattan furniture blends harmoniously
with the traditional *shoin* design.

Western "perspectives." The "artists of the Imperial Meiji household" were an elite group responsible for great achievements in a broad range of fields, many of which can be admired today in countless museums around the world.

Not only at Futami-kan is the *engawa*, the closed veranda bordering the living room and bedroom, a frequent site for the "East-West composition." While the *futon*, the traditional Japanese bed, is being made, the guests move to the veranda to chat, to watch the moon or for a sake night-cap. However, this is not an interlude on floor cushions but in a Western ambience with chairs and "coffee table." Passed on from the Meiji and Taisho periods, it finally became customary in the thirties of the last century, explaining the design of the furniture today. One is unlikely to find contemporary models but usually typical

European stylistic features from the turn of the century, the 1920s and 1930s, in many cases from Thonet, from Josef Hoffmann, or furniture inspired by the Art Deco movement or by Mies van der Rohe. Now and then, to Western delight and surprise, one comes across an original by the aforementioned designers or at least an object of the period.

Shoin – Formal way of dwelling and life

One of the special treasures the Futami-kan ryokan boasts is the spacious reception room, measuring 120 *tatami* mats. The ceiling of this impressive salon is a special structure called the *kisohiuoki* and is a classic example of Japanese carpenters' art.

Above
Futami-kan Hinjitsu-kan
View of the Imperial living rooms and the decorated sliding doors, the

chōdaigamae, and the *iko*, a stand for garments and decorative fabrics, with a precious brocade, *nishiki*. The rooms have an elaborately lacquered ceiling.

Opposite
Futami-kan Hinjitsu-kan
Brocade, *nishiki*, with aristocratic patterns from the state apartments of Emperor

Taisho (1912–1926), who resided at Ise while undergoing a course of curative treatment.

This coffered ceiling is made using the rare timber of a tree found only on Yakusugi Island. The ceiling of the circumferential corridor has been designed using timbers from an ancient tree on Yakushima Island. A further attraction of the ryokan are the state apartments on the first floor. This where the Taisho Emperor resided during a three-week course of curative treatment. The extremely valuable furnishings include among other things an elaborately lacquered ceiling and a brocade, *nishiki*, with aristocratic patterns. The "Imperial" character of the rooms is recognisable by the fact that they are maintained in a formal *shoin* style. *Shoin* means the former and yet at the same time "modern" residences of the aristocracy.

Shoin developed during the Muromachi period (1338–1573) from the *shinden* architectural style and the *shinden* way of life. Formative elements of the *shoin* style were found in the *kaisho*

halls of the *shinden* residential complexes and in the abbots' quarters, *hōjō*, of the Zen monasteries. The word *shoin* originally meant "study alcove." The residences of abbots' in religious orders often had a bay of the same name, which was used for scholarly discussions or study.

The fixed components of the most important formal room of a *shoin* building are an alcove for the display of art objects, *tokonoma*, with base, *jōdan*, graduated shelves, *chigaidana*, a built-in writing desk with a table function, *tsukeshoin*, and decorated sliding doors, *chōdaigamae*, although not all *shoin* accommodations contain all four features. The *shoin* style is also characterised by the *tatami* mats, which cover the entire floor, as well as by rectangular supporting pillars, some with slightly bevelled edges. Frequently there are coved or coffered ceilings, painted or unpainted sliding doors, *fusuma*, between the interior

Futami-kan Hinjitsu-kan
The ryokan has a impressive reception
room, which measures 120 *tatami* mats.
The ceiling of this colossal salon is a
special structure, a prime example of
Japanese carpenters' art. This coffered
ceiling is made of the rare timber of a tree
which only grows on Yakusugi Island.

Above
Futami-kan Hinjitsu-kan
The *tsukeshoin*, a built-in writing desk,
which functions as a table, in the
reception room on the first floor of
the ryokan.
The "Imperial" character of the room
is illustrated by the standardised *shoin*
style.

Right
Futami-kan Hinjitsu-kan
The graduated arrangement of shelves,
chigaidana, in the large room.

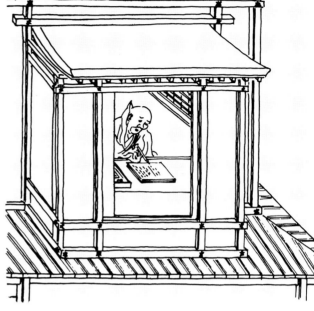

Above left
Sketch from the *e-makimono*, a picture scroll depicting stories, "Kasuga Gongen Miracles" from the 14th century
It can clearly be seen that at this period the graduated arrangement of shelves, *chigaidana*, was already a permanent internal fitting and not a moveable shelving system, as had previously been the case.

Above right
Sketch from the *e-makimono*, a picture scroll depicting stories, "The Picture Biography of the Monk Hō nen" from the late 13th century
One can recognize that at this period the *tsukeshoin*, the writing desk or table, was already common as a delimited place for reading and writing, although not a permanent component of the *tokonoma*.

sections of the room or the buildings, and *shōji*, white, translucent paper screens, strengthened by a wood latticework. They are protected in exterior areas by heavy wooden shutters, *amado*, which are installed at night or by stormy weather.

One can learn most about the continuous development of the four specific elements of *shoin* – embellished alcoves, graduated shelves, built-in writing desk and decorated sliding doors – from old picture scrolls. The earlier (around 1350) "decorative alcoves," in essence a sort of "cultural niche," were long and narrow and not more than two feet or 60 cm deep. Nowadays alcoves in traditional Japanese houses are of much greater depth, about one *tatami* mat deep, amounting to somewhat less than three feet three inches, or less than one meter, being termed also *tokonoma*. The earlier, narrower version is likewise frequently called a *tokonoma*, although using contemporary terminology it would correctly be termed an *oshiita*. To refine the nomenclature further, it must be said that the term *tokonoma* initially represented a whole room, fitted with one alcove. Usually one or more scrolls, with calligraphy or pictures, were hung in the wall recess, in front of which was placed a set of "three objects," *mitsugusoku* – the incense holder, the flower vase and the candle holders. The fourth of the decorative "standardised elements" of the *shoin* style are the graduated shelves. Originally, these shelves

could be removed from the room, by the late 14th century, as the old picture scrolls show, they had become fitted furnishings. The "spatially fixed" writing desk in the alcove, the third *shoin* element, usually juts out onto the veranda and, together with the more frequently used term *tsukeshoin*, is also known as the *idashifuzukue* – table to remove writing things. These "tables" were designed with the *shōji* in mind and attempted to capture as much light as possible. Further and last element of the *shoin* style are the painted sliding doors. Originally, they were the only means of access to an otherwise closed off and secured sleeping area, *chōdai*, meanwhile these doors are used for decoration and are aesthetic objects, likewise the shelves and the built-in writing desk. Together with the "decorative niche," they are part of the standardised qualities of the room in which they are still found today.

Art scene – Japan and the West

Without question, during the Meiji period, Japanese art and culture was subject to dramatic changes, and after initial reservations the government sent Japanese artists overseas to learn about the arts in other parts of the world.

Left
Futami-kan Hinjitsu-kan
kyō dai, a coiffeuse in Western style in the Taisho rooms. The traditional hair-dressing area with veiled mirror is replaced here by a French-inspired model.

Opposite
Eizan Kikukawa (1787–1867)
"Hime Yuujyo," ***Bijin-ga*, pictures of beautiful women**
Painting on silk
49 x 27 ½ in. (126.0 x 69.5 cm),
Nakau Collection, Japan
Eizan was one of the leading artists of the movement called *bijin-ga,* or pictures of beautiful women, and his representations were of seminal influence for the Nihonga School: Japanese motifs, colors and materials, combined with Western stylistic techniques.

Thus Japan learnt about the artistic schools and movements of the West, first and foremost those of France and the Americas. Initially, the concept of creating art for art's sake was registered with amazement because Japanese art had always been guided by religious or decorative aims – but before long the exotic Western, techniques were mastered, and were fused with deeply rooted traditional artistic skills to a new style.

This triggered an intellectual revolution, which polarised into two groups; on the one hand avant-garde protagonists of all things Western, and reactionary traditionalists on the other. The polemics arising offered fertile ground for the development of a lively artistic scene and the unfolding of two new painting styles: Nihonga and Yōga.

The actual meaning of the word Nihonga is "Japanese painting," but in the late 19th century the term was applied to a new kind of painting, which, although it used Japanese-style pigments and materials to paint Japanese themes, had proponents who were completely independent of all restrictions imposed by the established, traditional schools and who openly adopted new ideas from Western paintings to which they now had access.

Building on over 1300 years of experience, Japanese artists continued to excel in the working of wood and metal, though now in a Western style and with a Western sense of realism. Consequently, Western artists, who worked with true Japanese media such as stoneware, also increased their influence on Japanese design. The famous English ceramic artist Bernard Leach (1887–1979) maintained a lively exchange with Japanese artists and had a lasting influence on their work.

In other fields of applied art, as well, such as artistic cabinetmaking, it was not just a question of adaptation but also stylistic implementation. In the same way that the new perspective was received in painting, traditional furniture adopted Western "curves" and dimensions. At the threshold to the 20th century, however, especially in furniture art and also in architecture, influencing ideas tended to move in the opposite direction. Following World War Two, Japanese art liberated itself more and more from the West and the preconditions were created for an autonomous form of expression arising from Japanese tradition and the new "perspectives."

Left
Hanaya
View of *tsutsuji*, or azalea bushes, on the enclosure walls of the ryokan.

花屋

Hanaya, Bessho Onsen

Celebrated warlords and regional significance

The small town of Bessho Onsen grew up in the Heian Period (794-1185) around a collection of thermal springs and experienced its political and cultural heyday during the Kamakura Period (1185-1333) when it was the administrative center of the region. The majority of the temples from this period are National Treasures or National Heritages.

Nearby Ueda has been the capital of Shinano Province since the Nara Period (645-794). The Shida, *hojo* (major-domos) of the Kamakura Shoguns lived here and were instrumental in helping the whole area to flourish. During the Sengoku Period (1481-1573), which was a time of civil war and unrest, Ueda achieved political importance in affairs of state as well as considerable fame. The warlord Sanada Masayuki (1547-1611), who was a famous strategist, succeeded in defending himself against the Togukawa, which in those days in Japan was a real sensation. Ueda Castle, which he built in 1583, is a marvel of fortification and defence planning. It was this castle that withstood two attacks by the Togukawa Hidetada army (1605-1623).

Above
Hanaya
View of the drive to the main building and entrance.
The Hanaya has the architectural qualities of a lowland castle or *hirajiro*. This is the name given to a fortification that does not have a building with several stories tapering towards the top. Although the Hanaya is used as an inn, its architecture bears numerous features peculiar to Japanese castle building.

Opposite
Hanaya
View of the side wing of the main building to the right of the entrance. Striking examples of Japanese castle architecture are the high embrasures with narrow gaps, ideal for archers, and the pure white white-washed exterior walls, producing a stark contrast with the dark roofs, path surfaces and trees.

In the years of the so-called Osaka Winter and Summer Battles that followed, his son Sanada Yukimara (1567-1615) earned himself the nickname Nippon's "First Warrior" because of the vigour of his heroic feats. This legendary feudal lord was a great admirer of Ishiyu, one of the three "open-air pools" with hot springs at Bessho Onsen.

Today Bessho Onsen is still one of Japan's favorite places to go for an outing, not just because of the superb hot springs, but because of the possibility of combining bathing in the water of the thermal springs with indulging in the sport of skiing. The town is in Nagano Prefecture, which is also known as the "roof of Japan," and was the venue of the 1998 Winter Olympics. However, this could hardly be called mass tourism and there are more National Parks and Conservation Areas in Nagano-ken than there are industrial plants. Rich in fish, the clear waters of the river Chikuma flow through the Ueda basin, which is approximately 3850 ft. above sea level, to the Sea of Japan. The climate is relatively mild and the area is to a great extent spared the usual natural disasters of the island, whilst the rainfall is one of the lowest in Japan. In short, the landscape is full of natural beauty and rich in the splendor of flowers.

The Hanaya - an example of Japanese castle architecture

The time-honored ryokan of Hanaya is a reflection of both the history and culture of Bessho Onsen and of the flora around the town: the main house has been constructed in the manner of Japanese castles, surrounded by a sea of azaleas. The cottage-like guest quarters linked by covered wooden passages are situated in the extensive gardens, as are three pools fed by hot springs.

The mighty castles in evidence since the Asuka Period (552-710), but mostly constructed in the late 16th century to underline the power and greatness of the warlords who controlled the armed forces, the economy, politics and even, in many areas, the cultural life, belong to a particular trend in Japanese architecture. After Tokugawa Ieyasus came to power (1603-1605) and peace was restored, considerably fewer castles were built. There are three basic types of castle: *yamajiro* (mountain fortresses), *hirayamajiro* (lowland-mountain fortresses) and *hirajiro* (lowland fortresses). Inside the *honmaru* or keep of a mountain fortress there is always a building with several stories tapering towards the top, called a *tenshu* (watchman of the heavens), forming a pyramid structure that can withstand

Left
Hanaya
Part of the brilliantly constructed walls

surrounding the ryokan, which are completely plain apart from the complicated structure of the tiled roofs.

simplicity and the delightful *shachihoko*, or projecting tiled roofs decorated with curved dolphins, the crowning glory of individual stories and parts of the building.

Light and shade

[…] All common shadows have some color in them, they are never black or almost black. They have a visible radiant quality.
[...] It is a fact that shadows are made up of color, just as clearly as segments of light are.[13]
John Ruskin (1819–1900; freely translated by J. B.)

Japanese design makes considerable artistic use of the visual effects of light and shade. Brightness and shade are the means by which the senses can perceive something solid as floating, freeing buildings and ground from the force of gravity. One simple method is the use of nuanced contrasts, to be found in the case of buildings, for example, in the powerful effect of white surrounding walls or in snow-white woodwork on a fortress of dark stone. A dark roof against a transparent sky has the same effect. Far more refined, however, are the effects of light and shade produced by, for example, overhanging roofs which break solid matter up into many weightless layers. The individual roof sections are

earthquakes. Lowland-mountain fortresses also have buildings with several stories, but without exception they stand on steep walls in the middle of a plain. Lowland fortresses are "flatter," in other words they do not have a tall building in the center.

The Hanaya has the architectural features of a lowland fortress, and although it is used as an inn its structure shows many of the characteristics peculiar to the building of fortresses in Japan: for example, the high embrasures with narrow gaps, ideal for archers, and the otherwise windowless pure white white-washed exterior walls, producing a stark contrast with the dark roofs, path surfaces and trees; also ornate crescent-shaped roof ridges with window openings, and so-called *chi*-turrets, or v-shaped roof gables. Long corridors, or *ro*, link the individual parts of the building to one another.

The aesthetic features of Japanese castle building are what is most fascinating about the Hanaya: the inimitable construction of the enclosure walls with their beguiling separated by deep angles that gather shadows, with the effect of giving the segments the impression of being detached and appearing to sail in the air. Gravity seems to be lifted with surgical precision in the exact place where it appears to the eye to be particularly immovable and solid.

A whole range of openings increases this gliding effect. The system of tunnels, tiny crevices, holes and perforations seems surely to breathe and vibrate with the air, rippling as it were. Every framework, every burden is shaken off. The cascade of rooftops is broken up into individual floating parts, made pliant by the shadows and the overhangs and the roof tiles shimmering so, letting air in through every gap in such a way that the overall impression created is one of beating wings spread out in the air and laden with energy, perhaps the gesture of a bird or some other creature of flight.

The black, white and grey buildings are brightened up in places by the colorful brushstrokes of flowers. The buildings themselves are never painted, nature alone gives them colorfulness and in the gardens nature is reconstructed with great care, as true nature can be lost at any time due to earthquakes, volcanic eruptions, spring tides or typhoons. This is one of the reasons for such a fervent "display of flowers."

The azalea - "floral event" of the early summer

The flower of the town of Ueda, and its emblem, is the azalea, or *tsutsuji* and its flowering represents one of the high spots in the floral calendar of Japan. Admiration and contemplation together with lively celebrations are not reserved solely for the cherry blossom, but are an essential ingredient of Japanese culture, born out of the changing seasons and a great sensitivity towards nature. The azaleas and irises follow the cherry blossom in late spring and early summer. The variety of types of *tsutsuji* is overwhelming and the richness of their colors planned to contrast with the simple architecture and the variations of green found on the island.

With his tale "The mountain azaleas on the top of Mount Gira ," written in 1950, Yashushi Inoue (1907-1991), the doyen

Left
Hanaya
Detail of the covered entrance at evening.
Effects of light and shade are a distinctive and yet subtle feature of Japanese architecture. On the one hand overhanging rooftops cast deep shadows and on the other hand they catch the light on their glazed tiles. An impression of weightlessness is created and solid forms are broken up by this trick supported by nature. At night rice paper lanterns illuminate the thick walls, creating a further contrast and a floating atmosphere.

Above
Hanaya
Roof ridge of the main house with one of the so-called *chi*-turrets, or v-shaped roof gables, crowned with a leaping dolphin.

Above
Hanaya
One of the covered wooden passages in the garden enclosure of the ryokan linking the guest houses with one another and with the main house and the hot springs. The connecting

passages are made of cypress, hiba family and deciduous timbers such as mulberry and paulownia crafted using the best traditional techniques passed down through the years, a teaching model for the balanced combinations of wood seen in Japanese design.

of more recent Japanese literature, has set up a monument to the *tsutsuji* in the West too.

"When I traveled along the Kyoto-Otsu road today the azaleas were blooming in their unique splendor. Maybe the mountain azaleas on top of Mount Hira are also in full bloom. Somewhere on the slopes the white blooms are gleaming. The large white clumps are scattered over the entire mountain. Oh, what deep joy my heart would find if I could lie on the mountaintop among the sweet-smelling flowers. Already the mere idea of lying stretched out up there and gazing at the night sky fills me with happiness. [...] A very long time ago, when I saw the photo with the mountain azaleas, I thought that the day must surely come sometime when I would climb to the top of the mountain. Maybe today is that day. But today I cannot climb to the top, even if I want to." [14]

The Hanaya microcosm

The estate on which the individual guesthouses of the Hanaya are situated covers an area of 25,650 sq. yards. The green areas are laid out as a *tsukiyama* (hilly landscape garden), one of the three traditional garden types in Japan alongside the *kare-sansui* (dry garden) and the *chaniwa* (tea garden). These three basic types have a common feature in that they always follow the *shakkei* principle (the principle of the borrowed scenery). In the course of their training Japanese architects and gardeners learn to design and arrange walls and hedges so that less attractive outlooks are concealed and more pleasing views (for example neighbouring treetops or mountains) are left free. Thus a stay at the Hanaya leads to the belief that one is residing in a self-contained "garden cosmos," with nothing to offend the eye.

The Japanese-style landscape garden shows "natural nature" in miniature by using stones, rocks, bushes, trees, sand and water to recreate hills, ponds and rivers in a landscape scenario that is true to nature.

The beauty of the different seasons is accentuated by the way in which certain plants and flowers "shine forth" when in bloom from the overall image of the garden. In the extensive garden of the Hanaya it is the azaleas above all that bloom in all their glory in early summer, inviting the visitor to contemplate and enjoy the season. The treasured azalea *bon-sai* is an example of how the "miniature standard" of garden plants is lovingly and individually applied to azaleas.

"*Bon-sai*, or potted plants, are dwarfed trees, trained to show the beauty of large normal trees, or of ancient trees. The favorite trees for bonsai are pines (*matsu*), principally of the needle-leaf family, and a species of broad-leaf Mongolian oak (*keyaki*).

[…] Trees also used in bonsai are cryptomeria or Japanese cedar (*sugi*), maple (*momiji*), ground cypress (*hinoki*), cherry (*sakura*), and others. Some trees have two trunks, some a single trunk; sometimes a different species is grafted into the main tree. Some of these dwarfed trees, from one foot up in height, have all the characteristics of normal trees.

The usual method of producing these dwarfed trees is as follows: the main roots of selected seedlings of small trees, not more than 3 to 5 in. in height, are cut away, leaving only the small roots to continue to develop. This procedure is carried out periodically. Weights are hung on the branches in order to make them hang in downward curved forms and the branches are tied with string or wire to form them into artistic shapes. The treatment differs with each tree. The trees are kept in a shaded location. Six to ten years are required to produce a desirable tree. Bonsai for decorative and exhibition purposes are common all over Japan.

Bon-kei are tray landscapes representing in miniature natural scenery by means of stones and sand placed in a

Above
Azalea *bon-sai*
The highly treasured azalea *bon-sai* is an example of how the "miniature standard" is lovingly and individually applied to azaleas.

Below
Hanaya
View of the wooden passages that enable the guest to reach all areas of the ryokan and yet keep his or her feet dry.

Opposite
Plan of the layout of the Hanaya
The estate where the individual cottages are situated covers an area of 25,650 sq. yards. Most of the free standing "cottages" have been built in the teahouse, *shoin* or *sukiya* style. House number 21 is the former residence of a courtesan from the *karyukai* (blossom and willow district) of Niigata, the entertainment area of the prefectural capital in the north of Japan. The tastefully decorated *sukiya* design dates from the Edo period (1615-1868) and was used in the Hanaya park.

Next double page
Hanaya
The landscape gardens seen through the veranda, or *nure-en* of the main house.

Below
Hanaya
Entrance of guest house No. 72, which has its own open air bathing pool, thus enjoying complete privacy nestling amidst the charming scenery.

Above
Hanaya
The green areas of the ryokan are laid out as a *tsukiyama* (landscape garden), one of the three traditional garden types in Japan alongside the *kare-sasnsui* (dry garden) and the *chaniwa* (tea garden). These three basic types have a common feature in that they always follow the *shakkei* principle. In the course of their training Japanese architects and gardeners learn to design and arrange walls and hedges so that less attractive outlooks are concealed and more pleasing views (for example neighboring treetops or mountains) are left free. Thus a stay at the Hanaya leads to the belief that one is residing in a self-contained "garden cosmos," with nothing to offend the eye.

shallow porcelain dish or tray. Sometimes artificial trees and flowers, as well as tiny models of men, animals, houses and other objects are used in the composition, which in this case is called *hako-niwa*.

Sometimes *bon-kei* are designed to depict, in miniature, favorite mountain and seashore views. *Bon-kei* are used as decorative features in many Japanese homes." [15]

At the Hanaya ryokan an irregularly shaped, natural looking pond adds the finishing touch to this prime example of a landscape garden. So that all this can be enjoyed even when the weather is bad there is a system of covered wooden passages linking the guesthouses with one another and with the main house and the hot springs. The connecting passages are made of cypress, hiba family and deciduous timbers such as mulberry and paulownia crafted using the best traditional techniques passed down through the years, a teaching model for the balanced combinations of wood seen in Japanese design. The interiors of the "cottages" and the "castle" are designed and built with the same master craftsmanship. The

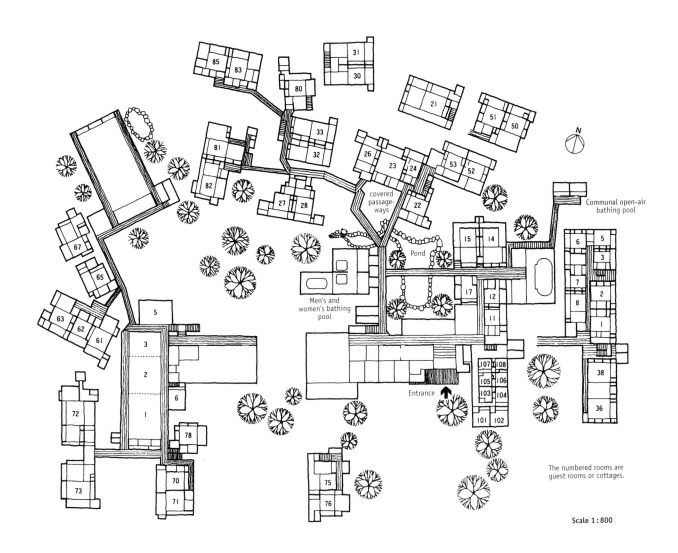

85 83
31
30
80
21
33
51 50
81 32
26 23 24 53 52
82 covered passage-ways 22
Communal open-air bathing pool
27 28
15 14
6 5
Pond 3
67 17 12 7 2
11 8
65
5 107 108
3 105 106 38
63 2 103 104
62 6 101 102 36
61 1
72 Entrance
78 N

Men's and women's bathing pool

The numbered rooms are guest rooms or cottages.

73 70
75 Scale 1 : 800
71 76

soft wood in warm colors is equally a feature of the elegant, yet muted contrast.

Most of the free standing "cottages" are in the teahouse, *shoin* and *sukiya* style. House No. 21 is the former residence of a courtesan from the *karyukai* (blossom and willow district) of Niigata, the entertainment area of the prefectural capital in the north of Japan. The tastefully decorated *sukiya* design dates from the Edo period (1615-1868) and was used in the Hanaya park. In this room one can soak up the atmosphere of the "fast-moving world," which elevated women with *iki* (chic) and men with *tsu* (*savoir faire*) to the status of idols. Another residence, No. 72, has its own open air bathing pool, thus enjoying complete privacy nestling amidst the charming scenery.

"Japanese living rooms are for engaging in contemplation and self-awareness and the conscious use of light and shade plays a role here, too. The overhanging roofs, which are to provide protection from the sun, let only a soft, dimmed light into the interior and create a half-lit area round the corners of the building. The rooms which lie deep inside the building are lit only by transparent shadows and resemble a peaceful, darkened holy room, stimulating both contemplation and quite ordinary concentration. The quality that we call beauty, however, must always grow from the realities of life, and our ancestors, forced to live in dark rooms, presently came to discover beauty in shadows, ultimately to guide shadows towards beauty's ends. And so it has come to be that the beauty of a Japanese room depends on a variation of shadows, heavy shadows against the light shadows – it has nothing else."[16]

Refreshment and a feast for the eyes.

A ryokan is of course not merely a place for quiet meditation and inner reflection; it also enables the guest to enjoy the pleasures of life in various ways and, if there is a hot spring bubbling nearby, there are health benefits, too. Before partaking of the exquisite, sumptuous meal provided the guest puts on the *yūkata* and strolls along to the communal bathing pool. Whether it is in the open air or under a roof, separated according to sex or "mixed," he or she can always expect a pleasurable and invigorating experience. The water temperature must be at least 25 °C and if the water contains precisely specified amounts per gallon of certain minerals a positive effect is ensured. There is a special spring for the slightest touch of gout and for every other ailment, and a bath of this kind is always relaxing.

"Japan is situated in a zone of active volcanoes and is therefore dotted with mineral spas, numbering over two hundred, which attract people from all directions at all times of the year. A hot spring is traditionally considered in Japan to be the best and most efficacious resort for curing a protracted illness. We have a saying to the effect that a disease will prove fatal that is not healed by taking the baths at a hot spring, sometimes five or six times a day, for three cyclic periods of seven days in three consecutive years. The orthodox Japanese, particularly in the rural districts, seem to rely more upon the efficacy of a mineral spring than upon the effect of modern medicine for the cure of a disease, though as a general practice one does not stay at a hot spring more than three weeks at a time, or, as they say, three cyclic periods of seven days.

Regarding mineral springs, there are in Japan 951 hot springs and 155 cold springs of sufficient importance to be listed – and more than 250 of them possess radio-activity. The majority of the springs have valuable medicinal properties.

Because many of these springs are remote from beaten paths, and have poor hotel accommodations, they are unknown to the average tourist, but now a national enterprise proposes to erect modern hotels at some of the springs in order to attract visitors.

These springs are classified as simple cold, thermal, and carbon-dioxated springs, earthy carbon-dioxated and alkaline springs, common salt, bitter, iron carbonated, vitriol, and sulphur springs.

As to radioactivity, our Masutomi cold spring ranks next to the famous water (909 ft. deep) in the Joachimsthal mine in Czechoslovakia (the ore from which produced the radium discovered by Madam Curie), and to that of Bramback, Germany.

Above left
Hanaya
Guest room "lit" by the filtered light of the *shoji* and a ceiling light with a paper lamp shade.
Japanese living rooms are for engaging in contemplation and self-awareness and the conscious use of light and shade

plays a role here too. The overhanging roofs, which are to provide protection from the sun, let only a soft, dimmed light into the interior and create a half-lit area round the corners of the building. The rooms that lie deep inside the building are lit only by transparent shadows.

Above right
Hanaya
One of the corridors or *ro* of the main house, which is modeled on a lowland castle.

Opposite
Hanaya
The mixed open-air pool, or *kon-yoku*,

fed by a hot thermal spring. Bathing in cheerful, uninhibited company – also of both sexes – to relax and cleanse oneself of the strain and stress of everyday life is one of the lasting experiences of staying in a ryokan, and one frequently wishes to return to the Japanese *onsen*.

Our Misasa hot spring ranks next to the Ischia, Italy, spring – the most radio-active hot spring in the world." [17]

Restored, relaxed and hungry the guest returns to his or her room. In the area around Bessho Onsen, country freshness and local specialties bring perfection to *tsukeba* cuisine – it never disappoints. The region's climate makes it ideal for fruit growing. In spring and summer a well-known local delicacy is *ayu*, a type of freshwater fish, which, in keeping with an old custom, is often eaten on the riverbank immediately after it has been caught. In autumn, *matsutake* mushrooms from the Shioda region are the specialty. Various types of whitefish and the familiar *soba* (buckwheat noodles) are also used in the different dishes.

The Japanese kimono

Just as Japanese cuisine is determined by the seasons, so the appearance of the kimono, the traditional Japanese attire, varies according to the time of year. The patterns, colors and choice of material allude to the domain of nature. Plum and cherry blossoms, irises and azaleas do not thrive merely in the landscape gardens, but also "flower" in endless variations on these traditional garments.

The Japanese word *kimono* means "clothing." As early as the Tumulus Period (250-552) the *haniwa* figures had decorative garments with irregular patterns, and the main items of female clothing in these early days were clearly a kind of coat and a shirt called a *kinumo*, or silk garment.

The first classic examples of textiles came to Japan from China via Korea, and during the Nara Period (552-794) the courtly garment revealed considerable Chinese influence and was made of silk brocade or silk gauze. Braided sashes and embroidered silk slippers were favorite accessories.

But fashion, the craft industry and architecture soon took on a Japanese character during the Heian Period (794-1185) that followed. The ordinary folk of the day already wore a simple, relatively short kimono with narrow sleeves. Ladies-in-waiting, on the other hand, were extravagantly clad in a "twelve-layer" kimono that consisted of several costumes worn one on top of the other, in different materials and colors and with splendid trains, and in addition a tightly belted, long pleated shirt.

During the Kamakura Period (1185-1333) courtly garments were also simplified and the many layers were "discarded" until the *kosode*, the former undergarment, eventually made its appearance as a top garment. At the end of this period a type of clothing called a *kosode-hakama* became popular. This was a pair of loose culotte trousers, *hakama*, worn over the *kosode*, which first had a band of cloth wound round it. During the Muromachi Period (1333-1573) the *hakama* disappeared for women, the usual female clothing becoming the *kosode* on its own. The *hakama* continued to be worn by men.

In the years that followed the *kosode* grew less and less reminiscent of an undergarment and evolved into an exquisitely patterned, carefully finished garment, eventually liberating itself to become the item of clothing that is today called a kimono.

Kimonos that have been handed down through the generations are often very costly garments with magnificent embroidery on lengths of silk cloth several yards long and frequently interwoven with metal. Each one of these kimonos is a unique item created with such extravagance that a modern copy would be absolutely unaffordable. The kimonos worn by actors and dancers were particularly striking. A simplified version that follows the old models, gathered at the sides and worn over a simple black undergarment appears nowadays as popular, sensational evening wear.

The kimono found in the room in every ryokan, as well as in most westernized Japanese hotels is, however, an exact copy of the *yūkata*, a cotton Japanese garment cut like a kimono and worn in summer by country folk with blue and white stencilled patterns. From the 16th century onwards the Japanese peasantry had always favored materials made of local plant fibers or cotton. In the hot summer months linen materials made of flax, hemp, or banana shrub fibers and supplied by the southern parts of the country and the Ryukyu Islands were popular with all levels of society. The peasant population of the remote regions wove coarser materials from the durable fibers of the local wisteria and mulberry tree, which also provided the raw material for producing paper.

The *yūkata* has also found many enthusiasts in the West replacing the conventional Western garment, the so-called dressing gown, in the domestic field.

"The 'cute little kimono,' as tourists call them, that the Japanese lass wears are not as simple as they look. Many visitors think that the clothes of Japanese women are not very expensive and base this deduction on the presumption that the *kimono* is 'quite a simple thing.' If they faced a jury of long-suffering Japanese husbands they surely would be sentenced to pay for a few of these 'simple things.'

There are more parts to the Japanese *kimono* than appear on the surface. Leaving aside those undergarments next to the flesh that, it would seem, the lass of every country affects, the first requisite of Japanese dress is a garment very similar to the *kimono*, which is worn under the *kimono*. It reaches from shoulders to ankles. After it has been put on, a wide band of cloth is wound around it, while above its collar is arranged a strip of silk. Her garment material thus far has cost from ¥30 up, inclusive of [*sic*] the undergarments. The cost of silk material for the outer *kimono* of the average woman is from ¥20 up. The long sleeves and the lower part of the *kimono* have to be lined with bright-colored cloth, and the cost has now clicked up another ¥8 or ¥10.

The *kimono*, by the way, is five or more inches longer than is necessary. Consequently, the wearer draws it up carefully until its hem is just level with her heels, arranges a silken cord around her waist and over it smooths down what may be called the 'slack' of the *kimono*. Then comes a very important part of the costume, called the *obi*, a long broad, stiff sash. The *obi* generally is about 4½ yards long and its minimum width is twelve inches. It is very heavy, owing to the thick lining it must have to enable it to retain its stiffness, and, in summer, it is an actual torment to the Japanese girl. The least cost of a decent *obi* is ¥20, but the cost of fine or *maruobi* may run into the thousands of yen [*sic*] because in place of a lining the *obi* material is doubled.

These are the most conspicuous parts of the Japanese woman's costume, but there are a number of minor details. The *obi* must have two cords to hold it in place. One of these, which is worn at the top and drawn through the bow at the back of the *obi*, costs from ¥2 up. Then comes the jewelry of the *obi-dome*, the ornamental front buckle or clasp, which costs up to the thousands of yen.

Thus the *kimono* and its accessories are not as cheap as some think, nor is the *kimono* as simple as it looks." [18]

Japanese Pagoda Architecture

A tour of Bessho Onsen and its romantic surroundings is associated with numerous cultural attractions that have been declared Japanese "National Treasures," because the temples built during the Kamakura Period (1192-1333) have mostly been preserved in their original state – a rare occurrence in Japan. Amongst these are the Taihoji and Zensanji temples. The balanced proportions of the Anrakuji temple's octagonal, three-story pagoda (National Treasure) make it a particularly successful example of Japan's highly developed pagoda architecture. Since Buddhism was introduced, the pagoda, as the symbol of the holy Buddhist realm, has been the central identifying feature of a Japanese temple, similar to the spires of Gothic churches in Europe. Their aspiring dimensions and unique outline are doubtless what has predestined them for this important role. The number of stories in a pagoda varies, as does the artistic form, because due to their unusual position in the temple area the structure has naturally over the centuries moved away from the puristic and become increasingly ornamental. The pagoda serves as a reliquary for holy treasures, such as, for example, relics of the Buddha, which are traditionally kept under the center pillar, called the heart pillar. At the same time the pagoda functions as a symbol for the path of truth and a pointer to the direction of heaven. In his novella *The Five-story Pagoda* written in 1891, Koda Rohan (1867-1947) chooses the pagoda as a simile for the immortality of artistic inspiration.

The archetypal Japanese pagoda is the Indian stupa; the stupa was the only type of reliquary or place of worship that the early Buddhists were allowed to have. Images of the Buddha and larger temples did not evolve until later.

The method of construction of the Japanese pagoda with its wooden skeleton and an overhanging roof on each story has had considerable influence on a distinctive shape that appears in the whole of Japanese architecture. The splendor of Buddhist pagodas and temples is above all a result of the inspired roofs and astutely crafted style, as well as of their carefully worked out construction.

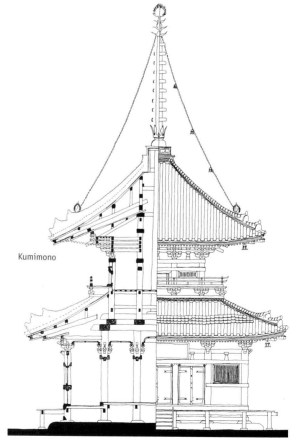

Kumimono

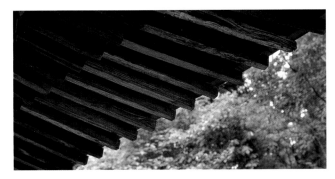

Opposite, left
The octagonal, three-story pagoda (National Treasure) of the Kamakura Period (1192-1333).

Opposite, right
Section and view of a pagoda Shikoku, Japan, 1618.

Above top, above and right
Detail views of the roofs of the Anraku-ji temple pagoda (National Treasure)
The system of consoles and overhangs used in building pagodas is the key to the distinctive quality of its structure and ornamentation, which went through numerous stages of refinement as it developed over many years.

The system of consoles and overhangs used in building a pagoda is the key to the distinctive quality of its structure and ornamentation, which went through numerous stages of refinement as it developed over many years. The Japanese console complex, *kumimono*, or *tokyo*, consists of two basic elements, the load-bearing block, *masu*, and the console arm, the *hijiki*. The load-bearing block is usually cube-shaped or right-angled and bevelled on the underside, on the plinth or *tojiri*. The latter, which is placed directly onto a pillar, is a so-called small block, or *makito*. The load-bearing blocks on the side supports usually have complicated bevelled carvings on the plinth and are logically called demon blocks or *onito*. External support for the console complex is provided by console arms. These are also bevelled at the protruding end and call to mind the shape of a human elbow, *hiji*, hence their name elbow timbers, or *hijiki*.

Although the console constructions in the Great Buddha and Zen styles are as countless as they are varied and very different in shape, the so-called Japanese style is still the starting point for all designs. A simple example of this is the boat-shaped console arm, the *funahijiki*, which directly bears the load of the beam lying on top of it, in contrast to the highly developed *demitsudo*, the protruding triple block. More and more layers are added to the console arms so that they can carry increasingly heavy loads. They divide into branches, are sometimes simply painted white, and sometimes in many colors, richly decorated and a masterpiece of style created by Japanese carpenters. As console arm construction became ever more elaborate, decorative wooden parts also appeared that were not necessary either from a structural or an aesthetic point of view, but were designed rather as a sort of puzzle. So the pagoda is in every respect a miracle of carpentry and joinery, for, although all the wooden parts are fitted together without the use of nails, it was possible to take into account the loads and stresses which might occur due to the weight of the roof, the changeable weather and the frequent earthquakes. The graceful shapes and curved lines of the pagodas blend into the surrounding landscape of pine forests, distant ranges of hills and endless sky.

In the classical (10th-12th centuries) and the medieval (13th-16th centuries) periods in particular, religious architecture took on a leading role in the introduction of pioneering construction features that were hitherto unknown.

石田屋

Opposite
Ishidaya
Porcelain plate with iris motif in the
kakiemon ware style, in front of a window
with a decorative bamboo latticework.

Ishidaya, Yatsu

The iris

"Japanese art turned to nature. It taught methods that perceive and express the most subtle changes in nature as the seasons change. The beauty of the object remains hidden to the mind researching analytically. Beauty reveals itself in the feeling that connects the heart and the object." [19]

The iris is one of the most beautiful and most frequently varied motifs in Japanese pictures and its representations have also had a lasting influence on art in the West. The theme is an expression of the Japanese affinity for nature and a notable synthesis of perception, life and the object.

The extraordinary iris garden at Ishidaya is reserved for the inn guests and delights the appreciation the Japanese have for nature with 250 different types of iris - a mythical member of the lily family. Enjoying the beauty and endless variation in

colors and the abundance of flowers is one the essential experiences when lodging at this noble ryokan. The Japanese iris has been cultured over a long period of time from the *Iris ensata*, a robust waterside plant which is native to large parts of Asia. Many years of selective breeding were necessary to perfect this special kind of iris whose striking bloom is balanced by the sword-shaped foliage; a highlight in summer in contrast to the calm surface of a leisurely flowing watercourse or the still waters of a pond. Especially delightful kinds are: *kozasagawa*, *nemuri-jishi*, *chiyo-no-haru*, *miyoshino* and *haru-no-umi*. As a further natural spectacle, Ishidaya offers an apricot garden which is in full bloom at the end of January. 200 trees yield fruit in June for the delicious, home-made pickled apricots and a house distilled, invigorating apricot brandy.

"The Japanese floral calendar. Each month of the year has its favorite flower or tree, their blooming seasons varying a little according to latitude and location in Japan's long stretch from north to south. January, the pine [and adnis]; February, plum; March, the peach and the pear; April, cherry; May, azalea, the peony, and wistaria; June, iris; July, morning glory; August, lotus [and lespedezea]; September has the 'seven grasses of Autumn'; October, the chrysanthemum [and narcissus]; November, the maples; and December, the camellia [and hibiscus]. The 'seven grasses' are the *hagi* (bush, or Japanese clover), *susuki* (pampas grass), *kuzu* (arrow-root), *nadeshiko* (wild carnation), *ominaeshi* (maiden flower), *fujibakama* (Chinese agrimony), and *hirugao* (convulvus – wild morning-glory)." [20]

Light and shadow - The pale glow of the *shōji*

The Ishidaya ryokan and its hot springs date from 1873. The complex comprises 14 separate cottages, each with two private baths, one covered, one in the open air. The architecture of the free-standing guest houses is a guide in itself to traditional Japanese construction styles, the interiors are largely a composition of the tea house and *sukiya* styles.

Left
Ishidaya
Iris in flower, *fujishiro*, one of the 250 different kinds of iris which can be admired in the garden of the ryokan.

Opposite
Ishidaya
The *tokonoma* in the *Shouba-an* (Iris Cottage) guest room. The supporting pillars have unfinished, non-bevelled edges, *menkawabashira*, and the *tokonoma* is a so-called *murodoko* where the back pillar is concealed.

All aspects of the rooms reflect rusticity and simultaneously refinement in the calculated use of the natural materials and the articulation of their inherent beauty and quality. The basic elements of the *sukiya* style tea house, such as the *tokonoma* with *jōdan* (alcoves), the *shoin* or *tsukeshoin* (built-in writing desk, functioning as a table), the *tana* or *chigaidana* (built-in shelves) and the *tatami* floor covering, are rounded off by an anteroom for the tea preparations, *katte*, and the *ro*, a type of hearth where the water for the tea ceremony simmers.

The supporting pillars have unfinished, non-bevelled edges, *menkawabashira*, and the *tokonoma* is in principle a so-called *murodoko* – a *tokonoma* where the rear pillar is concealed. All buildings and the furnishing of the rooms in the Ishidaya inn are characterised by a plain simplicity and puristic elegance. The textures of the wood and the plaster have been left in their original beauty as complementary elements to nature. The only decorations are delicately

Above
Ishidaya
Elaborate open-work in a wooden panel with rice paper background.

Opposite
Ishidaya
View from a cottage into the garden. To transform the view from the veranda of a temple or a residential dwelling into an object of meditation, the vague brightness must give way to a centered force field, requiring a frame. The segment of an opened *shōji* not only fixes the scene in an atmospheric, silhouette-like picture, but blends the diffuse view into a neutral background.

Left
Ishidaya
shōji in a guest room. "But for me the most exquisite touch [in the Japanese house] is the pale white glow of the *shōji* in the study bay; I need only pass before it, and I forget the passage of time." (Jun'ichiō Tanizaki)

structured segments such as latticework, trelliswork and small or round *shōji* windows with fragile patterns, *shitajimado*. Exquisite are the paintings, the flower arrangements (*ike-bana*), the dinner services, the picture (*kakemono*) and the calligraphy scrolls (*shō*) – in June always decorated with iris themes.

"The light from the pale white paper, powerless to dispel the heavy darkness of the alcove, is instead repelled by the darkness, creating a world of confusion where dark and light are indistinguishable. Have not you yourselves sensed a difference in the light that suffuses such a room, a rare tranquility not found in ordinary light? Have you never felt a sort of fear in the face of the ageless, a fear that in that room you might lose all consciousness of the passage of time, that untold years might pass and upon emerging you should find you had grown old and gray?" [21]

The transparency of the smaller paper windows, round or rectangular *shitajimado*, is increased unobtrusively by subtly projected shadows on the surface of the rear side. The latticework of thin reed, branches or bamboo casts finely spread, narrow lines on to the soft, snow-white paper, whose fibrous consistency clouds the picture somewhat more and so generates a type of strange liquefaction and monochrome blurring which is peculiar to water color paintings. Associations are formed with the photograms of László Moholy-Nagy (1895-1946) or comparisons arise with Man Ray's rayographs (1890-1976). The influence of Japanese "light paintings" upon the photographers Edward Steichen (1879-1973) and Arnold Genthe (1869-1942) cannot be underestimated. Inside a dimly illuminated room, the *shitajimado* form a kind of "shadow box."

During overcast weather on a densely wooded group of islands such as Japan the sunbeams are broken, an optical medium which makes everything appear soft and peaceful and which immerses the surroundings in an indirectly illuminated grey or white. At dawn the water-rich mantle of air changes the light into a pale, slightly glittering mother-of-pearl. To transform the hazy scenery from the veranda of a temple or a residential dwelling into an object of meditation, the vague brightness must give way to a centered force field, requiring framing. Openings in the trimmed foliage, the counterpoint of a white wall and the segment of an opened *shōji* not only fix the scene in an atmospheric, silhouette-like picture, but blend the diffuse view into a neutral background.

Preceding double page
Ishidaya
The guest cottage Amagi-Sanbou (cottage on Amagi Mountain). The interior is mostly a composition of the tea house and the *sukiya* styles. All aspects of the rooms reflect rusticity and simultaneously refinement in the calculated use of the natural materials and the articulation of their inherent beauty and quality. The basic elements of the *sukiya* style tea house, such as the *tokonoma* with *jōdan* (built-in decorative alcoves), the *shoin* or *tsukeshoin* (built-in writing desk, functioning as a table), the *tana* or *chigaidana* (built-in shelves) and the *tatami* floor covering, are rounded off by an anteroom for the tea preparations, *katte*, and the *ro*, a type of hearth where the water for the tea ceremony simmers.

Opposite
Utagawa Toyokuni
(1769-1825; active 1788-1824)
Woman with goldfish bowl
Ukiyo painting
approx. 67 x 19 in. (171.0 x 49.0 cm)
Nakau Collection, Japan

Left
Ishidaya
Kyodai (Japanese coiffeuse) with veiled mirror in a guest room in front of the *shitajimado*, a delicately patterned rectangular or round *shōji* window.

Nature worship and decoration on a "small" scale - goldfish and fans

To view, record and worship nature in all its guises in "excerpts" is a genuine form of Japanese art. The *ukiyo* painting "Woman with goldfish bowl" by Utagawa Toyokuni (active 1788-1824) clearly and artistically combines in one the different components of the admiration for nature. A young woman, balancing her iris-decorated fan, scrutinises devotedly a goldfish in its aquarium. Japan sees itself as the home of the *kingyo* (goldfish), and breeding goldfish and their popularity have here reached an intensity unknown elsewhere. Owing to their elegant silhouette and bright range of colors, goldfish are kept and improved by enthusiasts and businessmen alike and depending on the species and their appearance they change hands for astronomical prices. Competitions and auctions are held and there is not a temple, palace or domestic garden to be found that does not boast goldfish in a stretch of water or container. There are veritable libraries concerning the care and rearing of the fish, and when one takes a closer look at its decadent life, the lavish care and attention these "masterpieces" enjoy, reincarnation as a goldfish would appear a tempting option.

The *uchiwa* (round, non-folding fan) carried by the woman in the picture and the *ogi*, *sensu* or *suyehiro* (folding fans) are also an original Japanese attribute. While the *uchiwa* came from China to Japan, the *ogi* took the reverse route as it is purely a Japanese invention, attributed to a lady aristocrat, the widow of the youthful hero Atsumori. In the Mieido Temple in Kyoto where she stayed as a nun after the premature death of her spouse, she is supposed to have saved the life of a devout priest. With a folded piece of paper, she fanned the air to create a cool draught and prayed for him. Until this day, many stores specialising in fans have the name "Mieido." However, the Japanese fan was traditionally used less for cooling purposes and more for concealing the face of an aristocratic lady and therefore was frequently adorned with small calligraphy or painted artworks. If the decoration is the work of a well-known master craftsman, the paper or silk is removed from the bamboo ribs and framed as a picture.

The art of the "natural segment" knows no scale because every object and every existence contains the absolute, there is no "magnitude" or levels of dignity, whether in artistic or philosophical thought. Thus the iris motif is found reduced in size, but never debased, on a fan or a delicate sake cup and enlarged, though never monumentalised, on space-filling screens, *byōbu*, and *fusuma*, sliding doors.

The rhythmic composition of the isolated clumps of iris on a golden background draws its tension from the empty spaces between the diagonals of the virtually floating structure of the plants in powerful ultramarine blue and green on gold. The theme relates to a sequence from the Tales of Ise, the "Eight Plank Bridge" or "Yatsuhashi." Neither the figures nor the famous bridge are shown, leaving only the irises as a symbolic representation of the theme. This handling of the content distinguishes Korin both as a master of decorative style as well as a philosopher with the ability to represent the essence. The style and signature of the screens show that the artist must have painted the work when he was 45 or 46 years old.

Japanese screens - The "gilded" plant world

"Perhaps [Kōrin's] most famous work is the pair of six-panel screens that are displayed every May to June at the Nezu Museum in Tokyo, showing clumps of irises on a background of gold leaf. Kōrin used no outline to define the shapes of the plants and just painted the color directly on the paper: a flat green for the leaves and two shades of blue to give a certain three-dimensional effect for the flowers. At first sight, and especially in low lighting, the effect is one of seeing a silhouette of the forms against the glowing gold background, with the clumps of lowers forming an almost musical composition. The screens are always displayed as they would have been on the *tatami*-covered floor of a 17th century palace, standing in a zigzag with a 90-degree angle between the panels. The musical analogy can be carried further when one looks at the screens from either side; it is always a surprise to notice that the composition is still just as coherent and interesting when, viewed from this angle, only three panels can be seen from each screen.

[...] Screen paintings are essentially movable, folding walls, and were used to delineate space and create a special atmosphere for some household activity. For example, a pair of screens with paintings on a seasonal theme might be brought out to create a more intimate area in a large room, and to provide a dramatic background for entertaining and impressing visitors. They were made of paper pasted on a lattice-like wooden frame, with the painted front usually bordered with brocade, and the whole arrangement framed with a thin wooden strip that was finished with red or black lacquer. Usually screens were constructed with two or six panels (although occasional examples are seen with four or eight), which are hinged so that the screen can stand in a zigzag shape and also be folded flat for storage. Six-panel screens are almost always made in pairs with some contiguity in the design or painting. A pair of screens with paintings of landscapes for

Right
Katsushika Hokusai
(1760-1849; active 1779-1849)
Iris and meadow cicada
1832,
Nishiki-e,
color woodblock print
Yoko-o'ban-Format 10 ½ x 15 in (26.5 x 38.2 cm),
Hiraki-Ukiyo-e Museum, Yokohama

Right
Vincent van Gogh (1853-1890)
Irises
1889
Oil on canvas
approx. 30 x 36 ½ in. (71 x 93 cm)
Joan Whitney Payson Gallery of Art,
Westbrook College, Portland/Maine
Japanese color woodblock prints,
ukiyo-e (pictures of the floating
world), offer a compendium of "iris
reproductions" and, thanks to
Vincent van Gogh's famous iris
painting, have also helped this
picture motif to great popularity in
the West.

example, will usually depict different seasons but in viewing from right to left the composition moves from foreground to distance on one screen, and back from distance to foreground on the other. [...]

[G]old leaf was often applied for decorative effect – especially in screen paintings, where it was valued for the remarkable quality it has of picking up light from the weakest of sources and of gleaming magically in the deep shadows of rooms lit by candle or lamp." [22]

Japan and the West

Japanese color woodblock prints, *ukiyo-e* (pictures of the floating world), offer a compendium of "iris reproductions" and, thanks to Vincent van Gogh's famous iris painting, have also helped this picture motif to great popularity in the West; the most expensive painting ever auctioned is that of the irises by this ultimate exponent of the postimpressionist period.

The suggestive power Japanese culture had on Western culture at the turn of the last century is genuine and has countless facets. An eclectic range of perspectives comes to light: asymmetrical compositions, new motifs from nature

and society, respect for the void, that is, "love of the infinite" instead of "horror vacui" and the singular beauty of the line. In 1890, at the École des Beaux-Arts, as Samuel Bing presented 725 Japanese reproductions and 428 illustrated books and thus attracted artists from all over Europe, Japan as a model changed from being a source of inspiration for solitary painters to being the leitmotif for a whole generation of artists. The first recognition of Japanese art coincided with the World Expositions. "Japanese art is important as a teacher. With it, we learn for the first time clearly to recognize how far we have departed from the real models of organic nature through a continuous tradition of inherited form and through continuous imitation of fixed models; how necessary it is to again draw from the source; what a wealth of naive, exquisite beauty the human spirit is able to take in from organic nature instead of the pedantic decrepitude of a rigid adherence to forms." [23] As evidenced by the writings of Julius Lessing, it was not a bizarre or an exotic effect but the recognition that naturalness and directness had been "smothered" intellectually in Europe.

In his essay "Ver Sacrum" in 1899, Ernst Schur couples Europe's "art of the brain" with Japan's "art of the nerve." [24] The reception of Japanese art was not just one of perspective, it

also guided to depths of feeling and poetic inspiration. The passionate work produced by van Gogh – heroes of the classical modern period – was triggered by his acquaintance with Japanese color woodblock prints. In 1887 he wrote from the South of France to his brother Theo, "Here, my life is becoming more and more like that of a Japanese painter." [25] The natural light of the pale colors, the lines and dots resonant with rhythm, the intensified expressiveness of simplifying outlines and the embracing of decorative areas on the focal plane were what enraptured him about the *ukyio-e*.

Even Cézanne, stubbornly against the "Japan Trend," did not remain indifferent. Behind his crystalline homages to the Mont Sainte-Victoire, appears from afar, the influence of Hokusai's equally praised *fuji* series. The list of the painters directly or indirectly influenced by *ukiyo-e* reads like a "hit parade" of art between 1860 and 1910: Pissarro, Monet, van Gogh, Gauguin, Seurat, Signac, Redon, Ensor, Munch, Hodler, Toulouse-Lautrec, Bonnard, Vallotton, Vuillard, Beardsley, Klimt, Matisse and all those who have entered the halls of fame of art history. The turn to pure surface areas, the movement away to the edges, were not solely phenomena limited to the graphic arts in the Jugendstil or Art Nouveau movement, furnished space was also influenced. The consideration of the function, the material properties and the work process – features of Japanese handicraft – became the archetype for the design of object art around 1900. The vital style adopted by the Arts and Crafts Movement in England spread across the entire continent as a design revolution. The Jugendstil and Art Noveau movement also sought to eliminate the difference between "base, applied" and "higher, free" art; the Japanese craft industry offered a paradigm for this equal status. "What we want is that what the Japanese have always done," [26] explained Josef Hoffman in the working program of the Wiener Werkstätte. There was not a master craft studio at the turn of the last century, whether Gallé, Lalique or Tiffany, which did not implement its own image of Japan, likewise the ascendancy of book art and lithography would not have been possible without the spontaneousness of Japanese graphical art. The immediacy of the heart is a Zen principle and it replaces all forms of dogmatism, and this is probably where the relationship is furthest reaching, largely defying description – in an aesthetic lifestyle. "A Zen artwork also has no meaning, it simply exists. Form is emptiness. Emptiness is nothing but form. The circle is emptiness and fullness. The objects and the emptiness between them have the same status." [27] Zen teachings have also figured prominently in Western architecture. Frank

Opposite
Ishidaya
The iris garden at Ishidaya with a view of the tea pavilion. Against an evergreen background of plants and trees, the garden is blossoming into its full seasonal splendor in an almost artistic manner.

Above
Ishidaya
Tsukubai, a stone water basin in the landscape garden at Ishidaya. The natural basin, formed from a foundling, has a water pipe made of bamboo cane. On the edge of the basin rests the wooden ladle, traditionally used to clean one's mouth before the tea ceremony or a prayer.

Lloyd Wright and Josef Hoffmann have realised a free flowing mobility between interior and exterior space by means of a design that was compatible with the materials used. The receptiveness of the painters, craftsmen, designers, artist-architects and architects for vital forms and motifs, not least since Ruskin, derived from the yearning for a new spirituality through attachment to external and inner nature to counteract the life-threatening implications of a growing industrialisation. The Englishman John Ruskin (1819-1900) initiated the Aesthetic Movement which championed the artistic value of work by craftsmen contra the banal decorative forms of mass-produced arts which were considered profoundly disturbing.

The synthesis of garden, cult and living area

"Japanese art turned to nature. It acquired methods for perceiving and expressing the most subtle changes of nature as the seasons change." [28] On the one hand, the change of seasons is "put in the picture," on the other hand imitated with the same precision in the artificial nature of the garden. In front of an evergreen background of plants and trees, the seasons blossom into their full magnificence in a virtually artistic manner. Necessary additions, or those arising out of tradition, such as fences, gates, lanterns, *ishi-doro*, and water basins, *tsukubai*, are integral parts of the environment in both material and form.

"What a wealth of naive, exquisite beauty the human spirit is able to take in from organic nature instead of the pedantic decrepitude of a rigid adherence to forms." [29] The "organic" structures in the Japanese garden, likewise in modern buildings, include water. In the traditional garden it is found in all possible forms: calm, large ponds, short river courses, miniature waterfalls, water basins, *tsukubai*, to name just a small selection. In many multi-story buildings water plunges, tamed in channels, through the stairwell or floods a decorative wall; in modern Japan too, the babble and splashing of water is omnipresent in place and time. Water is one of the main elements of the Japanese archipelago and therefore also one of the revered "natural

Opposite
Ishidaya
One of the 14 *hanare*, the guest cottages, in the ryokan's spacious landscape garden.

Above
Ishidaya
A goldfish pond in the landscape garden with the valuable and adored *kingyo*, which are well-fed, lively dabs of color in Japan's numerous ponds and calm waters.

spirits," but also a point of focus for meditation, imparting calmness, contemplation and reverence. As an artificial manipulation it is used to create reflections, and the changing and often monotonous sounds of running water are a further source of contemplation.

The impressive guest houses located in the spacious garden at the Ishidaya inn are free-standing Japanese "homes," connected by covered passages. A study by the European Community a few years ago published the stunning and simultaneously defamatory result that the Japanese live in "rabbit hutches." As is always the case in such studies, the limited horizons of the indigenous yardstick are applied. Quite amazing: a Japanese family of four is satisfied to live cheerfully in a dwelling comprising 40 m² or 430 sq. feet, while the minimum area for four persons in Europe is 100 m² or 1076 sq.

feet. Conclusion: less than 100 m² for a family is comparable to animal husbandry. Or could we not counter here with the question: do we waste space? How do the similarly highly industrialised "Prussians of the East" thrive in such a small amount of living space? Obviously, the study overlooked that the volume of space depends decisively on the structural design and the organization of the architecture and moreover is crucially affected by cultural tradition. To illustrate these aspects there is no better example than the Japanese dwelling house and its various embodiments. The architectural inheritance in Japan developed under entirely different cultural and geographical conditions than in the West. Even today many Japanese hold on to a traditional lifestyle because it is at one with religion and customs. The contemporary Japanese dwelling house remains a Shinto or Buddhist building in terms of structure. Furniture plays a very subsidiary role because a shrine or temple simply does not have any furniture, and a dwelling minimalism developed from the frugal needs of the monks. Conversely, the West should perhaps also ask itself whether all the "artefacts" that clutter up Western residences really add to home comforts.

Different countries have different customs (2): "A Japanese house has hardly any furniture to speak of. Stoves, fireplaces, and stair-rails are conspicuous by their absence. Doors do not open, they slide in grooves. Doors inside the house are never locked, the rooms being intercommunicating, more or less.

Japanese pack away their pictures, curios, and ornaments, and have as little as possible in their rooms, in contrast to the Western custom. Pictures are hung in a certain order. The principal, and usually the only one in a room, is the *kakemono* or scroll picture, hung in the *tokonoma*, or alcove (the holy of holies), in the best room. Ideographs hold the first rank, then black and white pictures, lastly colored pictures. These are changed according to the season and they conform with fixed aesthetic rules. This order is in contrast to the Western way of hanging pictures wherever they will go, often with little artistic consideration." [30]

The Ishidaya guest houses provide the perfect study of the variety of *minka* (literally houses of the population): thatched roofs, high gabled roofs with half-timbering, hipped roofs, U-shaped roofs, stepped roofs, with wooden shingles or tiles. The living rooms show the *shoin* and *sukiya* styles, which were adopted by large swaths of the population at any early age. The traditional decorations used at Ishidaya and the harmonious balance of accessories changes with the seasons. The visitor is certain to come across a variety of atmospheres each time he or she lodges at a ryokan.

A classic architectural component of the Japanese lifestyle is the *onsen*, the hot bath, which refreshes the senses, lifts the spirits and promotes health and hygiene. The Ishidaya inn has its own thermal spring which supplies more than 33 gallons or 150 liters of hot water a minute at a temperature of 98°C. The water bubbles into the private inside baths, which are made of cypress wood, into the various outside baths, which are maintained in a "landscape style," and into the perfectly arranged common baths. The salina (thermal spring containing native salt) alleviates many aliments and in particular neuralgia, rheumatism and female complaints.

Refreshed and equipped with an umbrella, the guest can now take an evening stroll.

Kasa - The Japanese umbrella

"Japanese umbrellas are always of interest to foreign visitors, so
different are they from their western cousins – which the
Japanese call *komori-gasa* or 'batlike umbrellas.' *Kasa* are made
of bamboo and oiled paper or silk and are decorated with
painted designs, which vary. Many mercantile houses, inns, etc.
provide *kasa*, called *bangasa*, for the convenience of their
customers. These have the name of the house or their trade-
mark painted on them.

[...] The ribs of *kasa* are made of split bamboo, and a
circular piece of wood into which they are gathered at the top
allows the *kasa* to be opened and shut freely. Waterproof paper
or silk is stretched over the frame and a bamboo handle is
attached. They are made usually in shops which also
manufacture paper lanterns.

Kasa include umbrellas for rain (*ama-gasa*) and those for protection against the heat of the sun (*higasa*) – parasol-like *kasa*, lighter than the *ama-gasa*.

Kasa are heavier than the western umbrellas and are not so handy to carry about – when closed they are carried handle down by means of a ring or loop at the top.

[…] The standard size for men's use is about 20 in. in size with 40 to 50 ribs; for women, about 21 in., with 40 ribs. The oldest historical record of *kasa* is that during the reign of Emperor Kimmei, 539-71, when the King of Kudara, an ancient Korean province, sent, among other things, 'several gorgeous *kasa*' to the Japanese Emperor as tribute. Prior to that time large rush hats were used in place of *kasa*." [31]

The synthesis of the arts that Ishidaya represents is rounded off by the choice *kaiseki* seasonal cuisine which, depending on the season, spoils the guest with all the delicacies Japan has to offer, and in particular seafood. The synaesthetic experience is made complete by the exquisite dinner service which boasts a gamut of colors in early summer borrowed from the iris and whose ornamental decoration represents the original forms of the blossom in its countless variations. Caressed by the fragrance of the irises, given to the *audition colorée* of the iris fields and listening to the calming babbling of the water, all sensory impressions blend at an elevated aesthetic level to an indelible perceptual experience.

伊豆谷津温泉　石田屋

Left
Ishidaya
The synthesis of the arts that Ishidaya
represents is rounded off by the choice
kaiseki seasonal cuisine, *shun*, which,
depending on the season, spoils the
guest with all the delicacies Japan has to
offer, and in particular seafood.

Above
The Bay of Amanohashidate
The ryokan is situated on the pine-covered promontory called Amanohashidate (bridge of heaven), one of the "three most beautiful views" in Japan. The "bridge in heaven" is a 2¼-mile long sandbank, between 130 and 330 feet wide, on which the "exalted pine tree" flourishes in a particularly impressive manner.

松露亭

Shouro-tei, Amanohashidate

The pine tree lives for a thousand years,
The gentle breeze of morning only a day.
Yet both fulfil their destiny.

Zen poem, anonymous [freely translated by J. B.]

Natura Naturans

Leaving aside any religious theories based on analysis or speculation, it was without doubt from time immemorial a dynamic faith that dominated, and at the same time unified, the Japanese national subconscious. A creed completely in accord with a nature that manifests itself as divinely all-embracing – in trees, in every organic form of life, in the soil and in the natural phenomena of birth, growth and decay.

The island kingdom of Japan is often described as a land of forests and trees. The intense feelings held by the inhabitants for trees, wood and plants, and their inner affinity with them, are not only legendary but also part of everyday experience, as

is seen from the local saying "plants and trees all have something to tell us." The Japanese believe that nature is inhabited by spirits, and they see *kami* divine beings of nature in the trees. Trees are at the heart of the Japanese people's sensibility towards nature and so it is not surprising that the indigenous architecture is based on construction methods using timber. Architecture is also another way of glorifying nature and holding on to its beauty and strength. The way in which a bunch of pine needles is attached to a branch, how this branch stands in relation to the proportions of the tree, how its roots support it, all this shows the simplicity and at the same time the elegant proportions of nature through the analogy of a pine tree.

"The real beauty of the pine tree can be seen only in Japan. In other countries, however large the trees may grow, shapely ones are very rare. Not a few pine trees in Japan are over 800 years old. During a long period of time the climate and other natural causes have combined to form the picturesque pine tree. Especially has this been the case with trees not growing in forests but standing alone, probably because their branches have been bent by the winter winds and thus formed into artistic shapes.

Pine trees are always to be found in Japanese gardens. A very special art is required in the shaping of these trees. In late spring a gardener climbs the tree and trims the young sprouts by picking off the imperfect sprouts and allowing the tree to concentrate its nutriment on the perfect sprouts. From five to seven years are given these sprouts to grow into graceful shapes. While still very young the tree is formed into a desired shape by means of a system of strings or wires. The 'Sailboat' at the Kinkakuji Temple, Kyōto, is a good example of the artificially shaped trees. It is made out of one pine tree and about a hundred years is supposed to have been spent in its making. When the tree was young a branch was bent into shape by means of strings and left for several years in that condition. The branch formed the hull of a boat. Then the central trunk was allowed to grow and was formed into the sail of the boat. Seventy or eighty years were needed for this operation. It is presumed that at present the tree is about four hundred years old. 'Hair dressing,' or trimming, has been practised on the tree every spring during these four hundred years." [32]

The Shouro-tei ryokan is situated on the pine-covered promontory called Amanohashidate (bridge of heaven), one of the "Three most beautiful views " in Japan. The other two are the "swimming" *torii* on the island of Miyajima and the Bay of Matsushima with its islands overgrown with pine trees. The "bridge in heaven" is a 2 ¼-mile long sandbank, between 130 and 330 feet wide, on which the "exalted pine tree" flourishes in a particularly impressive manner.

Opposite
Shouro-tei
View of the façade with the entrance to the ryokan surrounded by massive pine trees. Very restrained and intentionally unadorned, the building fits in with the austere coastal landscape. The bamboo fence, the stonework plastered with clay, the cane work and woodwork and the grey glazed tiles of the roof are as it were a structured repetition and extension of surrounding nature, without diminishing it in any way.

Below
Shouro-tei
The reception room in the ryokan with "Western" seating, where the welcoming tea is served. The art of making and drinking tea is inextricably associated with mental discipline, physical control and aesthetic sensibility. The bare tea cottage with its rough walls and open ceilings contributed greatly to a precept of rustic simplicity, which is found again in a different form in *sukiya* houses.

Opposite
Shouro-tei
Garden seating: the stools and table are
made of ceramics glazed in natural colors
and are placed on a bed of gravel with a
bamboo border, thus furnishing a perfect

example of the creation of decorative
items using natural materials and relying
on composition and shades of color rather
than on colors and effects.

Above
Utagawa Hiroshige
(1797–1858; active approx. 1818–1858)
**The 53 stations of the Tōkaidō,
40th station, the horse market**

around Tenpō 4–5 (1833/1834),
Nishiki-e, multicolored woodcut,
Yoko-ō̄ban format, 10 x 15 in., (detail),
Publisher: Takeuchi Magohachi

The promontory closes off Miyazu Bay, forming the charming Aso Lagoon. According to a long-established custom, the visitor must turn his back to the spit of land and bend down to look through his legs and enjoy one of the finest views in Japan.

You can also enjoy a wonderful, romantic outlook from the Shouro-tei, which is situated right by the sea, without having to perform any gymnastics, as the gardens were created according to the *shakkei* principle of the "borrowed" scenery and mercifully conceal some ugly sights such as more recent hotel bunkers. The special significance of the pine tree is also clear in the choice of the "three most beautiful views" in Japan, for two of them were selected because of their magnificent pine trees.

Architecture and anthropology

The ideology of nature and wood is continued in the buildings "borrowed" from nature, in which natural materials are used in perfect harmony so that nature is as it were reconstructed. This has been achieved in the most diverse ways, from the impressive structural engineering designs of the castles through the magnificent *shoin* rooms right down to the almost spartan tea houses. The basic principles are always the same, nature

and ritual, as the physical details are determined less by practical and economic requirements than by ritualistic requirements, etiquette and an extremely disciplined way of life. The simple design of the tea-room is therefore in harmony with a premise that can be described as a natural law. Timber is largely left in its natural state as a block or as bark, the walls consist of a mixture of aluminium oxide and straw; everything is without facing or embellishment, any "decoration" is provided by the grain, the unevenness and the knotholes in the wood, the rough surfaces of the walls and the combination of materials from various natural products such as straw, bamboo, linen, wicker, and various timbers, mainly Japanese cedar, chestnut and pine. This purism also serves ceremonial purposes: the few objects – the picture scroll, the flower arrangement and the tea utensils – are more striking against the "natural" background of the rooms.

The four forces, namely society, ritual, religion and art, were bound together into one completely worldly everyday action, which created the unusual environment of the *cha-no-yū*, or tea ceremony. Unusual because its purely artistic character is concealed behind strict ethics. "What Shinto expresses is really no religion; its gods are no gods. In principle it means the culture of the imagination and nothing else. Shinto binds the imagination to reality thus making it fertile. This creates productive aesthetics, all the more productive as they are united

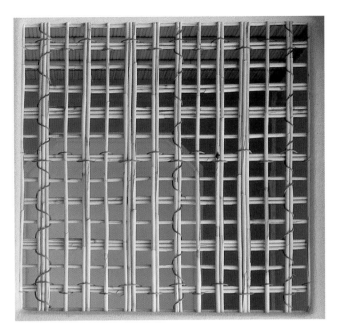

to nature, that is, to reality. [...] [The painter's] material, wood metal or stone is alive to him, which means that he sees beginning and end, youth and age, in it. The wood that has become beautiful by age is not simply beautiful because it is beautiful but because it has gained a sort of life experience." [33]

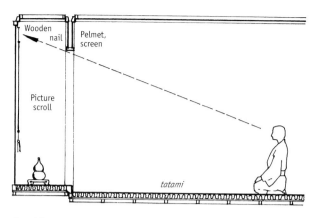

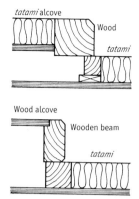

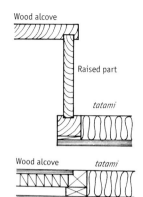

Above left
Section of a *tokonoma*
For the observer in the traditional Japanese sitting position a projecting screen conceals how the picture scroll is suspended.

Sketch from: *A Japanese Touch for your Home*, New York, London, Tokyo 1992, p. 58.

Above right
Section of the base of a *tokonoma*
The base of the *tokonoma* forms a podium. There are various methods of creating the difference in levels, but usually a wooden

beam is used as an edge and for levelling. Sketch from: *A Japanese Touch for your Home*, New York, London, Tokyo 1992, p. 58.

Architecture and the aesthetics of tea

The influence of the "aesthetics of tea" on the architecture of residential buildings was overwhelming. The basic features of the layout, such as *tokonoma* (in a residential building a built-in decorative alcove), *shoin* (in a residential building *tsukeshoin*, a built-in writing podium, which can be used as a table) and *tana* (in a residential building *chigaidana*, built-in, graduated shelving) were taken from the tea-rooms of the Zen priests. The *tokonoma* was originally used as the priest's private altar, when a votive candle and an incense burner would burn on a low wooden table under a Buddhist scroll. *Shoin* was a small, raised alcove before the window where the priest could study. The *tana* was finally a place where sacred scrolls and Buddhist relics were kept.

The fixed features of a traditional Japanese living room developed from the *shoin* style (Muromachi Period 1333–1573): decorated alcoves, *tokonoma*, with a substructure, *jōdan*, graduated shelving, *chigaidana*, a built-in writing podium, which can be used as a table, *tsukeshoin*, and decorated sliding doors, *chōdaigamae*, although not all *shoin* lodgings displayed all four features. The *shoin* style is also characterised by the *tatami* mats covering the entire floor and by square supporting posts, some with lightly bevelled edges. Often there are vaulted or coffered ceilings, painted or unpainted sliding walls, or *fusuma*, between the internal sections of the room or building, and *shōji*, white, transparent paper panels, reinforced by wooden latticework. Outside, these are protected by heavy wooden shutters, *amado*, which are hung in front of them at night or in bad weather.

The traditional Japanese door is a sliding panel. The *shoji* consist of a wooden frame with rice paper stretched over it to create spatial intimacy whilst at the same time letting in the daylight. Some *shoji* have small glass insets in the centre of the lower part of the sliding door. These "windows" can be slid across to air the room or so that the person sitting on the floor can see into the garden, but can also be closed off with rice paper for privacy. The *fusuma* also have a wooden frame, but this is covered with wood, cloth or some other strong, non-transparent material. There are often decoratively fashioned lattice girders, *kuroshoin*, fitted with lattice screens, *ramma*, above the *fusuma*, to ensure that there is ventilation between the individual rooms.

The dimensions of the "doors" are determined by the size of the *tatami*, their height corresponds exactly to the length of one *tatami*.

Alongside the formal type a variation developed in the *shoin* style: supporting posts with rough, unlevelled corners, *menkawabashira*, exquisitely structured sections and "understatement decoration" for the more dignified fittings of official *shoin* rooms. Intimacy and intuition were the maxims of this *shoin* type, which is frequently called the *sukiya* or *sukiya-shoin* style. In this too can be seen much of the flair that is typical of the essence of *sukiya* and is borrowed from the ideas of the structural creation of the tea ceremony. The art of making and drinking tea is inextricably associated with mental discipline, physical control and aesthetic sensibility. The bare tea cottage with its rough walls, open ceilings and surrounding garden contributed greatly to a precept of rustic simplicity, which is found again in a different form in *sukiya* houses.

The courtyard lies covered
Under the needles
Of the pine trees.
No speck of dust moves
in the air
And my soul is at peace!

Senno Rikyū (1521–1591)
[freely translated by J. B.]

Above left
Shouro-tei
Part of a tree left in its original state as a "link with nature" in the communal pool.

Above right
Shouro-tei
Changing room at the communal pool.

Here, too, the closeness to nature is expressed in a decorative style, the colors of the linen curtains are in shades of earth tones, which harmoniously complement the different types of wood in the room and the *midare-bako*, or kimono baskets, made from woven wickerwork.

Opposite
Shouro-tei
Corridors connect the guest rooms with one another and with the communal facilities of the ryokan. The corridors are not straight for, contrary to ancient China's preference for symmetry, the *sukiya* favors asymmetry, as in it lies a source of creativity, whereas

symmetry does not allow for any further develop-ment. However, the corridors are not just for the purpose of linking the different parts of the ryokan, but are also intended as rooms. A great deal of care is devoted to their design and furnishings. Views of the garden invite the guest to linger.

Buildings and rooms in the *sukiya* style attach importance to simplicity and straight lines. The textures of wood and plaster are left in their original state of beauty to complement nature. The décor is kept to a minimum with nothing more than latticework and wickerwork, *shitajimado*, subtly patterned paper and the sparing use of ornamentation on mountings and handles.

The picture scroll, flower arrangement, and a decorative ceramic dish in the *tokonoma* of the guest room impress not because of any flamboyance or bold combination of colors, but owe their exquisite charm rather to a symbiotic affinity with the natural materials of the room and their relation to the colors of the landscape: sea blue.

The *sukiya* villas also served the purpose of providing the occupants with the opportunity to relax informally whilst surrounded by nature. Providing this facility is also the main objective of all exclusive ryokan. The Shouro-tei possesses an exquisite garden: its character fits in harmoniously with the surrounding landscape and the adjoining bay, and yet it displays a carefully thought out combination of trees, shrubs, stones, moss and sand. Its design is based on the modest elegance of the tea garden. Trees and shrubs protect the house from unwelcome eyes, the inner and outer gardens are separated from one another by miscanthus (Japanese silver grass), *kayamon*, or bamboo trellis gates, *agesudo*. The fences are also made of bamboo or wickerwork. The stepping-stones are arranged harmoniously, varying in size, type of stone and coloring. Other features of the garden are elaborately shaped stone *ishi-doro* and wooden lanterns, as well as ponds, *tsukubai*.

"Natural products" in all spheres of life

In order to discover and admire the garden from your room you slip on the *geta* that have been placed there ready for you.

"Japanese footgear attracts the immediate attention of foreign visitors – as does the peculiar click-clack sound of *geta* on the pavement. The most distinctive feature of Japanese footwear is the Y-shaped cord or thong which passes between the big toe and the second toe – and it is a constant feature, since there is a great variety in Japanese footgear itself. However, all kinds may be roughly divided into two main classes, those for hard wear and those for easy wear. The former are known as *geta*, the latter as *zōri*.

Geta may best be translated as 'clog' or 'patten.' It is an oblong wooden piece raised on a crosswise support. A thong passes up through a hole in the forward end of the piece. This is attached to an ornamental cord whose ends are fastened down at either side of the wood. There are two main types of

geta – one consisting of the oblong piece with two thin wooden cross-pieces under it, and one carved out of a solid block of wood. The former type is the most common. For rainy weather the cross-pieces are 2 or 3 or more inches high, lifting the foot well above muddy ground. Such *geta* have a toe cap of stiff oiled paper or leather. Well-nigh endless are the different styles of *geta* – some are lacquered, some have their tops covered with finely plaited rushes and the thongs are of velvet, silk brocade, cotton or velveteen, in many colors. *Geta* are only worn outdoors.

The *zōri* is a sandal, not intended for such rough wear as the *geta*, though a coarse straw *zōri*, selling for a few sen each, is made for mountain climbing and coolie wear. The ordinary *zōri* is made of straw or reeds. There are many grades and styles for wear outside and inside the house, but even so the latter are never worn on the soft surface of the *tatami*, or thick straw mats which cover the floors of rooms – only bare or stocking-covered feet being allowed to touch the mats. The word stocking gives a wrong idea, for the Japanese do not wear stockings. They wear a sort of sock, known as *tabi*, which has a separate division for the big toe. It reaches just above the ankle and is fastend [*sic*] at the back by means of an overlap having metal hook tabs which engage with thread loops on the inner side. Above the *tabi* the legs are bare." [34]

In contrast to Chinese tradition Japanese rooms were never painted for decoration nor were the textures ever covered up with artwork. It is the antithesis of the Chinese and Korean view of art, the "raw material" being left in its natural opulence, as it embodies beauty per se. Contrary to ancient China's preference for symmetry, the *sukiya* favors asymmetry, as in it lies a source of creativity, whereas symmetry does not allow for any further development.

So in the Shouro-tei the corridors are not straight, the passages are created in different *tatami* dimensions and patterns are irregular. The wooden floors are a display of living asymmetry, the grain having been carefully fitted together to produce a natural design.

It can be said without exaggeration that in traditional Japan all aspects of daily life, and the customs and needs arising out of it, are inextricably linked to nature and that this natura naturans view is reflected in the entire ambience of living. Even in the changing room of the communal pool and in the *onsen* of the Shouro-tei the closeness to nature finds effective expression. The colors of the linen curtains are in shades of earth tones, which harmoniously complement the different types of wood in the room and the *midare-bako*, or kimono baskets, made from woven wickerwork. Part of a tree in its original state takes centre stage in the wood panelled pool.

The delicacies served after the refreshing bath create another link to the surrounding landscape. They are served on exquisite china with glazing and patterns that reflect the colors of the pine trees and the sea, or in elaborately woven tableware, clear glass with pieces of silica enclosed in it or on polished wooden plates. The dishes themselves cover the entire spectrum of seafood: giant prawns, a regional speciality, lobster, mussels, sea snails, fish of every kind, the latter sometimes still very much alive in a special spiced drink.

Above
Chikutei Yagyu-no-sho
Shōji windows with an arrow-shaped bamboo lattice in the entrance area of the inn. The
Shōji, which shed a filtered, subtle brightness, are translucent screens and were and still
are a characteristic design element of every traditional Japanese room and
representatives of a puristic and elegant design principle of Japanese arts and crafts.

竹庭　柳生の庄

Chikutei Yagyu-no-sho, Shuzenji

The Yagyo-no-sho ryokan is situated close to Shuzenji on Izu Peninsula. Of the numerous hot springs on the peninsula, the thermal bath at Shuzenji is one of the most popular. Alone the proximity to Tokyo makes the whole region an excursion destination with a high visitor frequency – with the fastest rail link hardly more than one hour from the capital. "The hot-spring of Shuzenji, Shizuoka Prefecture, is attributed to the discovery of Priest Kobo during the era of Daido (806–809). During his stay here, the priest put into the ground his cane of the judas-tree, which he had brought from China. The cane took root, and became what is now called the Katsura-tree (judas-tree) of the Shuzenji Temple, after which the River Katsura is named." [35]

Although it is located in a region popular among visitors, Yagyu-no-sho is a "Hortus conclusus" of Japanese tradition and culture. Enclosed by a bamboo grove, it is a fund of Japanese standards, traditional architecture and courtly etiquette. Hardly any other site in Japan allows the visitor to experience such authentic *kaiseki* Kyōto cuisine and learn about the rituals of the tea ceremony. In every room there is a kiriro, a small stove, on which the maid prepares the fresh miso soup for breakfast every morning. Further outstanding features of the ryokan include the site amid a bamboo grove and the extraordinary architecture. The Yagyu-no-sho inn was modelled on the *dōjō* of a famous swordsman from Nara and has a classic kendo training hall. The ingeniousness of kendo bamboo stave fencing is also found in many variations, such as in the decoration and in the ornaments. Above all, however, it is the spirit of the *yagyu-shinkage-ryu* swordsmanship schools and their dignified courtesy which have virtually set up a "branch office" in the hospitality of the ryokan.

Shibui konomi – An elusive phase of Japanese aestheticism

"The Japanese have given the word *shibumi* to a quality which is literally a 'rough or stringent taste,' i.e. the opposite of 'sweet taste.' Its adjective, *shibui*, is derived from *shibu*, an astringent quality. Japanese-English dictionaries define *shibui* as simple, unaffected, tasty, or elegant. None of these words, however, gives more than the barest hint, if any at all, of what shibui really is.

Like all transcendent qualities, the word *shibumi* eludes definition. To the Japanese, those externals which soothe and satisfy the spirit are *shibumi*. These things are instinctive, not shaped by reason and not easily put into speech, but *shibumi* suggests art appreciation, culture, ultra-refinement, quiet tastes, and a great consideration for others. "Nothing too much" is in it, and the word is in itself a protest against ostentation. There is something in it which conforms to the traditional appreciation of serenity, introspection, modesty, formality, nobility and reserve, and conservatism, and, as the antithesis of bizarre, it is opposed to everything that is garish, gay, loud or noisy, or sensuous.

No single English word exactly describes *shibumi* as the Japanese understand it. By an artistic foreign visitor *shibumi* has been described as 'the acme of elegance and refinement – the result of the use of restraint in the highest sense.' Japanese speak of *shibui* in relation to customs, houses, rooms, decorations and ornaments, persons, dress, as well as to the tone of voice. It marks the character of the old order of things, and sometimes of the new. In short, the parts must be related to the whole, and the whole must be seemly to place and circumstance. *Shibumi* is found in all the arts of Japan – that esoteric quality introduced into Art by the Zen Sect of Buddhism. It is the art that conceals art.

Opposite
Chikutei Yagyu-no-sho
Bamboo sprigs in the bamboo grove at the ryokan. They are decorated each year on the 7th of July on the occasion of the Hoshi-matsuri festival with strips of paper containing love poems. The festival commemorates the tale of love between the heavenly Princess Shokujo, the Weaver Princess Star, and Kengyu, the Herdboy Star, and their meeting on the evening of the 7th of July on the bank of the Amanogawa river, the Milky Way. They were so much in love that they neglected their duties, weaving and herding the cows, and were separated by the Celestial King. They were only allowed to see each other once a year, but because there is no bridge over the Milky Way, it was impossible for them to meet. The beautiful princess wept so bitterly that she roused a magpie which spread its wings with other magpies and formed a bridge. The legend says, however, that if the eve of the 7th of July is rainy the magpies will not form the bridge and the unhappy lovers must wait another year.

Below
Chikutei Yagyu-no-sho
View of the private garden of a *hanare*, a guest cottage, and the formal rooms illuminated in the evening.

Above
Chikutei Yagyu-no-sho
Suzuri-bako, lacquer writing box, with
artistically packed Japanese paper for
poetry and calligraphy, which every guest
will find in his or her the room.

Right
Chikutei Yagyu-no-sho
Jochū-san or maid in the corridor of the
main building, on her way to serve one of
the many dishes of the *kaiseki* menu in
one of the guest rooms.

Opposite
Chikutei Yagyu-no-sho
The shade of a floor lamp in the "lobby" of
the ryokan in front of the *renjimado*. It is
not alone the soft light of the *shōji* which
lends Japanese rooms their delicate
quality, illumination with artificial light is
a further manipulation in the interaction
of light and shadow. The lamp shown here
is a prime example of the principle of
simplicity in Japanese design: the shade is
made using only a rolled sheet of rice
paper.
A purely aristocratic "attribute" of the
shinden style were the *renjimado*, windows
comprising narrow horizontal wooden
strips allowing nobility to see the common
folk outside without being viewed
themselves. This feudal element is also
found in Yagyu-no-sho.

Perhaps a liberal rendition of the meaning of *shibui konomi* would be: An inherent appreciation of the elements, properly arranged and balanced, that enter into art, and into one's life and personality." [36]

The "properly arranged elements" which characterise *shibui konomi* also include spiritual and ethical discipline, above all self-control and humility. The legendary Shogun Ieyasu established the still highly respected rules and principles of conduct, for instance: consider anger your enemy. Ieyasu (also:

A certain color scheme is essential in producing a *shibui* effect. A sculptured piece of white marble, for instance, cannot be *shibui* because it is devoid of color, but the prevalence of brilliant or bright color is antagonistic to *shibui*. The color of bran, the outer coat of kernels of rice, wheat, etc., is commonly called *shibu-kawa* (meaning astringent skin), and this color, or that of various shades of chestnut or russet in an art object is usually essential in securing a *shibui* effect. The color of ashes, unpolished silver and gold, and other colors, constitute factors for producing a subdued and tranquil effect in an art object and it is the artistic employment of such colors or combinations of colors that imparts to Japanese art an indescribable *shibui* effect. A careful study of a guest-room in a Japanese house will reveal that the color scheme is obtained by the contrast of the colors of the walls, ceiling, pillars, and other parts of the room. In no part of it is there a color which departs from the traditional color that makes that room *shibui*.

A Japanese, in commenting upon a woman's kimono, might say: 'Look at her *shibui konomi*' – meaning that the woman was dressed with discrimination in silk material of the traditional color, not showy, but rich in quality. In speaking of a voice as *shibui*, reference is made to its quality through the cultivation and training it has received.

I-e-yasu; 1542–1616) established the Tokugawa Shogunate, which ruled Japan from 1603 until 1867. He is one of the most enigmatic figures of Japanese history and his mausoleum is found in Nikkō at the Toshogu shrine. During the 264 years of Tokugawa rule, the fine arts flourished in Japan as never before.

Take – Bamboo

"The most useful plant in the world: The uses of bamboo are almost numberless, but 1400 ways of its use in Japan have been listed. It gives the Japanese chopsticks, umbrellas, building and fencing materials, fans, arrows, *fude* (writing brushes), baskets, pipes for conveying water, besides many other things of utility and value. It is also carved for ornamental purposes. Edison, when he first produced electric lamps, used bamboo filaments obtained from Yawata, a town situated between Kyōto and Osaka.

Bamboo is a grass; from a botanical point of view it is a tree grass. The biggest specimens come from Java and India, where the giant bamboo has been known to reach a height of 120 feet. There are about 490 known species of bamboo. The main plant runs underground, the canes as they grow up are only branches, therefore a bamboo grove may be only one plant and anything that affects a part of it will affect the whole.

Take-no-ko (Baby Bamboo or Bamboo shoot) first comes up very slowly, generally in the spring and autumn and only occasionally in the summer. Its growth then gradually increases more rapidly until it reaches half of its full height, after which the growth is less rapid. It has the most rapid rate of growth of any plant known. At maximum speed its growth is 49.5 to 50 centimeters (19 ½ to 20 in.) in 24 hours. Its greatest record growth is 91 centimeters (about 36 in.) in 24 hours. It has wonderful strength, elasticity and extreme hardness. It is so hard that some of its species, if struck by a piece of steel, will give off sparks. This is due to the amount of silicon it contains.

Take-no-ko supplies a delicate foodstuff which is sliced and cooked in various ways; cooked with rice it is called *Take-no-ko Meshi*. Some restaurants make a specialty of this dish.

Left
Chikutei Yayu-no-sho
View of the main room of the Matsuno-o cottage.
Proportions, decorations and details of the room are maintained in the exquisite sukiya style. The aesthetic of the *sunoko-tenjō* ceiling is particularly notable – asymmetrically divided by bamboo sashes, made of wooden boards and woven bamboo leaves.

 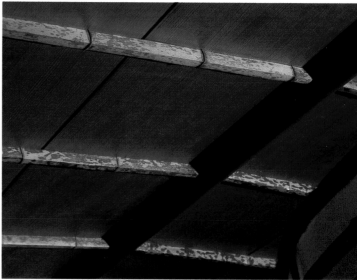

Above left and right
Chikutei Yagyu-no-sho
Two detail views of a baldacchino-like and a coffered ceiling with bamboo sashes, wooden boards and bamboo cane.

Opposite
Chikutei Yagyu-no-sho
View of the guest room of the *murodoko,,* a *tokonoma* which has a concealed back column. The brocade trimming of the *tatami* mats is exquisitely patterned and structured.

Bamboo flowers, but only rarely. There is a saying in the Far East that it only flowers in time of famine, and instances of this have been recorded.

A bamboo forest is worth much money and brings good return for the care and trouble given. At the time of a severe earthquake such forests are considered safe ground on account of the matted roots." [37]

Bamboo does not belong, as frequently incorrectly assumed, to the tree family but is a grass. Nonetheless bamboo is used in the same way as timber as a construction material although an alternative method of fastening must be used as nails cause bamboo to splinter. Bamboo is therefore often fitted into a rectangular mat woven to exploit the design advantages offered by the elasticity of the material. "Weaving" bamboo instead of using plastic or metal fastenings means that the composition remains "organic" and is integrated perfectly into the natural environment.

Traditionally bamboo growing on a plot of land is used as a fence for the estate. The idea of self-sufficiency and modesty this represents and of using almost solely local materials for building has a model character. Moreover, a bamboo fence does not have the intimidating effect of a wall or a metal railing but is more of a design element. The pattern of the woven bamboo is a delightful mirror of the landscape.

Bamboo is also used as a wall skeleton which is encased by a mixture of agrillaceous earth, sand and straw fiber, or also hydrated lime from limestone or oyster shells.

All Japanese houses are constructed using a net of bamboo or timber which provides support for the large variety of positions of walls – for lest it should be forgotten, in a Japanese house walls are functional but are not bearing structures, they "draw" rooms, without supporting the house. The flexible structure of Japanese houses, which owes its greatest debt to the bamboo, causes them to "wobble" during natural phenomena such as whirlwinds and (mild) earthquakes and thus avoid collapse. This flexible style of construction again demonstrates the universal close links the Japanese people have to nature. The Western architect typically prefers rigid structures which pit themselves against the natural elements, while the Japanese master builder acts according to the principle: better to give way to the wind and the trembling earth than be destroyed by it. "Outside the city there are also large houses with courtyards, and close study will reveal a number of gardens planted with bamboo. This is a symbolic touch. Bamboo is an evergreen, flexible plant that bows but does not bend, a symbol of durability and adaptability. As a pictorial motif, bamboo is suitable for the display of a variety of brushwork techniques, and it was also part of the flora and fauna that were the favorite subjects of Academy painters." [38]

The representation of the "physical environment" in Japanese architecture can be explained very well in stories and poems which present analogies with forms that occur in nature. To ascend a flight of stairs is like climbing a mountain. Many small window apertures scatter light in a similar way to the broken light on the forest floor.

The pine tree
Struggled many years
In order to grow.

In the hard winters
It was made to twist and turn
Because the snow and the wind
Tormented it.
The pine tree was patient and endured
The restlessness of the climate.

Alone the bamboo
Grew in the hot
Humid, tropical months
Of summer
It grew unbelievably quickly
Think, many bamboo plants
Grew three inches in one
Single day.

The summer was short
So the bamboo grew
Straight upwards
Toward the sun.

Soon there were fields of
Bamboo high over
Our heads.

The bamboo was
Quick and
Impetuous.

Traditional, anonymous
[freely translated by N.C.]

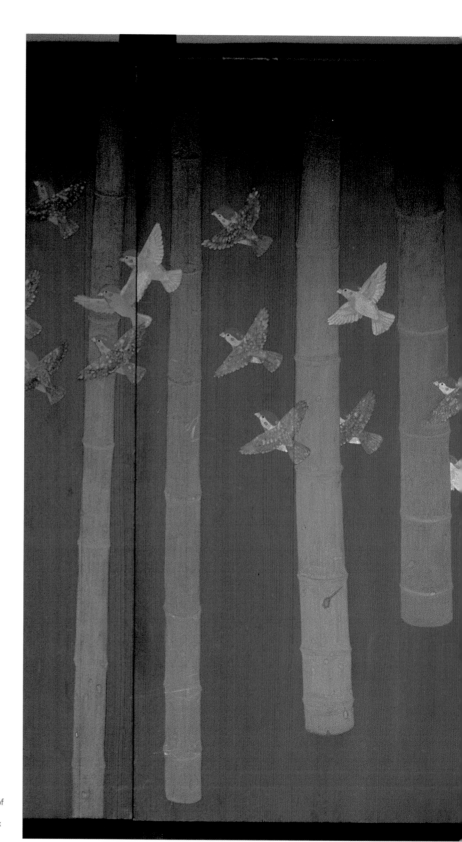

Right
Chikutei Yagyu-no-sho
Decorative wall panel in the reception hall on the right-hand side of
the entrance to the ryokan.
Painting on wood and inlay work, approximately 67 x 118 in. (170 x
300 cm).

Left
Chikutei Yagyu-no-sho
Bamboo canes in the ryokan garden.
"The most useful plant in the world. The
uses of bamboo are almost numberless,
but 1400 ways of its use in Japan have
been listed. It gives the Japanese
chopsticks, umbrellas, building and
fencing materials, fans, arrows,
fude (writing brushes), baskets, pipes for
conveying water, besides many other
things of utility and value. It is also
carved for ornamental purposes. Edison,
when he first produced electric lamps,
used bamboo filaments obtained from
Yawata, a town situated between Kyōto
and Osaka." (*We Japanese*)

Opposite
Chikutei Yagyu-no-sho
Covered passage in the garden of the
ryokan which connects the main building
with the guest cottages. The passage is
built in an elegant, rustic *sukiya* tea
house style.

The extreme climate in Japan with the subtropical summers and the bitterly cold winters has a produced an environment of contrasts, which are also reflected in everyday life. Long ago poets and artists discovered these contrasts in the unusual comparison between the pine tree and the bamboo (see page 152).

The bent pine tree and the upright, but impetuous bamboo are two fully different markers of the Japanese landscape. Both, however, teach how to survive in the Japanese climate.

The slow growth under natural conditions may have inherent delays and twists and turns – as the pine tree demonstrates. Under favorable conditions on the other hand a plant like the bamboo can react with enormous spurts of growth – which however do not make it particularly resistant to important influences. To always be reminded of the lessons nature offers, the Japanese design parts of their houses in such a way as to emphasise the qualities of the leaning pine tree and the upright bamboo. Bamboo is found in quantities in the Japanese house and every year a new harvest is brought in. Pine is valuable and is used sparingly, for luxurious and ceremonial objects only. The Japanese consider the pine tree and the bamboo master teachers and at the same time they respect their natural world through careful use of the materials as a resource.

Yagyu shinkage-ryu, *dōjō* and *budō*

Yagyu shinkage-ryu is one of the earliest swordsmanship traditions in old Japan. This special sword technique came into being when Kamiizumi Ise no Kami, a master of the *shinkage-ryu* style, met Yagyo So'uemon no Jo Muneyoshi on the battlefield. Muneyoshi was defeated by Ise no Kami a number of times in single combat using split bamboo swords after which he knelt before Kamiizumi and begged him to become his pupil. Muneyoshi received a master's licence in the *shinkage* style of swordsmanship. As a *daimyō* (lord of a province) in the Yamoto plains, Muneysohi was involved in countless battles and wars of the period.

When Muneyoshi demonstrated his specially developed version of the *shinkage-ryu* style to the Shogun Tokugawa Ieyasu (1542–1616, founder of the Tokugawa dynasty, in 1603 raised to the hereditary shogun by the tenno) at Kyōto's Takagamine mountain, Ieyasu surprisingly attacked the more than 80-year old, barehanded Muneyoshi after the official presentation. The aged warrior disarmed the shogun with ease and threw him to the ground. Ieyasu was so impressed by Muneyoshi's strength that he tried to enlist his services. However, owing to his age, Muneyoshi sent one of his sons, Munenori, to be placed in the shogun's service. At the Battle of Sekigahara (1600), Munenori and Ieyasu were in command of the army camp, and legend has it that he saved the shogun and his generals against a murderous attack by enemy intruders by cutting down at least ten men at once, causing the others to flee. This heroic deed enabled his glittering rise through the ranks: he became the Tokogawa Shogun's swordmaster and in later years a *soh-metsuke*, overseer of the *daimyō* throughout the country not allied with the shogun.

Munenori founded the Edo Yagyu line of the Yagyu family, which resided in the capital Edo (now Tokyo). His son Hyogo no Suke Toshiyoshi Myounsai in turn formed the Owari Yagyu branch of the family. His son Renyasai was also a famous swordsman and a practitioner of the fine arts. Soon after his father's death Munenori's son Jubei was immortalised as a master swordsman in numerous wood carvings and legends.

The Owari Yayu family is still involved in training pupils in the art of *yagyu-shinkage-ryu* swordsmanship and has *dōjō* in Tokyo and Nagoya.

"A *dōjō* is a place where the way *dōjō* is practised (*dō* – way, *jō* – place). Practising the way (*geiko*) gains in meaning and clarity if there is an honest connection between the learner (*deishi*) and the *dōjō*. Therefore the *dōjō* in the theory of the way (*oshi*) is not a training room but a holy place which is also called the "Room of Enlightenment." The designation *dōjō* means the room in which the exercises take place but it is a symbol for the learner's deep relation to his art.

The word *dōjō* has its origins in Buddhism and means a place of self-knowledge and meditation. Later it changed its meaning into the place where the martial arts are practised. But the sense of the word remained as it was before. For every serious learner the *dōjō* is a place of meditation and concentration, even today. An honored place of learning, of brotherhood, of friendship and of respect. It is more than just a word – it stands for the way of the martial arts in a symbolic manner.

In the philosophical sense, the word *dōjō* can refer to any place where a person within the meaning *budō* concentrates his mind and body in practising the way. Moreover, the type of relationship the learner maintains with his own *dōjō* characterises his efforts to attain correct thinking and correct composure. The correct relationship to the *dōjō* is a part of practising the way itself. It consists of striving to serve the spirit of *budō* through selfless dedication and the personal

Right
Chikutei Yagyu-no-sho
Connecting passage, *rō* with *shitomi-do,* reticulated shutters made of wood and rice paper, hinged at the top and flipped up or down.

progress that a learner makes in a *dōjō*. For the genuine learner (*deishi*) the *dōjō* is his second home. Through such a relationship with the *dōjō*, a compensatory value is created by which the individual matures and the *budō* spirit (shin) can flourish. Egotistical people who only use a *dōjō* as a training room cannot participate in this process. A *dōjō* lives through the concessions made by the learners to the ideal of the martial arts. Only in this way can a learner find access to the way.

In every *dōjō* there is a *sensei* and several advanced learners (*sempai*), some of whom are also masters. The students of a *dōjō* who wish to learn the martial arts do not join the group of learners (*yudansha*) until they understand and learn to respect the profound meaning of the *dōjō* relationship (*shitei*) through their composure (*shisei*). There are no advanced learners who take more from a *dōjō* than they give. In this point, the *dōjō* of the way differ from the sports hall. The physical training (*shosa*) may be the same, but only the correct composure (*shisei*) enables progress on the way." [39]

Film producers show *dōjō* as a humorous form of acrobatics, combined with a ridiculous plot, and sportsmen practise *budō* as an exotic possibility for collecting cups and becoming the European champion. Consequently *budō* is misunderstood and incorrectly interpreted by most Europeans.

Budō means "way of the samurai" and was the life philosophy of the rulers of Japan from 1160 to 1868. The ability to do combat with or without different samurai weapons is the visible part of *budō* while the "invisible" part which is the philosophy is far more important and the main reason why *budō* still has an important and accepted role in Japan. The philosophy of life associated with *budō* teaches virtues, for example, courage and determination, which can be acquired through combat training. The ever present thought of improving oneself in these characteristics is the motivation for constant training. Although one can progress as regards the combat technique without improving in the above characteristics, this is not the way of the samurai. If physical and spiritual development diverge too far one will soon no longer enjoy training and one becomes a burden on the other students.

Kendo – The way of the sword

The original meaning of kendo is "the way of the sword" and it relates to the traditional Japanese art of fencing as developed and practised by the *bushi* (warrior class) and the samurai. This special style arose from the numerous styles of swordsmanship and was brought to real mastery through centuries of combat, training and study. The aim of kendo is not solely to train physical skills and "combat readiness" but above and beyond that to perfect moral and spiritual aspects of the struggle and also to better master the challenges of everyday life. In Japan, kendo is still one of the most popular martial arts and the number of followers of this quintessential Japanese discipline is growing notably world-wide too.

Left
Chikutei Yagyu-no-sho
A variety of the traditional *andon*, the interior room lantern on an asymmetrically laid natural stone floor.

The room is divided by *shōji* which are modelled on the *shitomi-do*, a reticulated, hinged window protection used in *shinden* and *shoin* residences.

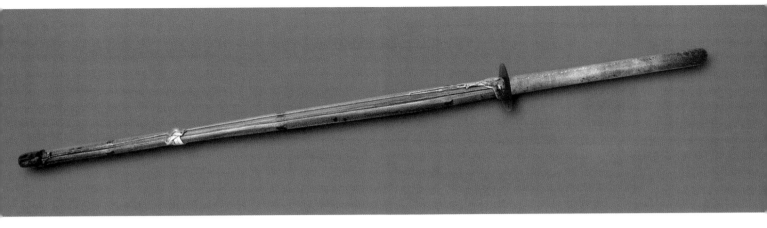

Shinai, bamboo fencing stave
Length 43 inches,
Japan
The uses of bamboo appear
endless. It not only serves
a building material, but has
medicinal uses and is a
potent "sword."

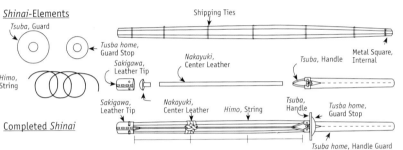

Shinai-Elements

Tsuba, Guard

← *Tusba home*,
Guard Stop

Himo,
String

Sakigawa,
Leather Tip

Shipping Ties

Nakayuki,
Center Leather

Tsuba, Handle

Metal Square,
Internal

Completed *Shinai*

Sakigawa,
Leather Tip

Nakayuki,
Center Leather

Himo, String

Tsuba,
Handle

Tusba home,
Guard Stop

Tsuba home, Handle Guard

Left
Detail drawing of a *shinai*, a bamboo fencing stave
The kendo sword is a bamboo fencing stave, *shinai*, made of four well-finished lengths of bamboo bound together at both ends by a leather tip and a leather handle. The equipment used consists of the protective clothing, *bogu*, the mask, *men* which covers face, neck, the upper part of the head and the temples, the chest and stomach protector, *do*, the waist protector, *tare*, and the padded gloves, the *kote*.

The sword came from the Asian mainland to Japan around 200 B.C. as a ritual object. It was less a weapon and served to symbolise the power of the wearer.

As time passed, however, swords replaced traditional war instruments such as the bow and the sling and they were forged in Japan from the 7th century onwards. As the *bushi* class was constituted from the 9th century, the prototype of the legendary Japanese sword, the *nihon-to*, was developed. This more than 6 feet or approximately 2 meter long weapon dominated the battlefield during the following centuries. The civil wars which threw the country into turmoil from the 14th century onwards led to the establishment of numerous kenjutsu schools (schools for the art of the sword) by master swordsmen who taught their own special styles. As peace slowly returned to the country, the moral and spiritual side of swordsmanship was strengthened, borrowing from Zen Buddhism and *bushi-dō*, the way of the warriors. Although only the samurai were allowed to wear a sword, it nevertheless represented the spirit of the *bushi* whose philosophy is Confucian in origin.

It was not until the second half of the 18th century that protective clothing was introduced and the *shinai*, the bamboo fencing staves were used, both playing a decisive role in the development of kenjutsu. As the realisation grew during the final days of the Tokugawa Shogunate (1615–1868) that national defence would be required, kenjutsu grew immensely in popularity even among the common folk.

Modern Japan after 1867 disenfranchised the warrior class and it was only the superior might of the Western nations that renewed interest in kenjutsu and as one started to concentrate on native virtues. The nascence of kendo was 1912 as the different kenjutsu lines were unified in a single teaching system, which became part of the sports curriculum in schools. For obvious reasons the triumphal march of kendo was again interrupted at the end of World War Two and was in fact banned by the Occupation Authorities.

In 1957 the still numerous kendo enthusiasts formed the All Japan Kendo Federation which emphasised the training of spirit and discipline over the combat aspects.

Shinai – The bamboo fencing stave

The kendo sword is a bamboo fencing stave, *shinai*, made of four well-finished lengths of bamboo bound together at both ends by a leather tip and a leather handle. The equipment used

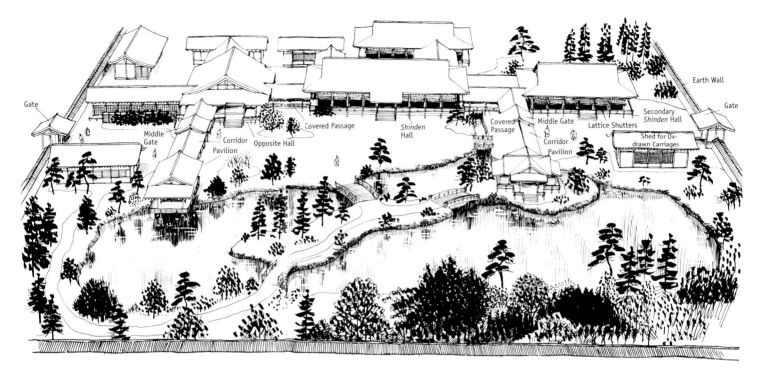

Labels on image: Gate, Middle Gate, Corridor Pavilion, Opposite Hall, Covered Passage, Shinden Hall, Middle Gate, Corridor Pavilion, Covered Passage, Lattice Shutters, Secondary Shinden Hall, Shed for Ox-drawn Carriages, Earth Wall, Gate

Above
Top plan view of a *shinden* complex
Shinden is the term used to designate the residences of the Heian nobility (794–1185).
Life in a *shinden* residence can only be reconstructed from picture scrolls as not

a single *shinden* complex has survived. Although excavations allow us to piece together the location plans and the gardens, for the elevations and the interiors other sources have to be consulted such as the *e-makimono*, the narrative picture scrolls, and the

literature of the period.
Drawing from: Kazuo Nishi and Kazuo Hozumi, *What is Japanese Architecture?* Tokyo 1985, p. 64

Opposite
Chikutei Yagyu-no-sho
View across the *engawa*, the veranda of the guest cottage Matsuno-o and the interior garden to the study room of the cottage with two main rooms arranged in a horseshoe shape.

consists of the protective clothing, *bogu*, the mask, *men* which covers face, neck, the upper part of the head and the temples, the chest and stomach protector, *do*, the waist protector, *tare*, and the padded gloves, the *kote*.

The kendo match and the execution of the blows and thrusts with the bamboo sword are subject to strict rules. A successful blow requires precise mental co-ordination, the correct grasp of the sword and perfect physical movement. Kendo training comprises many different exercises which are aimed at developing power and skill. The continuous repetition of individual moves is intended to produce automatic, unconscious movements because a kendo fencer has to be able to parry an attack directly and intuitively when the opponent makes the slightest movement. Besides the intellectual sensitivity, apodeictic etiquette plays a significant role as the instruction aims to develop personality characteristics such as confidence, courteousness and respect for the opponent – the basic virtues of the samurai.

The residences of the Heian nobility – *shinden*

The starting point or better the "genius loci" of all formal and ritual architecture are the residences of the Heian period (794–1185), and the mental discipline and the highly imaginative aesthetic lifestyle of the Heian aristocracy.

The *shinden* style, *shinden-zukuri*, acquired its name from the central structure of such a complex. The word originally means "hall for sleeping." Although every known *shinden* complex has its own unique aspects, most face south on an interior courtyard where ceremonies and entertainment events were held. South of the courtyard there was artificial pond with an island in the middle which could be reached by bridges. The banks of the pond frequently had a small hill planted with trees which were formed using the earth from the excavation of the pond. Playing with little boats on the pond was a particularly popular form of relaxation for the lucky residents of such aristocratic dwellings.

The *shinden* hall was the residence of the head of the household during the Heian period (794–1185) and the place where he received guests and presided over rites and special celebrations. From one or more sides of the *shinden* hall there extended wide covered corridors, *watadono*, which led to subsidiary living quarters, *tainoya* (original meaning: opposite fought-over halls) and which were raised about a foot above ground. Most were reserved for family members and the servants. Corridors, *rō*, extended from the *tainoya* to the pond, ending in small fishing pavilions called *tsuri-dono*, or fountain pavilions called *izumi-dono*. Half way along these southern corridors there were middle gates, *chūmon*, through which one entered the complex and which were accordingly called "inner gate corridors" or *chūmonrō*. These corridors were quite spacious and housed the residence management offices.

Shinden residences were usually constructed on single block plots of land (144 sq. yards) although some double block plots were built from north to south. The land was enclosed by thick earth walls called *tsujibei* which were faced with boards and crowned on both sides by tiles. Gates were integrated into the east and west walls, one being the main gate, the *seimon*, and the other the back gate, the *uramon*. The gates were large enough for ox-drawn carriages – these elegantly decorated vehicles were the preferred means of transport for the Heian nobility. The gates were also living quarters for the escorts and the servants of the guests. Almost all buildings were interconnected by means of hall passages or corridors. The terrain was lower on the southwest side and the pond was fed by a river which came from the northeast. Running water built up in the southwest of Heian (Kyōto) and this explains the steaminess and naturally the unpopularity of this district of the city.

The interior rooms of the *shinden* residences were sparsely furnished and could be modified at will, allowing mobile intimacy. Sliding doors, hinged walls, moveable shutters and panels allowed large social or small intimate rooms to be created as required. The enclosed space could be transformed into a type of loggia through removal of the wooden shutters.

Kai-awase and uta-karuta – Art and games

The popular drawing-room game *kai-awase* originates from the Heian period (794–1185) and by the end of the Edo period (1868) had become particularly popular among young girls from aristocratic families. Not alone the game with the shells but equally the cultivated nature of the pastime are an expression of an aestheticising lifestyle which had devoted itself to distinguished leisure and beauty. The beautifully patterned shells were compared and then poems were written about the design, and these poems then became the object of a further competition.

After the Muromachi period (1392–1573) the game was played differently, with greater focus on the play aspect while the poem writing competition was increasingly neglected, and the poetry became part of the game. This version was known as *uta-kai* and consisted of shells each with half a poem which had to be linked to the other half. To be successful at the game required on the one hand wide reading but also wit and imagination as it was usual to write poems that related to the exalted courtly life and its intrigues.

The 360 shells for *kai-awase* come from a special hard-shelled clam called *hamaguri*, from which no two shells are the same. The shells are divided between the two players. The bigger and bulgier the more valuable they were considered. Characters and scenes from "Genji-monogatari" and "Ise-monogatari", landscapes, mountains and rivers, and flowers and birds were the most popular themes of the miniature paintings inside the shells, painted by masters of the *yamato-e* style, the traditional form of Japanese painting. Identical pictures were painted inside matching shells and one player now turned a shell and if the opponent had the other matching half, she won the whole shell. A further version of the game involved one player turning a pair of shells at the same time and the winner was the player with the greatest number of matching shells. During the Meiji Restoration (1868–1912), this courtly amusement also evolved into the currently very popular *hana-awase*, a flower card game.

Further elements of the game set such as fans and the *kai-oke*, the caskets for storing the shells, were beautiful artworks of exquisite elegance. Apart from the shells, the accessories were extremely expensive and therefore only girls from rich and aristocratic families could hope to possess such a superb pastime. *Kai-awase* is an echo of an age which was dedicated to the perfection of form and a life of creative idleness.

Left
Poet card game *uta-karuta – ogura hyakuninisshu*
Wano-sato
Game set with 200 cards, consisting of 100 *waka* poems from 100 different poets during the Heian period (794–1185).

Above left
Two matching shells of the game *kai-awase*, "courtiers from the Heian period"
"Genji-*monogatari*" and "Ise-*monogatari*" were books of morals for young girls from Edo. Although sometimes on the list of forbidden books of the Confucian School, the life of the Heian nobility that was described was shown secretly in the shells.

Above center
Two matching shells of the game *kai-awase*, "grasses and trees/flowers and birds"
Flowers and trees flourish and birds sing during the sequences of the year – symbolising the four Japanese seasons – at the same time the paintings were intended to portrait the sound of running water and the wind, even if these elements were not represented.

Above right
***Kai-oke*, lacquered casket for the shells used for the *kai-awase* or shell matching game**
Chikutei Yagyu-no-sho
Kai-oke are costly lacquered caskets, round but also hexagonal or octagonal, frequently provided with ornamental metal fittings and closed with a lavish silk cord.

Also based on the shell matching game *kai-awase* was the 16th-century poet card game called *uta-karuta*. It consisted of 200 cards based on the collection of poems called *ogura hyakuninisshu*, an anthology of 100 poems from 100 different poets. Each poem is divided onto two cards which must be pieced together by the players. All the poems are *waka*, today also called *tanka*. A *waka* consists of 5 lines and 31 syllables divided into the five syllabic units: 5-7-5-7-7. The *waka* from the *hyakuninisshu* are courtly lyric poems for which the *waka* form was used exclusively from the earliest period of Japanese poetry, until the 17-syllable *haiku* poems gained in importance in the 17th century.

It is said that the *hyakuninisshu* was compiled in 1235 by the famous poet and critic Fujiwara no Sadaie (also known as Teika). The 100 poems collected chronologically from the 7th to the 12th century for the "Hyakuninisshu" are all by celebrated poets from the Heian period (794–1185).

The card game *uta-karuta* is still extremely popular in contemporary Japan, whereas *kai-awase* and other traditional games from the Genroku period (1688–1704) are nowadays only fostered by a few exclusive circles in Kyōto and Kamakura. The traditional aristocratic games also include guessing types of incense (see introduction) by sense of smell. Aside from the

tea way *cha-dō* and the flower way, guessing games and various board games are Japanese disciplines which combines amusement, a sense of beauty and competition. Especially popular was and is among sophisticated circles an arrow range competition game *yakazu-kō*, a rendering of the famous archery contest at Sanjūsangen-dō in Kyōto. In this game, two persons or groups competing against each other are symbolised by figures of horsemen. The horsemen advance one field at a time on game boards with holes and usually 15 or 20 fields after the player has successfully identified a scent, thereby arrows and standards are inserted into the holes.

The floors were made of smooth wooden floor boards which were covered by straw mats as and when required. Earlier *shinden* buildings still lacked permanent features such as the *tokonoma*, the rooms were "multipurpose halls." During the course of the Heian period, however, the need for privacy, more informality and distance increased. Accordingly the functions and structures of the interior rooms in the residences changed. The central space, *moya*, of the shinden hall came to be used mainly for ceremonial functions and the secondary spaces, *hisashi*, were used for daily living. These changes in the *shinden* lifestyle were related to the rise of the warrior class.

The evolution from *shinden* to *shoin* was gradual and had fluid transitions. Until this day, *shinden* has not been entirely replaced by *shoin*. *Shinden* still exists in Japanese architecture as a symbol of an aristocratic culture. The *chūmon-rō*, the covered entrance arcade, became the *genkan*, the vestibule of every ryokan. This space continues to signify the division between public and private spheres. However, completely replaced were the hinged wall panels, *shitomi*, and the swinging doors, *itakarato* by *shōji* and *fusuma*. Whenever they are still found, they signify an exquisite, distant past life.

A purely aristocratic attribute were the *renjimado*, windows slatted with horizontal strips of wood, which allowed the nobility on the interior to view the common folk without being viewed themselves. Likewise, the round *shinden* post was replaced by square posts because the *shōji* did not make a tight joint with the round posts. However, there are still residences and public buildings to be found today which have round posts as a symbol of a past aristocracy.

It is frequently assumed that two-sided symmetry was the ideal for *shinden* structures. However, the real examples we know of do not appear to have been constructed in this way. A possible reason for the aforementioned hypothesis might be the orientation of the main hall to the south, but by virtue of the garden and the pond, the main entrance was on the side and thus the opposite side was automatically the rear side. The rooms are arranged strictly from east to west, because the buildings were oriented southwards, irregularity not symmetry was the result.

We can only reconstruct life in a *shinden* residence from picture scrolls because not one single *shinden* complex has survived to the present day. Although excavations allow us to piece together the location plans and the gardens, for the elevations and the interiors other sources have to be consulted such as the *e-makimono*, the narrative picture scrolls, which without doubt are the best basis. Some contain texts with instructions and reports about the pastimes pursued by the members of the Heian and medieval aristocracies.

For example, we learn that aesthetic competitions among the nobility were the order of the day. The picture scrolls tell us about events and the participating guests. They wore the court dress, *sokutai*, with long trains, which they draped over the railings. The longer the train the higher the rank of the wearer. White was fixed for the winter and brown, *suō*, or double indigo, *futaai*, for the summer. While observing this custom, nevertheless individual tones and preferences were encouraged. A further vivid source of information about the *shinden* are diaries from the Heian period, for example, *The Tale of Prince Genji*, written by the female aristocrat Murasaki Shikibu (978–1015). The amorous adventures of Prince Genji are one of the most important prose works of Japanese literature.

Kaiseki-ryōri – Courtly cuisine

The aestheticising of life during the Heian period also included the stylisation of food to artworks. From the Heian period (794–1185) until the Kamakura period (1185–1333), indigenous Japanese cuisine was developed first and foremost at the Imperial Court and by the samurai class. During the Edo period (1615–1868) this cuisine was also served during "tea parties" which accompanied the tea ceremony. These types of banquet functions were formative in establishing *kaiseki-ryōri*.

From the starter to the dessert with fish and crustaceans, accompanied by seasonal vegetables and fruit, the hallmark of this cuisine are the subtle arrangement, the color combinations and the materials. The dishes are carefully selected for the specific foods, and so as to match the interior decoration, the occasion and the season. It is of overriding importance to reveal the season in the meal; the changing seasons are reflected by the table.

Kaiseki today means a course of dishes from a luxurious Japanese banquet, yet it remains a centuries old type of feast which over time developed into a separate form of art, synaesthetic in nature and addressing the panoply of the senses – the eye, the palate, the sense of smell, also the Eros because here special attention is paid to the ingredients.

Kaiseki-ryōri is also combined closely with the surrounding architecture and arts and crafts to ensure complete authenticity. A substantial spiritual element of the seasonal *kaiseki* cuisine

Opposite
View of a *shinden* residence through the "blown-off roof", *fukinuki yatai*, a convention used in *yamato-e* paintings from the Heian period (794–1185)
Attributed to Tosa Mitsunori (1583–1638), Sumiyoshi, No. 25, from the second tale about Prince Genji.
Byō'bu, folding screens, painting and gold leaf on paper.
The "romantic adventure" albums produced during the Momoyama period (1573–1615) were created by painters from the Tosa School (from the 15th century onwards) as so-called Genji-e (a special genre of Japanese painting), after the hanging picture scroll "The Tale of Genji", mid 12th century.

Right
***Sunoko-en*, "hurdle veranda", and *hisashi*, peripheral chambers, of a *shinden* residence (794–1185)**
Also seen are the typical bamboo blinds, the veil-like curtains and the *tatami* floor.
Reconstruction line drawings from: Kazuo Nishi and Kazuo Hozumi, *What is Japanese Architecture?* Tokyo 1985, p. 66

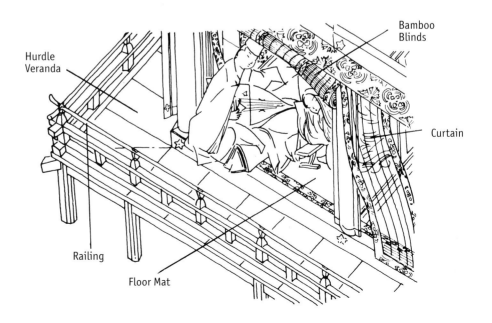

Hurdle Veranda

Bamboo Blinds

Curtain

Railing

Floor Mat

has its roots in the tea ceremony of the monasteries. Here accompanying the "way of the tea," plain, strictly seasonal vegetarian meals were served.

A further characteristic of *kaiseki* cuisine are the numerous small portions of prescribed meals which are proffered at suitable intervals.

The host must be sensitive to the mood on the premises and leave sufficient time between the courses to create an atmosphere which balances anticipation and satisfaction.

A *kaiseki* meal is not simply a certain sequence of courses, numerous rules also have to be followed to avoid mishaps, especially the following: no tradition-conscious Japanese will serve one or three items of a food because *hito-kire* (*hito*=one, *kire*=piece) also means "kill somebody" and *mikire* (*mi*=three, *kire*=piece) is ambiguous and can mean "kill me," in this case *mi*=person, while *kire* is the imperative form of the verb to kill, "kill yourself." It is therefore considered an absolutely fatal omen to be served one or three pieces of a food. Two or four

Below left and top right
Chikutei Yagyu-no-sho
Three different courses from a summer *kaiseki* meal which comprises more than 20 courses in total, served in exquisite ceramic dishes, *oribe* and *kyōyaki*, and a lacquer bowl, *wan,* all served on a lacquer tray, *bon,* adorned with bamboo motifs.

Above
Chikutei Yagyu-no-sho
Menu with the individual courses shown in calligraphy which each guest receives decorated with his or her own name at Chikutei Yagyu-no-sho.

pieces can be proffered with impunity, although four slices are also not a good sign as four is homonymous with "death" – *shi* – and is generally considered an unlucky number and consequently avoided by the Japanese as far as possible.

芭蕉

大橋屋

Ohashi-ya, O-aza Akasaka

The moon shows the way;
Take this path to my house,
This is the invitation
from the landlord of a wayside guesthouse.
Matsuo Bashō (1644–1694)
[freely translated by J.B.]

Mr. Kazuhiro Aoki, the present owner of the Ohashi-ya, is the 19th descendant of the founder, and according to his view every guest at the Ohashi-ya is making a journey into the history of Japan. "People visit this ryokan because it is the Tōkaidō's only remaining historical guesthouse. After the national railway line was built in 1889 there was a dramatic fall in the number of our guests and the station town became deserted. When the railway line was opened there were 64 guesthouses in operation, but the rapid growth in railway traffic destroyed the Tōkaidō road in an instant." The Tōkaidō line's Shinkansen is without question the swiftest and most efficient way to travel, but the

scenes and impressions afforded by earlier, more leisurely journeys are lost. And yet even today there are people who prefer to saunter through the little town, wherever the wind takes them, looking up at the moon. At twilight it already grows dark on the old Tōkaidō road, making it a real delight to gaze at the late summer or autumn moon from the Ohashi-ya.

Matsuo Bashō (1644–1694), the famous *haiku* poet, was also a guest at the Ohashi-ya, choosing it on several occasions as a place from which to view the moon. In his introduction to his cycle of poems "On narrow paths through the hinterland," which originated from an excursion to central Japan, Bashō writes: "The years and months are our traveling companions, and the people who come and go are travelers too." [freely translated by J.B.]

Noren – The sign
The guest enters the Ohashi-ya by passing through, or better still "under" a *noren*, which even today gives a traditional character to the appearance of streets in Japanese towns.

"The Noren [*sic*], which literally means a 'warm blind or curtain,' [...] is found at the entrance of a commercial house. Originally means [*sic*] for keeping the wind, heat, cold and dust off, the Noren was made of cloth of some kind or often of matting, or even of rope, though blue cotton seems to have been popularly used. There is no fixed size for the curtain, but almost invariably it has the name, mark or brand of the firm dyed on it.

When the Noren was first used is little known, but it was in vogue about the middle of the Shogunate reign (1338–1573) of Ashikaga, and it was very extensively used by most of the leading merchants during the Tokugawa Shogunate (1603–1867), so that one could tell the business of a shop by just looking at the Noren.

During the era of Genroku (1688–1703), a short Noren became so fashionable that a longer Noren was used at dry-goods stores, dryers' shops, public baths, barbers' shops, licensed houses, apothecaries, etc. In this way the Noren became almost as binding as the foreign 'goodwill,' and it sometimes changed hands. A clerk or apprentice who had served his term was privileged to 'share the Noren' by establishing a branch of the firm where he had worked.

During the Tokugawa Shogunate, a restriction was placed on certain branches of business. The number of dealers in calendars, for instance, was limited to 81 in the era of Genroku (1688–1703); that of exchange brokers to 600 in the era of Kyoho (1716–1735); and the permits issued to hair-

Opposite
Ohashi-ya
Detail of the tiled canopy with the *noren*, or "warm blind or curtain," which preserves the house from the iniquities of the weather, and a *takahari-chochin*, a lantern, most often oval in shape, and usually suspended from the top of a tall post or under the eaves of the house. People carry these lanterns before them in lantern processions.

Below
Utagawa Hiroshige
(1797–1858; active approx. 1818–1858)

The 53 stations of the Tōkaidō, 36th station, courtesans in the street in Goyu
around Tenpō 4–5 (1833/1834), *Nishiki-e*, multi-colored woodblock print, *Yoko-ōban* format, 10 × 15 ins., Publisher: Takeuchi Magohachi Bashō (1644–1694), the famous *haiku* poet, wrote: "The summer moon, which rose near Goyu, now stands over Akasaka." [freely translated by J.B.] Goyu is the Tōkaidō station before Akasaka and is just over a mile away from it, making these two stops the closest together of all 53 stations of the Tōkaidō.

The Japanese townhouse and business premises

Since the wealthy Genroku Period (1688–1703) there have been three trends in living accommodation that are very distinct from one another. Thanks to the new tools and techniques that were spreading across the entire country, the houses of the simple townsfolk became more lasting and improvements turned them into solidly built constructions with clear structural engineering and a quantum leap in quality. The samurai class built increasingly in the *sukiya* style, thereby signalling a breakthrough to simplicity and plainness in house building, an architectural form that from the end of the 19th century gained general recognition as a model for Japanese house construction. In addition the town houses were compact and developed their own significant style. Even the houses of the wealthy obeyed the common building regulations and were not scattered around on individual plots of land as in earlier times. Most houses in the town were narrow and stretched back a long way because of the high frontage costs and even lower status samurai who were not very well-to-do lived in similarly laid out townhouses. In their endeavours to create the optimum living space on small plots a second and third floor were added, if approval was given. Imagination knew no bounds at all when it was a question of creating space.

In pre-modern settlements and towns, where almost all transport was on foot, the problem of space led to the development of compact houses. Strings of small businesses and dwelling houses packed close to one another can be seen lining the street on medieval Japanese picture scrolls. There was not much space between the individual houses and the street, a style that continued throughout the entire Tokugawa Period (1603–1867). As it was essential for businessmen to have frontage onto the main street, a universal pattern arose for town living: blocks of buildings with businesses on long, narrow plots of land, which looked out onto a thoroughfare, and workshops as well as small, mostly one-room apartments in long buildings, or *nagaya*, the Japanese equivalent of tenement buildings. Whether small or large, the business premises had a characteristic shop, *mise* at the front, where sales were made or trade was carried out. The living quarters for the family and employees were behind the shop and at the back were the stores and stockrooms. In Kyōto buildings had the unique feature of a kitchen with an earth floor housed in a side passage, or *tōriniwa*, leading to the back of the house, whereas in Edo there are no side sections on townhouses.

In urban estates, the method of construction, the arrangement of space, and the interior furnishings differed only slightly from the way the *minka* was built, and the more the townsfolk began to imitate the lifestyle of the Samurai,

Above
Kawamata Tsuneyuki (active 2nd half of the 18th C, during the Edo Period 1615–1868)
Young woman
Nishiki-e, multi-colored woodblock print, *Ōban* format, 15 x 10 ins. (detail)
Kawamata Tsuneyuki was a successor of Miyagawa Choshun (1682–1752), who was famous for his hand paintings, or *nikuhitsuga*, of beautiful women. The original of the woodcut illustrated here

is assumed to be Kawamata Jogyo's "Street at evening."

Opposite
Ohashi-ya
Street frontage of the ryokan.
There are few streets left in modern Japan with closely packed houses and shops. However, it is always worth turning off into a side street, where you may suddenly come across a block of old town house buildings that has remained intact.

dressers in the era of Manji (1658–1660) numbered a little over 600, which increased in 1730 to 967 permits owned by 770 hair-dressers, some of whom operated several barber-shops. A hair-dresser, by the way, means one who dressed the hair of samurai or warriors, for they wore top-knots in the feudal days of Japan. So the Noren was a sort of patented permit, which was sellable and to own it cost several dozen or even hundred pieces of gold.

The Nawa-noren or rope-curtain, which is now seen in Tokyo, indicates a bar or cheap eating-house, so that 'to go under the rope-curtain' means to get a cheap drink or meal." [40]

Above
Ohashi-ya
View from the *dōma*, or ground floor room out onto the adjoining street.
The prototype of the divided ground plan of a Japanese house shows the space divided up into an upper living and sleeping section and a lower working area, the ground floor room or *dōma*. The higher part or *hiroshiki* is fitted with floorboards or covered with grass mats. The lower part is a household workroom and kitchen. Conventionally the floor there is flattened earth. This room is often also called *niwa*, which means garden or yard.

the more widespread the *sukiya* architectural style became. Certainly there were differences in design and intended use in urban areas, especially with regard to the garden area, living habits and size, but the basic architectural features always remained identical.

"The Japanese word for town is identical with the word street. This fully expresses what we have pointed out above, namely that a contrast between town and country has never existed. A number of houses where trade was carried on and which in consequence of greater traffic had settled on both sides of the crowded road was simply called 'town' as opposed to 'village.' To a certain extent it was only the farmhouse itself, a little changed and differently grouped, which had multiplied at such spots. [...] I might well say that of all things in Japan the astonishing endless line of shops stretching along almost all the streets (except the narrow sideways) made the greatest impression upon us."[41]

Engelbert Kämpfer – a German naturalist on the Tōkaidō

In his book *Geschichte und Beschreibung von Japan* (History and Description of Japan), published in 1728, the German naturalist Engelbert Kämpfer (1651–1716) described the increase in "tourists" on the Tōkaidō as follows: "Every day the major highways of this country are crowded by an unbelievable number of travelers, and at certain times I found more people here than in the capital cities of Europe." Kämpfer, who twice ventured to travel along the Tōkaidō from Nagasaki to Edo during the Genroku Period (1688–1703), undoubtedly broke his journey in Akasaka, staying at the Ohashi-ya.

In 1683 Kämpfer had been called to Moscow in his capacity as secretary of a Swedish embassy that was supposed to establish trade relations with Russia and Persia. From there he continued his journey to take in Nisabad and Isfahan, Persepolis, India, Siam, Java and finally Japan, where he stayed for two years (1690–1692). On 9.24.1690 Kämpfer entered the Dejima (Nagasaki) trading post and started to work with the Japanese scientist Imamura Genemon Eisei. He made his first journey to the Edo court between 2.13.–5.7.1691, arriving on 3.13.1691 and found lodging at the Nagasaki House

(Nagasakiya). He was granted an audience with the Shōgun Tokugawa Tsunayoshi as early as 3.29.1691. On 4.5.1691 Kämpfer left the eastern capital, reaching Nagasaki on 5.7.1691, from where on 3.2.1692 he set off on his second journey to the court. After arriving in Edo on 3.31.1692, he was again admitted into the presence of the Shōgun Tokugawa Tsunayoshin on 4.21.1692. Kämpfer set out on the return journey on 4.27.1692, reaching Nagasaki after just four weeks on 5.21.1692. In the same year he left Japan, heading for Batavia and returning to Lemgo in 1694 via Batavia with a stopover at the Cape of Good Hope and a stay in Amsterdam.

His work would certainly have been scattered over the entire world if the English doctor, botanist and writer, Sir Hans Sloane had not bought up Kämpfer's manuscripts from his heirs. They are now in the British Library in London, where they are accessible to every scientist. [42]

Top
Ohashi-ya
A simple variation of the *kendai* or *bondai* on the *hiroshiki*, the part of the *dōma* that is covered with floorboards. The Japanese desk for books, *kendai*, dates from the Nara Period (645–794) and was once reserved for members of the imperial household and the priesthood.

Center
Ohashi-ya
Noren to the *nando*, the closed side room of the *dōma*, which was formerly used for storage or for sleeping in. Above the *noren* are masks from a traditional ritual dance.

Below
Ohashi-ya
View looking into the ground level entrance room.

Above
Ohashi-ya
View looking into the open ceiling with wooden joists.

The roof space is often left open above the ground floor section so that the joists of the roof structure, which have been left in their natural state, can be seen. "In watching the building of any Japanese house, such as are erected in quantities to-day [sic], one can observe an unusually rough and clumsy tree-trunk [sic] put on top of the upper ceiling, on which the timber for the ridge-lead is very simply stood. [The intention is probably to] avert in this way a possible inclination of the roof. This beam supports the roof, the weight of it equally distributed above and in the middle, the essential construction of a span-work being unknown and generally not even used to-day [sic]. Any bending of this beam would immediately be visible in the room, as the ceiling is hanging from it.

Thus the house is so flexible that it bows to every wind or earthquake shock down to the smallest oscillations." (Bruno Taut)

The Tōkaidō

Akasaka is the 37th station of the Tōkaidō, which starts in Nihonbashi in Edo, now Tokyo. At the height of the Edo Period (1615–1868) about 1.5 million people traveled the Tōkaidō each year, and this already impressive figure rose notably in subsequent years. At that time the town had 360 estates and was a very lively place, but unfortunately after the great fire of 1709 only 80 houses were left intact. By 1716, only six years after the catastrophe, the Ohashi-ya had been rebuilt true to the original. The town of Akasaka recovered quickly too, and when Hiroshige immortalized the Ohashi-ya in his woodcut (1833), the little town had triumphed completely over the destruction.

At this time the Ohashi-ya was called "Iemon-Koiya" and the cycad tree, which adorns the picture in Hiroshige's portrayal, was later planted when fully grown in the grounds of the Josen-ji temple nearby.

"In feudal times the magnificent baggage trains of the *daimyō* (local feudal lords) used the Tōkaidō road on their way to and from Yedo (Tokyo) and Kyōto. This road was the main route in the east of Japan, and before the railway was constructed a constant stream of traffic surged along it. A Shōgun edict dictated that the *daimyō* had to spend certain times in Yedo with their retinue. This measure was intended to prevent the idea of rebelling against the shogunate occurring to the powerful local rulers in spite of the watchful eye of the Shōgun. Not least the vast sums of money eaten up by these journeys the *daimyō* made (the numbers of their servants ran into the hundreds) put a stop to any possibility of accumulating the funds necessary for equipping and keeping armed forces. There were 53 stations in which the *daimyō* would stay overnight. They were immortalized in Hiroshige's series of color prints *The 53 Stations of the Tōkaidō*.

The road is also famous for the pine trees lining it, in some places touching each other overhead to create tunnels of trees. Because of the increasing population, and the consequent need to widen the road, there has been a decline in the number of trees, but enough of them have been spared for the traveler to realize how beautiful the road must have been in feudal times and what interesting things revealed themselves all along the route to the numerous people who made their way along it, mostly on foot.

The 53 Stations of the Tōkaidō – tōkaidō gojūsan tsugi no uchi: In the year Tenpō 3 (1832) Hiroshige (1797–1858) first had the opportunity to travel the *Tōkaidō*. Under the orders of the Shōgun government he accompanied one of the annual delegations that paid homage to the tenno, wishing to present him with the gift of a horse. Hiroshige was supposed to record this journey in pictures. On returning to Edo Hiroshige secured the support of the big publisher, Tsuruya Kieimon and brought out the sketches of this journey under the auspices of the newly founded Hōeidō publishing house. Hiroshige had given such a vivid portrayal of the impressions he gained on the journey that many people showed increased interest in traveling the Tōkaidō. His book *Tōkaidō Chūhizakurige* from the Juppensha Ikku publishing house and other pictures of the Tōkaidō sold like hot cakes.

At this time trade and traffic were on the increase in Edo. More and more guesthouses and means of transport such as horses and sedan chairs were available. Pilgrimages to Ise and Shikoku, and pleasure trips too, were becoming ever more popular. Above all, admiration for the capital city Kyōto increased. As the Tōkaidō was the chief route between Edo and Kyōto, the publication of the views in the *53 Stations of the Tōkaidō* came at just the right time. Meanwhile the Hoeido publishing house was dealing exclusively with the publication of the Tōkaidō, and that is why these became known simply as *Hōeidōban* (*Hōeidō* prints) in order to distinguish them from other Tōkaidō series, so that the name of this otherwise small and insignificant publishing house is well-known even today. The pleasing views lend a lyrical atmosphere to the journey, but also have their humorous moments. They also found particular favor because they show popular subjects such as snow scenes, scenes by moonlight, or in the rain and mist, and also changes in nature and its forces.

Below
Utagawa Hiroshige
(1797–1858; active approx. 1818–1858)
**The 53 stations of the Tōkaidō
37th station, courtesans in the ryokan
at Akasaka**
around Tenpō 4–5 (1833/1834),
Nishiki-e, multi-colored woodblock print,

Yoko-ōban format, 10 x 15 ins.,
Publisher: Takeuchi Magohachi
In Hiroshige's time the Ohashi-ya was called "Iemon-Koiya" and the cycad tree, which adorns the picture in Hiroshige's portrayal, was planted later, when fully grown, in the grounds of the Josen-ji temple situated nearby.

Hiroshige also frequently used the popular *fukibokashi* style, in which the paint for the background is washed onto the printing plate with a cloth. In this way not only the Japanese people's feeling for nature but also the color moods peculiar to Japanese landscapes found excellent expression and inspired many painters in subsequent years to depict scenery from across the entire country. Of the views included in Hiroshige's *53 Stations of the Tōkaidō* – he was known simply as the Tōkaidō painter – the 30 or so that were published by Hoeido can definitely be classified as masterpieces. These works achieved the absolute best-seller record in the history of the *ukiyo-e*, with over 10,000 copies being printed. Due to the frequent reprints the shape of the prints changed several times, and some of the printing plates had to be recut. Later editions differed from the first impression, especially in the color." [43]

With his Tōkaidō series (1833/1834) Utagawa Hiroshige (1797–1858) achieved fame and a reputation as the best landscape painter in Japan. He created his masterpiece with his portrayals of the area around the Tōkaidō in all four seasons and of the daily life of the people living there. However, in addition to landscape scenes and the celebrated "100 views of famous places in Edo," *Edōkinkō hakkei,* Hiroshige's extensive work also includes excellent portrayals of birds, flowers, and poetic subjects. His reputation spread with the first exports of Japanese color woodcuts – unexpectedly in the Western world too – and Vincent van Gogh made use of many of Hiroshige's works as designs for his own paintings. This sensitive, "avant garde," and yet fundamentally Japanese artist has provided the Western classical modern age with essential stimuli.

Matsuo Bashō – the "Saint of *haiku*"

Taken sick on the journey:
Over parched fields
Your dreams wander on.
Matsuo Bashō (1644–1694)
[freely translated by J.B.]

It was Bashō who wrote: "The summer moon, which rose over Goyu, now stands over Akasaka." Goyu is the Tōkaidō station before Akasaka and is just over a mile away from it,

Right
Ohashi-ya
The upper part of the *dōma*, the *hiroshiki*, with floorboards and covered with *tatami*. In the foreground is a *hibachi*, a fire container, which is more for the purpose of warming one's hands than for heating the room. "The *hibachi* creates a cozy effect and in Japan is generally considered to be typically the comfortable place where the members of the family gather together to chat whilst warming their hands over the glowing coals in the pan." (*We Japanese*)

Above
Ohashi-ya
The "suite of rooms" consisting of the three guest rooms. The sliding doors are open and give a clear impression of the flexibility of Japanese accommodation, the size and function of the rooms being variable according to need.

Opposite
Ohashi-ya
The three upper guest rooms looking out onto the street are reached by the old, steep staircase. Nothing has changed since the travelers stopped here on their way along the Tōkaidō to the capital city, and the rooms have kept the atmosphere of those days as if in a dream. In one of these rooms Bashō, the famous *haiku* poet, lost himself to his thoughts, and the German naturalist Engelbert Kämpfer (1651–1716) stayed here on his way to see the Shōgun.

making these the two stops which are closest together of all 53 stations of the Tōkaidō. Bashō particularly loved the moon, which on short summer nights accompanied the travelers as they hurried to and fro on the short stretch between Goyu and Akasaka. Maybe, too, he was comparing his life, which he felt was not likely to last that long, with the ephemeral summer moon.

The room in the Ohashi-ya where Bashō stayed has been preserved. The guest enters the ryokan across the floor of flattened earth, to reach the next room with a wooden floor and then another room with a fireplace, which, although small, receives a wonderfully intimate light from the rays of the sun as they stream through the latticework of the lintel. The three upper guestrooms looking out onto the street are reached by the old, steep staircase. Nothing has changed since the travelers stopped here on their way along the Tōkaidō to the capital city, and the rooms have kept the atmosphere of those days as if in a dream. In one of these rooms Bashō, the famous *haiku* poet, abandoned himself to his thoughts, and one of Bashō's pupils expresses in a *haiku* the desire to have once more the opportunity of returning to the Ohashi-ya so beloved by him.

It can be said that the tradition of the particular literary genre known today as the *haiku* goes back to the poet Matsuo Bashō (1644–1694). This unique form of the art of Japanese poetry, so typical of the Japanese intellect, still enjoys great popularity today.

The *haiku* was originally called *hokku*, meaning much the same as the first verse of a *renga* (chain poem), the historical predecessor to the *haiku*, and served as a link between *waka* and the latter. The *haiku* was born when the first verses of the chain poem were allowed to stand independently. So the *haiku* consists of a sentence (or sentences) of 17 syllables, divided up

Opposite
Ohashi-ya
Built-in shelving – one of the main features of *shoin* architecture – in the *hiroshiki* of the main room.

On the bottom shelf is a collection of sake bottles.

Above
Ohashi-ya
View into the lit ryokan in the evening. "I might well say that of all things in Japan the astonishing endless line of shops stretching along almost all the streets (except the narrow sideways) made the greatest impression upon us." (Bruno Taut)

into 5/7/5 syllables, in form therefore being the exact equivalent of the top stanza of a *waka*.

The striking feature of the *haiku* as a poetic form lies in the fact that, just as with the *waka*, it is extremely short – even shorter than a *waka* – and that cutting back the linguistic unit to the most extreme limit assists the creation of a timeless, poetic-linguistic field.

Certainly there was a string of important predecessors to Basho; and from a historical point of view he was nothing more than the founder of one of the many schools that left their mark on history as Bashō schools. But it was precisely this Bashō who, after freeing *haiku* poetry from the playful, mischievous aura that had been characteristic of this type of literature for centuries before, placed it resolutely on the footing of the metaphysical and existential experience of *wabi*. Thus he

elevated it to a position that can be justly considered as an art form equal to the other art forms such as *waka* poetry, *nō* drama, the tea ceremony, kendo and others.

Bashō who is traditionally called "Saint of the *haiku*," was not merely a poet of standing, but also an original thinker who opened up a completely new field to the school of thought on the aesthetics of poetry. [44]

鱒の家

Masu-no-ya, Oshigusa

... Transported away by the wind
The vapour from Fuji
Evaporating on the firmament
Where do they go, nobody knows,
The yearnings in my dreams? ...

Saigyō Hōshi

[freely translated by N.C.]

Located at the foot of *fuji-san*, Japan's incomparable sacred mountain, is the Masu-no-ya ryokan, representative of a world almost lost. Since the 17th century, this unchanged agricultural estate with fish farm has been owned by the same family. The guest house is a traditional *minka* whose rooms were once used for silkworm breeding, and in these original rooms the visitor can still experience traditional Japanese customs. The inn is fabulously situated in an enchanting "landscape strolling garden," *chisen-kaiyu*, with a small lake and an old mill.

The traditional minka

The word *minka*, literally "houses of the population," describes a large spectrum of Japanese dwellings – from the residences of rich merchants to the humblest abodes of farmers. The term is frequently also applied to the houses of Shinto priests, lesser nobility and the samurai, in short all dwellings of the population not belonging to the very upper echelons of society.

Above
Masu-no-ya
View across the landscape garden, *tsukiyama*, with hills, a pond and an old mill.

Opposite
Masu-no-ya
The waterfall in the fish pond has three levels which represent the sky, the earth and human beings. In the foreground there is a stone lantern, *ishi-doro*.

Originally only found in the gardens of temples and shrines, above all as devotional objects and votive offerings, the stone lanterns gradually evolved from being religious objects and since the Kamakura period (1185–1333) have been used to provide light and for secular purposes. Nowadays *ishi-doro* are also popular in the West as exotic garden decorations, and are available in numerous speciality stores.

Above
Masu-no-ya
The old thatched mill is driven by the force of a water source on the property of the ryokan, which also supplies constant fresh water to the fish farm. In front of the mill is a composition of several rocks which reminds the viewer of a turtle or a crane, both animals symbolising health and a long life.

The *minka* type itself is as diverse as its occupiers and over the centuries has undergone numerous changes in line with the needs of the different occupants. During the Edo period (1615–1868) more and more *shoin* elements were adopted in the *minka*, especially for the design of the *zashiki*, the main living room, where official visitors were received. Nonetheless a clear difference remained between the dwelling houses of the nobility and the *minka* owing to the numerous laws prescribing house designs and so maintaining class distinctions.

"It is interesting to note that in the Japanese language the word for a home is *katei*, which is written with the combined characters for a house (*ka*) and garden (*tei*) – a telling indication of how inseparable the two used to be in the Japanese mind. Housing is obviously born out of our coping with our environment, both topographical and climatic, and in the areas of Japan where most people live the land is hilly or mountainous, and the weather, except for the tropical summer, is usually temperate. Until the postwar years, the Japanese built with this warmer weather in mind, the general philosophy being that one can put up with anything during the short winter, but a house that is not built to provide relief from the summer heat would be simply unbearable. [...] Houses were raised above the ground to avoid dampness and to allow for the circulation of air. They were built on an ingenious modular system, with sliding doors that could be opened up (or even removed) to make space flexible for family and social functions, and to take advantage of the cooling summer breezes and views of the greenery outside. As a result, every Japanese lived close to – and was acutely sensitive to – all of the subtle signs and moods of nature: the sounds of birds and fall insects, the breeze whispering in the pine-needles, and the smells of the earth after a summer rain shower. In Japan there were no dangerous predators to guard against, and apart from a few mosquitoes, which could be screened out, nature is soft, welcoming, and seductively beautiful.

Country houses were usually more spacious than those in the city, and apart from having to house a large extended family might also, in some parts of the country, be used for raising silkworms. Traditionally, roofs were thatched, [...] but as this kind of roofing has to be replaced every few years, increased wealth in the countryside has seen thatch replaced with tiles, which are longer lasting and less of a fire risk. Farmhouses were built mainly of wood with a system of interlocking posts and beams that is strong and flexible enough to withstand the force of frequent earthquakes and the fall typhoons. Despite the discomforts of poor heating and a smoky atmosphere, Japanese *minka* (farmhouses) have a captivating and homely character that is welcoming and honest; they provide the sense of satisfaction that can only be achieved by living close to natural materials, namely wood, straw, and paper. They have served their owners well through the centuries and it is regrettable to see that so many are now being destroyed, only to be replaced with mass-produced modern houses made of synthetic materials that have no redeeming architectural features whatsoever." [45]

Below
Masu-no-ya
The bridge spanning the pond in the garden.
These bridges are known as moon bridges. Aside from trout, the pond also contains *koi*, a type of goldfish. Usually reddish, they are living dabs of color that symbolize strength and courage.

Right
Masu-no-ya
A stone path across the pond.
The natural stepping stones are arranged in angular, free lines. The stones differ in size, nature, quality and coloring.

The "room" in the Japanese house

The Japanese language does not have a word that corresponds exactly to the Western concept of "room" in the sense of chamber, even if the character *ma* is the term for "room." Whenever we speak of rooms in a Japanese house, we understand the room to be a place or space. The walls which delineate a room in Western houses are moveable partitions in Japan which subdivide space as needed.

If one looks at the plan of a Japanese house the bearing elements are clearly defined but closed spaces are not evident. Rooms have functions but are not structural in the sense of Western rooms, they localise space, but do not provide the structure with static support. The basic layout for the *minka* is a three-room arrangement which evolved during the 18th century into a four-room concept which varies in turn according to the landscape, region and the social class of the occupants.

Irori and jizai-kagi

"The *irori* (hearth) is no longer found in a modern-style house in Japan. It is a fire-place [*sic*], which suggests the old-time home-life of Japan better than anything else does. Nothing is considered to be as entertaining as a chat around an old *irori*, black with soot, on a cold night after a hard day's work. The *irori* is the heater or stove of a room as well as a cooking place. It has what is called the *jizai* (literally, elasticity) made of bamboo, a contrivance for hanging a tea-kettle over the charcoal of the *irori*; so named because it can be "freely" stretched out or contracted."[46]

For centuries the *jizai-kagi*, the adjustable hearth hook, which can be constructed of wood, metal and bamboo, was a familiar sight and eye-catcher in every *minka*. The hanger or hook is secured to a girder of the timberwork and hangs down from the ceiling to just above the open hearth. Near to the kettle suspended over the hearth is a large horizontal balance made of wood, frequently a sculptural masterpiece. Especially popular motives were colossal hooks, propeller blades or fish – lucky symbols. Below was the iron hook for the soup pot or the kettle. Depending on the degree of heat required the *jizai-kagi* is raised or lowered to simmer or boil the water for tea or to cook the food. There is no firm evidence regarding the origins of the *jizai-kagi*, however, we can assume that its beginnings are prehistoric as almost all old cultures had counterparts.

Likewise the *irori*, the open hearth, is the oldest heating system in Japan, for all classes and all dwelling houses. It is located in the center of the main room as a square opening in the floor, has a wood or stone lining and is filled with ash. The whole day wood or charcoal is burnt here and this fireplace is the "heart" of the *minka*, the family "communication center," and during the cold winter a cosy place to sleep.

The picturesque thatched roofs on old Japanese houses are the visual and practical equivalent to the *irori*, both keep away the cold and the smoke dries the reeds and discourages insects. Many roofs are several hundred years old. Today they are only permitted in the countryside because they are highly inflammable and a considerable fire hazard.

Silkworm breeding in the *minka*

Until World War Two, raw silk was one of Japan's most important export commodities and met 60% of the global demand. Japan was the main international source for raw silk because a large proportion of the mainly rural population living on small farmsteads earned a secondary income to rice cultivation with silkworm breeding. The entire family dedicated itself on alternating shifts day and night to the intensive care required by the okaiko *sama*, the "honorable" silkworm, and the time-consuming manual labor involved in reeling the filaments. Participation in this lucrative secondary income required an investment in an "egg card." The eggs were placed under newspaper into which small holes were cut and through which the hatched worms crawled attracted by the light. One also required mulberry leaves. Because, however, about 10% of the cultivated land in Japan is dedicated to mulberry trees the leaves were not in short supply. The women and children of the farmer's family had the task of picking the best and most tender leaves of the *kuwa*, the mulberry tree, and also the laborious job of drying the leaves.

Each time it sheds its skin the voracious silkworm greedily digs into large quantities of mulberry leaves. The thousands of worms on their straw beds are fed only the most tender leaves, pre-sorted according to the age of the worms. If it rains, the leaves are carefully dried before being fed to the worms as moisture could damage the silk threads. The noise that the creatures make when eating is said in Japan to be reminiscent

Left
Masu-no-ya
The *zashiki*, the formal guest room, with half-opened *fusuma* and *shōji*.
   The influence of the *shoin* style upon rural minka architecture becomes evident in the beautiful zabuton, the floor cushions, and the large root timber table. Tables were a rarity in Japan and developed from the low altar tables on which foodstuffs and flowers were placed as offerings. On the circumferential console below the ceiling is the *kamidana*, the household Shinto shrine.

of falling rain. With the technical perfection of an engineer, the satiated worms spin their silk thread on a single straw stem or a bundle of straw stems to anchor the cocoon. The silk is won from the cocoon of the caterpillar of the domesticated silkworm, a moth with a yellowy white color and three delicate brown stripes across the wings, which originally came from China and India. The oyster white caterpillars, with a darker head, reach maturity after they have shed their skins four times, and live for about seven weeks, eating nothing but mulberry leaves and finally pupating in a long round cocoon. To spin the cocoon, like all silkworms, they use a fine liquid which is produced inside two glands close to the head and which is secreted from two pairs of spinnerets below the mouth and then combined in a single filament which hardens on contact with air and is extremely fine. The caterpillar first creates a spacious, fine envelope to anchor the cocoon and then spins the cocoon in a circular form using a single filament that is around 1150 feet in length and then covers the cocoon from inside with a sticky liquid. After about three weeks the fully grown moth pushes its way out of the envelope to mate and then to die (the males of the species die immediately, the females after laying about 500 eggs).

The most difficult task, also requiring the greatest care, in producing the silk is the reeling of the silk filaments. This has to be done at the right time as otherwise the moth may leave the cocoon, breaking it and making it unusable. After the

Below left and right
Masu-no-ya
Closed *fusuma*, wooden sliding doors and *shōji* windows covered with mulberry tree paper with an aperture at eye-level (one sits on the floor cushions!) allowing a view of the garden.

Opposite, top
Masu-no-ya
A *fusuma* painted with a pine tree in the style of Kanō Eitokus (1543–1590); forceful and generous the design extends across the individual panels of the screen which is used to partition space. The artistic quality of the painting evidences the appreciation of beauty and the lifestyle of the family which has owned Masu-no-ya for centuries.

Opposite, bottom
A farmer's wife tending to the silkworms in the *minka*
The *okaiko sama*, the honorable silkworms, are placed on a type of woven "baking tray" for the molting process and are fed the best leaves of the mulberry tree, *kuwa*, at an optimum temperature.
Line drawing from: *We Japanese*, Fujiya Hotel Ltd. (publisher), Miyanoshita, Hakone 1949, p. 120

cocoon has been spun, the pupa is therefore killed through heat, the best method is to use steam or hot water into which the cocoons are thrown and which at the same time removes the gummy substance from the cocoon (degumming). Then the outer cocoon is wound off, which yields a lower quality silk, and the actual silk filament is reeled from the interior. Usually twelve cocoons are reeled simultaneously to obtain the desired thickness. For one pound one requires some 200 cocoons and 12–14 pounds of cocoon yield one pound of pure silk which, however, differs in quality as there are three types of caterpillars which spin respectively white, pure white and yellowish silk. [47]

The home of silkworm breeding is China where the art was closely guarded for thousands of years. About 200 B.C. silk production reached Korea and from there Japan. Around 550 A.D. monks are reported to have brought silkworm eggs to Byzantium in hollow canes. From here silk production spread to Spain, Italy and France.

"Baldabiou knew all these stores. Especially he was aware of the rumour that appeared time and time again in the tales of all those who had been there. It said that on that island (Japan) the most beautiful silk in the world was produced. This had been done for more than one thousand years according to rituals and secret recipes which had attained a mysterious precision. For his part, he believed it wasn't a rumour but simply the truth. Once he had held a piece of cloth that had been woven from Japanese silk. It was as if he had held nothing in his hands." [48]

A young Chinese Empress called Si Line-shi is supposed to have "discovered" silk about 5000 years ago as she unwound the delicate filament from a caterpillar that was spinning its cocoon and obtained an exquisite spun thread. The name of the innovative small empress lives on in the Chinese, French, German and English words for the costly cloth: *si, soie, Seide* and silk.

Perfect elegance in straw, reed and bamboo

Not without good reason is the claim made that the beauty of Japanese houses lies in the combination of the straight and curved lines of the roofs.

These roofs are a key expressive element of the architecture as a whole because they are the only diagonal features in the frame of an otherwise vertical and horizontal design. Even the *minka*, the plain Japanese dwelling and farmhouse, discloses a surprising wealth of designs: broad hipped roofs, steep, sharp gables, roof dormers and ridges in numerous artistic variations, made of a wide range of materials, partly puristic in design partly sumptuous.

Four different types of roof structure can be differentiated: *kiri-zuma*, the gable roof; *schichu, yose-mune* or *azumaya*, roofs where the roof slopes in four directions from the ridge pole without forming a gable; *irimoya*, a roof consisting of two sections, a *kiri-zuma* and a *shichu*; and *hogyo*, also a roof sloping primarily in four directions, but more from a vertex, a pyramidal roof. Ingeniously designed eaves are a further picturesque feature of Japanese roofs. However, they are not just gracefully curved decorative features but protect the house against adverse weather, heavy rain and the heat of sun, and allow the house to be kept open no matter what the weather.

The most important materials for roofing are straw, reeds, the bark of the *hinoki*, ceramic shingles, sheet bronze, slates, clay tiles, and bamboo. The type of roofing depends on the region, the type of building and its purpose. *Minka* are usually thatched and lend this basically plain form of house incomparable grace. "[...] Although they talk of disagreeable insects that like to nest in the straw, it can not [sic] be denied that this straw covering is the very best protection against heat and cold, besides being of an uncommon beauty." [49]

The thatched roof is mostly very thick and is folded and tucked in the most elegant of curves which are cut using shears and which decorate the corners and eaves of the roof. The straw is applied in individual layers from the bottom upwards and bamboo poles are used as temporary supports. All in all bamboo has a fundamental role in the structure of roof. Horizontal in relation to the sloping beams of the roof structure, the bamboo poles are lashed together at intervals of 8–12 inches and are covered by a woven mat comprising thin bamboo or reeds. This net remains in the halls as a visible surface and the different tones of the bamboo provide a particular pattern and decorative feature.

Special attention is paid to the roof ridge, which boasts numerous individual decorative designs. Japan's "principle gable," the gable of the Ise Shrine, is decorated with caps made of solid gold. What the "*minka* ridges" lack in monetary value they make up for with their highly imaginative designs. Transverse, uncut or neatly trimmed layers of straw tower up above the roof vertex, decorated and held in place by woven strips of straw. Bamboo poles in different variations and arrangements are disposed at the ends next to planks, slats and marginal boards cut in curved lines like a ship's bow. In addition one finds gable crosses reminiscent of European farmhouses. They often contain a free floating pole in the same way as round transverse beams are "levitated" into place on board supports. The imaginativeness displayed by the roofers, who in the main were also farmers, witnesses to this day the natural handicraft skills that were applied to form and material.

Fuji-san

Walking along the coast at Tago
I saw the snow falling
Perfect whiteness
On Mount Fuji's lofty peak
Yamabe no Akahito (8th century)
[freely translated by N.C.]

"Mt. Fujii may be seen in whole or in part, more or less distinctly, from 22 prefectures, but nowhere in Japan are the views of this regal mountain so beautiful or varied as those of the Hakone District. The perfect, majestic conical peak of Mt. Fuji, rising in sublime grandeur 12,395 feet (3,778 metres) above sea-level, is the highest, as well as the most famous mountain in all Japan. It is the 'National Mountain,' regarded as sacred by Japanese and it has been the Mecca for over 1,000 years for pilgrims and other folk who have climbed its slopes during July and August, the only time in the year when the mountain's robe of snow is laid aside.

Opposite
Masu-no-ya
Detail elevations of the roofs of the buildings of the *minka* ryokan Masu-no-ya. From left: thatch with superposed "ventilation roof"; *kiri-zuma*, gable roof, thatched; crossed rafter arrangement above the ridge; bearing tie beams; carved gable of a collar beam roof; ridge cap above the roof dormer; gable roof with double roof frame and large window. This kind of roof was used for breeding silkworms, which was usually carried out on the top roof story; the gable decoration of a dome-shaped roof.

Following double page
Masu-no-ya
View across the *tsukiyama*-style garden that includes all of the most important elements of the landscape garden: hills, water, garden plants, rocks, trees and bridges. Embedded in the "naturally landscaped nature" are the elegant thatched roofs of the *minka*. In the background is *fuji-san*.

MASU-NO-YA, OSHIGUSA

It extends into three provinces: Suruga, Kai, and Totomi. At its base it is about 100 miles in circumference. Peerless Fuji-yama defies description. You may read about it, see scores of pictures of it, hear what other travelers say about it, but when you see it in its varied aspects, never twice alike, you will realize that the real Fuji is far beyond anything you have ever imagined. Sometimes it appears in faultless white and silver against a blue sky, sometimes its perfect crest seems to float phantom-like above the clouds, and sometimes at sunset it lifts its purple mystery into a rosy sky – and its charm graces all the arts of Japan and appears in countless Japanese and foreign writings, and poems." [50]

"The sun shone bright and the air was clear. Never had we seen Mount Fuji so distinctly before. There was just a little snow on the summit; a delicate cloud was soaring in front of it, casting a light shadow. The silhouette of the mountain could be followed far down its extremely elegant lines.

It would be impossible to embellish the form of this mountain. It is a work of art, although of nature. When we compare it to other peaks these seem naked, rugged, elemental. All but a very few of the people in our compartment stood watching the mountain, gazing at it as long as it could be seen. And we said to each other: This is Japan; this is the Japanese spirit in clear shape. And the people, admiring in this mountain the crown of their country, must inevitably strive, whether they will or not, to attain in their art and life the same purity as it demonstrates before their eyes." [51]

Left
Masu-no-ya
The majestic *fuji-san*, Japan's sacred mountain, seen from Masu-no-ya. Phantom-like and always unpredictable, the incarnation of a mountain in the Platonic sense appears before our eyes.

Its magic decorates all Japan's arts and it is immortalised in countless Japanese and other international publications and poems. The legend says that if a person has the unexpected luck to see *fuji-san* in person he or she will return to Japan.

ダン林

Opposite
Dan-bayashi
During the summer months the mossy,
thatched dormer roof of the former
samurai residence unites with the lush
green landscape to create a charming
picture. "In country areas the compact
thatched roof of the traditional house
is common. Thatch has an excellent
insulating effect and is very economical.
Moreover, if brought to creative
perfection, as in Japan, it is of a
beauty that cannot be equalled."
(Bruno Taut; freely translated by J.B.)

Dan-bayashi, Kuta Sakyo-ku

The revered, old samurai residence of Dan-bayashi is situated in enchanting rural surroundings not far from the former capital Kyōto. During the summer months the mossy green roofs combine with the lush green of the landscape to create an idyllic picture. In tranquil and romantic surroundings the exquisite form of the Dan-bayashi ryokan, which reflects the spirit and lifestyle of the samurai and has been preserved like this for centuries now, astounds and inspires the visitor. The imposing gateway, the spacious entrance area with a *tokonoma*, or picture alcove, and the wonderfully painted *fusuma*, sliding doors, as well as the elaborately carved *ramma* in the interior – all these treasures nestle in surroundings left in their natural state of informal charm.

For Japanese architecture the garden and the surrounding countryside are not merely creative accessories, but also essential components, as both freely growing nature as well as the structured garden, reflect numerous aspects of Japanese history, traditions which have remained alive to the present day and find their form in a constantly renewing nature, imbued with life.

The appearance of the garden and of the landscape changes with the cycle of the seasons, illustrating the respect the Japanese people have for the realm of nature. Each of the four seasons is given space to unfold, so that the observer is inspired to reflect on what has been, whether this occurs

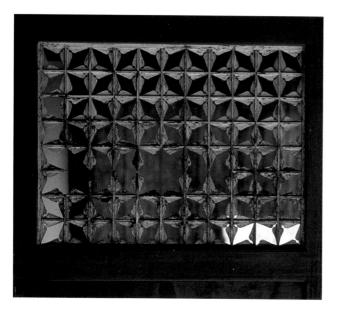

through what he sees, or through smell, touch or sound. An appeal is made to all the senses so that Japanese traditions may be experienced; this is also true of the sequence of dishes on the *kaiseki* menu.

Shintō, the way of the gods, with its deep respect for the natural world, which is valued as a sacred domain, finds expression in the gardens and in the way in which nature is worshipped, so that the visitor can relate to the genuine spirituality of the people.

A particular aspect is emphasised in each season, arousing an explicit feeling in the onlooker and maybe even providing an answer to his personal inner state. In summer it is not the fullness of the blooms and the color, but the gentle green of the meadows and mountains, as well as the "Seven Grasses" of late summer: *hagi* (Japanese clover), *susuki* (silver grass), *kuzu* (arrowroot), *nadeshiko* (wild carnation), *ominaeshi* (toad flax), *fujibakama* (Chinese agrimony), and *hirugao* (field bindweed). Grasses have the same status as the mighty pine trees or the glowing azaleas and they are transposed onto picture scrolls and screens with the same artistic care, even if they are less spectacular.

Japanese summers are hot, with many showers and therefore humidity is high. In this hazy ethereal atmosphere the rays of the sun are broken up – creating an optical medium that makes everything appear soft and peaceful and bathes the surroundings in a grey or white light that shines from within itself. A trick of nature, which characterizes much of that which appears "Asian" to us by mood. In summer, too, the countryside joins in with the creation and stage-management of space, feeling and art.

The Way of the Samurai

The rise of the samurai began in Japan in the 9th century, when the central aristocratic government was increasingly losing power to the big land owners, who employed their own troops. The leaders of these troops were called *bushi* or samurai, and the majority of them were descendents of the old *uji* clan. The samurai were responsible for giving general ethical views and moral standards, and were the keepers of the peace for centuries. These warriors followed their own code of honor, developed their own standards and rules of conduct, called *bushi-dō*. These were handed down orally, remaining in force for generations.

Opposite
Dan-bayashi
Decorative open-work in wood,
"light screens" on an external sliding
door, *amado*, literally "rain door."

Above
Dan-bayashi
Approach to the ryokan through the
estate, which has been left in its natural

state. The transition from outside to
inside, along with its implied antithesis,
does not exist in a Japanese house. The
natural world that surrounds a house is
part of its "own four walls" and the
absence of fixed doors and windows –
all are sliding and adaptable –
intensifies our awareness of these less
tangible parts.

The following lines were written down in the 17th century by a former samurai, who later became a Zen monk: "The Way of the Samurai is found in death. When it comes to either/or, there is only the quick choice of death. When pressed with the choice of life or death, it is not necessary to gain one's aim. We all want to live. And in a large part we make our logic according to what we like. But not having attained our aim and continuing to live is cowardice. This is a thin dangerous line. To die without gaining one's aim is a dog's death and fanaticism. But there is no shame in this. This is the substance of the Way of the Samurai. If by setting one's heart right every morning and evening, one is able to live as though his body were already dead, he gains freedom in the Way. His whole life will be without blame, and he will succeed in his calling. Being a retainer is nothing other than being a supporter of one's lord, entrusting matters of good and evil to him, and renouncing self-interest. If there are but two or three men of this type, the fief will be secure. Loyalty is said to be important in the pledge between lord and retainer.

Though it may seem unobtainable, it is right before your eyes. If you once set yourself to it, you will become a superb retainer at that very moment. The person without previous resolution to inevitable death makes certain that his death will be in bad form. But if one is resolved to death beforehand, in what way can he be despicable? One should be especially diligent in this concern.

If one were to say in a word what the condition of being a samurai is, its basis lies first in seriously devoting one's body and soul to his master. And if one is asked what to do beyond this, it would be to fit oneself inwardly with intelligence, humanity and courage. The combining of these three virtues may seem unobtainable to the ordinary person, but it is easy. Intelligence is nothing more than discussing things with others. Limitless wisdom comes from this. Humanity is something done for the sake of others, simply comparing oneself with them and putting them in the fore. Courage is gritting one's teeth; it is simply doing that and pushing ahead, paying no attention to the circumstances. Anything that seems above these three is not necessary to be known. As for outward aspects, there are personal appearance, one's way of speaking and calligraphy. And as all of these are daily matters, they improve by constant practice. Basically, one should perceive their nature to be one of quiet strength.

If one has accomplished all these things, then he should have a knowledge of our area's history and customs. After that he may study the various arts as recreation. If you think it over, being a retainer is simple. And these days, if you observe people who are even a bit useful, you will see that they have accomplished these three outward aspects." [52]

"Shigenari Kimura, a typical samurai of old: Shigenari Kimura served with the Toyotomi dynasty (1585–1603) in its declining days. He died at the unripe age of 21 years, but he may be said to have lived longer than the average span of human life if his life could be measured by its usefulness, for he was one of the most important samurai during the last years of the Toyotomi family. He was a typical samurai of old and died as such.

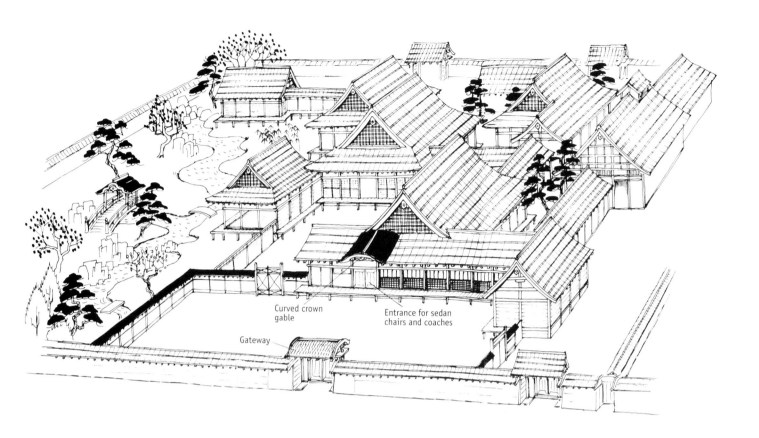

Curved crown
gable

Entrance for sedan
chairs and coaches

Gateway

In 1614, when peace was concluded between Toyotomi and Tokugawa, Kimura, just out of his teens, was sent on an important mission of getting the peace agreement signed by Iyeyasu, the ex-Shogun of Tokugawa. On his arrival at the Shogunate Palace, young Kimura saw all the Shogunate dignitaries sitting on both sides of a long passage-way he had to pass along, but he walked straight on with dignity, but no sign of fear, without even returning the greetings of the Shogunate lords, until he came into the presence of the ex-Shogun, whose signature he received. When he retired from the ex-Shogunate's presence, Kimura bowed politely at every Shogunate lord and said: 'Last time when I passed along this hall, I carried an important mission in representation of my lord, Tyotomi, and so I did not return your greetings. I ask your forgiveness.'

Peace was soon broken between the two Shogunate families, and Kimura was aware that he was not going to return alive from the battle they were to fight against each other, and he ate much less than usual at meals.

'I want to save myself the disgrace' Kimura answered when his worried young wife asked why he ate so little, 'of having undigested rice in my throat when my head is cut off by the enemy. Early in history, I am told, a certain warrior was shot dead with an arrow, which hit him on the throat [*sic*], when rice that he ate at breakfast ran out [*sic*].'

That night his young wife, 19 years old, retired into her chamber. She wrote a testament [*sic*]. 'Man has a time for everything,' she said among other things, 'and it will be a disgrace to survive the time of death [*sic*].' And she committed suicide.

On the morning of the battle, which totally ruined the Toyotomi family in 1615, Kimura took a bath, washed his hair cleaner and dressed it neater than usual, and showed such presence of mind that he sang a favorite *no* drama before his retainers. Then he held his helmet over burning incense to give it its fragrance before his departure for the front.

Top
Top view of the residence of the Hosokawa samurai clan in Kyōto
Late Muromachi Period (1392–1573)
From: Kazuo Nishi and Kazuo Hozumi, *What is Japanese Architecture?*
A survey of Traditional Japanese Architecture, Tokyo 1985, p. 71.

Opposite, left
Dan-bayashi
View of the entrance area, looking towards the inner garden.
Traditional Japanese houses are often built on stilts or pegs, on stone bases, sometimes with wooden open-work facings. This was to raise the building above the ground and protect it from rotting. A reason dictated by ritual was to avoid disturbing the earth by driving deep foundations into it.

Opposite, left
Dan-bayashi
Natural stone base, to secure the building and at the same time a link with the earth.

Above
Dan-bayashi
View of the *engawa* closed off with an *amado* (literally: rain door), under the moss-covered protruding roof. *Amado* are wooden latched or sliding veranda and outside shutters, which protect from rain, the night and the cold.

Opposite
Dan-bayashi
The *engawa*, or veranda running round the building, before closed *shōji*. The covering on these moveable walls is made of paper, obtained from the wood of the mulberry tree. Unlike a door that can only be opened in one direction, the *shōji* can be moved in any direction, like curtains, only without the "glass shutters" in front.

Shigenari Kimura was killed in a battle against Noataka Ii, a lord on the Tokugawa side. When his head was brought for inspection, Iyeyasu admired his samurai-like death and bade his attendant lords smell the helmet, which he said Kimura made scented because his head would soon smell bad in hot summer, in which the battle was fought. Naotaka Ii, who killed Kimura, was so much touched with his samurai-like death. He buried Kimura's head in his clan, and built a head-mound over it offering a prayer for the repose of his departed soul. Kimura is indeed looked up to as a true samurai." [53]

Samurai residences

The most influential medieval warlords organised their residences and their way of life using the model of the descendants of the Heian aristocracy, who, although they had lost power and political influence, still enjoyed enormous prestige on account of their past and their culture. High ranking samurai therefore adopted the *shinden* style for their residential complexes and gardens, or, to be more accurate, a modified version of *shinden* style, as this had already been transformed in previous centuries into a more formal *shoin* form with functional use of space. A major development was the *kaisho*, a separate building for official receptions, bringing greater intimacy to the arrangement of the living area. In any case from this time onwards the different parts of the building were organised individually according to their use and not just according to a strict code of etiquette. The variations on the samurai house range from palatial buildings with richly adorned tiled roofs to thatched houses in simple, yet formally elegant grounds. The samurai residence in particular combines the individual construction styles of Japanese dwelling houses from the *sukiya* right down to the *minka* type, from the townhouse to the teahouse style, in an exciting way. Even with all the differences in the individual designs the common elements inherent in all Japanese building and living can be seen in the samurai house. The characteristic features of living are generally founded on the need for a life of religion and ritual in keeping with nature and on the creation of an environment appropriate to this. Modifications are merely a result of diverse locations and of the class differences manifest in Japanese society.

Life in the Japanese house

Conventionally it was ritualistic needs rather than practical ones that structured life in a Japanese house. Here, too, one must not succumb to the temptation to classify this simply as far-eastern exoticism. Japanese ethnography, which was greatly influenced by European folklore, showed very similar structures in both Japanese and European agrarian rituals, particularly before World War Two. The best way for us to

understand the Japanese situation, or rather the relationship between autochthonous *shintō* traditions and imported Buddhism, is to imagine that we in Central and Northern Europe had maintained our heathen cultures alongside Christianity and churches with their appropriate liturgies right up until the present day. They would not, however, have degenerated completely to the level of just customs, as in many places in Europe, but would have remained as relevant village institutions from prehistoric agrarian cultures. At the heart of these ecstatic rituals there would still today be the cyclic renewal of the territorial marking system. The amazing thing is that such cults are not at all primitive, as the history of conversion to Christianity tried to make us believe. They are based on a traditional philosophical edifice, which is essentially orientated towards the harmonization of contrasting categories in the local environment. Everyday life

adapts itself, is merely a secularized form of ritualistic actions. The ritualistic routines cast a net joining places of ritual and entrances and accesses, between which the open free space, the space for ritual, or the entire interior of the house appears to be arranged hierarchically as if in a *shintō* enclosure or a temple. In other words, in spite of different architectural forms, Japanese ritualistic and residential building are alike as regards spatial structure. This interpretation of space is confirmed in archaic semantics in which both the house and the *shintō* shrines are "decorated" for festivals; in fact places of ritual and access gates are marked.

The *shintō* ritual system in Japan has its roots in prehistoric times. Basically it goes back to pre-Buddhist agrarian rituals, *ta no kami / yama no kami* and tribal or territorial cults, *uji, ujigami*. From here too comes the impression that Japanese living has retained ancient spatial concepts. Architectural research has not yet given us any information

about these connections because in it the building is seen not so much as vessel for human beings to live in as something that has been constructed, created: as architecture, designed for a life whose details it always considers as general knowledge. Precisely this silent assumption about the needs of the common people proves highly questionable in the example of Japan. For example: looking at the path/place pattern from a methodological point of view, the purely architectural consideration clearly gives a completely false picture, or better still, it projects its own framework onto reality as it was experienced in the Japanese house. By failing to take notice of the ritualistic, ascribing it to religion, it overlooks what is most important about the Japanese house: the Japanese people's very own way of reading, feeling and celebrating it. Social science, too, overlooks the ritual bonds of Japanese living: it merely penetrates everyday life with preconceived methods (the family as a fundamental social unit, the economy). It would in any case assign ritualistic behavior to religion, but then again from a metaphysical standpoint it differentiates it from the purely spiritual, applying hardly any understanding to the practical significance of the cults. In traditional Japan the spheres of social organization, economy, religion and aesthetics are

Opposite
Dan-bayashi
View of the *tsubo-niwa*, or inner courtyard garden, and of the parts of the building belonging to the former samurai residence, connected by covered corridors.

Top
Dan-bayashi
Heavy rain during a summer typhoon. The overhanging roofs protect the inside of the building from the heavy downpours that strike the group of islands in late summer. Even the rain is a typical Japanese "image of the seasons."

Opposite
Dan-bayashi
The *okuzashiki*, the inner day room, in
the style of a formal *shoin* room.
Worth noting are the round "light
screen" with decorative interlaced
pattern and the *fusuma* adorned with
shō. The sliding doors and walls mean
the room can be divided up or left
completely open, so not only the
requirements, but also the mood can be
altered accordingly.

Right
Dan-bayashi
Detail of the *okuzashiki*, the inner
day room.
The elaborate *ramma*, the open-work
wooden beam that is an essential
feature of rooms in Japanese residences,
can be seen clearly. On the one hand
ramma serve the practical purposes of
ventilation and providing a source of
daylight between the various sections of
the room, and on the other hand they
are decorative features of the internal
space, being embellished with latticework or open-work carvings of animals,
birds, flowers, and clouds, as well as
religious and mythological motifs.

closely interwoven with one another, both ideologically and practically. It is only we in the West who perceive a conceptual division between these spheres. And architectural research has unfortunately not yet understood what an important knot in the complex net that we call culture it holds in its hands in the shape of building and living. Ritualistically, the residential building in Japan is regarded as a domain that the occupier inhabits, marks, and locates perennially in cycles. In psychological terms he understands the house to be a domain which, despite its fragile construction, feels secure because it stands within the wider framework of a *shintō* system of values that in Japan is conventionally sanctioned by and large, and which expresses itself in the festive marking, in the social obligation of coming together before the place of ritual, and in the performance of certain actions — a domain that the occupier of the house therefore places in spiritual and emotional opposition to everything in life "outside" that seems uncertain and insecure. As already mentioned, the essential places of the house that are marked at New Year, for example, but also at other festivals, are on the one hand the outside gateway, the entrance to the anteroom, *genkan*, and possibly other accesses, and on the other hand the place of worship in the house or farm appropriate to the ritualistic festival. As a rule, markings in pairs indicate entrances and individual objects inside the building indicate the sacred place. Marking therefore obeys a system of antitheses, which we will here call the path/place pattern. Both the path/place pattern and also the antithetical/harmonious pattern in general are, in conjunction with the *shintō* rites that have been handed down, the true rationale behind the creation of everything, but also in particular of the earliest shrine styles.

The frame of reference for living in Japan is completely different to that in the West. The traditional dwelling house in Japan is neither a functional nor a formal whole. Roof, ground plan, places of worship, ritualistic pillars, hearth are relatively independent features, individual "buildings within a building," that have largely developed disparately, but each with its own harmony, and which have found themselves together in the typical traditional dwelling house. In short, the Japanese dwelling is an accumulation of heterogeneous elements. The basic pattern of traditional Japanese living is not folk "design." The forms are a result of centuries of old developments. They do not follow any functional or rational design principles, but rather are indebted to archetypal patterns rooted in anthropology, as for instance the cyclically marked path/place pattern, or in the wider sense, the antithetical/harmonious pattern for structuring formal and spatial features. The space is not conceived of as homogenous, but rather expresses itself in non-homogenous units. Sacred places lend a particular value to certain parts of the room. They are the focal points for traditional customs set in ritual, which are connected to the fundamental aspects of traditional rural existence. Living in Japan is not just about architecture, for

beyond the merely constructive and formal it lays bare a markedly spiritual dimension of human behavior. The residential house is also a social crystallization point, the nucleus of rituals performed cyclically and always in the same way.

Speaking in methodological terms, in order to understand the Japanese house one must look into what we call religion. We Europeans have difficulty understanding these structures. European cultural history has proceeded on a rational basis since the Enlightenment. If at a particular time something rational is considered right, then it is reproduced on all levels as of the new "spirit of the times," even if – over and over again – it turns out in the long or short term to be wrong. This is also particularly true in the case of more recent architecture and urban development. Man is at the mercy of the designer. In this way what is archetypal is always buried under what is most recent. In Japan, however, man does not have a pluralistic and individualistic view of himself, with his freedom in the individual act of thought as a starting point, as does the "enlightened" European in *cogito ergo sum*. He sees himself as a social being, who takes his identity with others from their communal cultural history. Accordingly, prehistoric traditions and history are never discarded. The new is

Above
Samurai helmet with neck guard, *eboshi kabuto*, **and samurai short sword,** *wakizashi*
Helmet: Lacquer on iron and gilt. The sheath, *saya*, fits into a brocade case, on the sword handle is a silk cord, *sageo*, for attaching the sword to the *obi*.

Opposite page
Dan-bayashi
Fusuma with *shō* ink drawings. The art of *shō*, Japanese calligraphy, is to be found on the hanging scrolls of the *tokonoma* and the *fusuma*, the moving wall panels, in which the "art" does not stand so dominantly in the foreground, but the content of the "writing" is also supposed to strive stylistically for "artistry," i.e. perfection.

Right
Dan-bayashi
Hikite, embellished handles of a *fusuma*. The elaborate details on handles and metal mountings, *kugikakushi*, which conceal nail heads are often the only decorative accessories in Japanese "interior decoration."

placed alongside the old, complementing it and becoming harmoniously fused with it. It would never occur to the Japanese to build modernistic *shintō* shrines, like our modern concrete churches, for they are the opposite of the present. They represent what is constant, what is primeval in the mundane course of life, and in many places they also formalize the appeal of the tension between past and present. Even in the most modern districts of Tokyo *shintō* shrines remain close to the archetypal. Religion in Japan is always the past in the present, and is therefore subject to strict conservativeness. Japan has always maintained continuity as the centuries have rolled by, and it may well be the ritualistic character of the Japanese house that has kept the tradition of Japanese houses almost unchanged to this day.

Ritual should not be read here as in the Western sense of metaphysical primacy, but be understood as humane tradition, which has maintained certain routines and behavior throughout the ages. In the social obligations of ritualistic encounters the individual feels socially elevated in his own house. The formal element of the ritual interrupts the everyday life of the inhabited space by allowing the past to enter into it. A ritual celebration brings a totally different drama into the house than that of, say, a modern television film: when the past penetrates the living present in the form of traditions, a strangely irrational tension comes into being that can only be described with difficulty. Perhaps it is best compared to poetry, where the use of ancient ideas and expressions creates a strange lyricism.

From a social point of view, ritual unites the individual/family space to the universal whole, while from a philosophical point of view the arrangement of the room has a spiritual quality. Without exception, an apparently very old philosophy of life shines through in everything, uniting opposites and bringing harmony. This philosophy embodies a principle that has grown out of the depths of time, and which advocates that everything should be harmoniously rooted in the spatial and social environment. Thinking and creating in antitheses that are at the same time harmonious and complementary is an essential feature of the Asiatic way of existence. The Japanese residential building therefore always stands in the center of an ordered system that interacts with the immediate environment, the whole of society, and finally also the cosmos. So it is perfectly easy to see why, under certain circumstances, people in Japan seem to be content even with very little space. The word comfort is used completely differently, not in the sense of just a feeling of physical well being, but in the spiritual sense. Needs are not focused on quantifiable space. It is principally a question of quality, again not in the material sense; it is a question of the historically or traditionally structured space, the archetype. In Japan personal well-being depends on this, but so does the awareness that one is part of a culture that has grown traditionally and historically. Anyone who talks to the Japanese about their culture will soon notice that the words "we" and "our" occur very frequently.

Left

Dan-bayashi

Painting on a *fusuma,* landscape in the Chinese style, ink and paint on paper (section).

There is no room for error when painting with ink, as there is no chance to correct mistakes. Each brush stroke must therefore be executed with precision. Against this background it is in no way surprising that many samurai warriors devoted themselves to the noble art of painting in ink, for anyone who is so well trained in the use of a sword, which must be wielded with deadly accuracy in order to overcome one's opponent, is also skilled in the use of a brush and ink.

Opposite

Dan-bayashi

Susuki, Silver Grass, one of the "Seven Grasses" of late summer. Zen philosophy states that a grass has the same status as the mighty pine trees or the glowing azaleas and deserves the same respect, attention and high regard.

This, too, is to quite a large extent due to the tradition of the Japanese house. Have we Central Europeans maybe turned into wasters of space because we frequently lack this complex understanding of the home as a social dwelling place with links to history, and therefore as a spiritual home? [54]

Shō and calligraphy

Another elemental artistically creative feature in the Japanese room is the art of *shō*, Japanese calligraphy. It is to be found on the hanging scrolls of the *tokonoma* and on the *fusuma*, in which the "art" does not stand so dominantly in the foreground, but the content of the "writing" is also supposed to strive stylistically for "artistry," that is, perfection.

"It is important to remember that every Zen painting has a meaning and a message, and was never created just for the purpose of decoration. Almost without exception they are painted in ink on paper in the small hanging scroll format that would be suitable for hanging in the *tokonoma* of a tea-room [...]. Many at first sight look like amateur doodles, but there is always a forcefulness in the brush strokes that cannot be faked and close examination of some of these paintings under a microscope has revealed that the particles of ink in a genuine Zen painting (in other words by an experienced monk), are much denser and more closely clustered than in other works. In calligraphy particularly, the Zen energy is an important part of the creation, and it is said of one master that he would never accept the work of any pupil who did not get drenched with sweat through the spiritual exertion of writing." [55]

How does the Western eye view this "art," what can it mean to anyone who cannot "read" these signs? Here, too, one must take the spontaneous path, the "Zen Path." One can simply allow the form to take effect, the beauty and intensity of the lines of ink, the balance between the dark brush strokes and white surfaces, which can suddenly open out into a space. To those in the West *shō* paintings are abstract works of art with no subject. It is permissible to approach it with naivety and objectivity, for on closer inspection the "content" will be recognized, without "reading." The lines, the rhythm, the broadening and narrowing of the strokes, the consistency of the ink – whether it be intensely black, wispy, dry or a delicate grey – become for us something akin to an atmosphere, which wishes to communicate the word in the written sign, to allow us to experience it, and maybe even its deeper meaning and intention.

Above
Choju-kan
Detail of the roofs of the oldest ryokan buildings; wooden shingles weighted down by
bamboo poles and overgrown with moss in the unmistakable "smoky" autumnal
moods of Japan.

長寿館

Choju-kan, Hōshi Onsen

The completely hermitical and secluded location of the venerable country ryokan Choju-kan, already a modern legend, is situated in the "wilderness" of Gunma prefecture, in the midst of a bizarre mountain environment, close to the popular skiing region of Naeba. Some 1200 years ago, the Buddhist monk Kukai, also known as Kōbō Daishi (744–835), is supposed to have discovered the hot springs at Hōshi, although it was another eleven hundred years before Choju-kan was constructed to provide guests with overnight lodgings.

Already in the misty past, Hōshi Onsen was a popular resting place for travelers crossing the Mikune Mountains on their journey along the Mikunikaidō road to Edo. At the Mikuni Tunnel on Mukuni Pass, according to legend, three deities are in attendance: Akagi, Suwa and Yahiko, who represent the provinces of Gunma, Nagano and Niigata. This venerable place is known as Mikuni Gongen. On clear days one can see the temple at Nikkō from the highest point of the pass.

Hōshi, surrounded by mountain ranges, is comprised of just the Choju-kan ryokan on the banks of the River Nishi. There is hardly a more appropriate place to experience the beauty and symbolism of the Japanese autumn. Journeying along a narrow mountain ridge one can take the time to view the rugged charm of the surroundings. To reach the building of the inn crouched in the landscape, one crosses an old wooden bridge and is once and for all is transported back to an age one thought never to experience again: the *onsen* community" strolls between the radiant colors of the leaves in kimono and *yūkata*.

Golden-red vanitas splendor of the Japanese autumn

An autumn eve:
See the valley mists arise
Among the fir leaves
That still hold the dripping wet
Of the chill day's sudden showers.
Jakuren Hōshi
[freely translated by N.C.]

Right
Choju-kan
Built among rugged wooded mountains, the Hōshi onsen and the Choju-kan ryokan are aglow with the quintessential Japanese image of a golden red opulence against a weathered grey background. Thanks to the proximity of the "thermal river," the healing springs are able to bubble into the wooden pools of the bathing house without the help of piping.

The end of summer is signalized picturesquely by the transition from a rich green to a blazing red, particularly in a country like Japan where the glowing maple dominates nature during autumn, and where in spring the pale pink clouds of the cherry blossom command the landscape. When in April the cherry trees appear to be bursting with blossom and the mantle of air is tinged pink, one knows that the earth has revitalized itself and winter is passing.

The glowing red atmosphere of the Japanese autumnal foliage is not only an expression of a transitory moment but the hyperbole of destruction and creation. Red is a synonym for heat, the lifecycle, the experience of high temperatures, a daily recurring natural spectacle of a burning, setting sun, and autumn symbolizes the powerfully flickering and glowing nature and simultaneously its temporary death.

In artistic nuances, closely interlinked and frequently visible, one can perceive the adjacency of the gray and black and white shadows of Japanese rooms and architecture, and a subtle golden flair. This specifically warm shade of the golden autumn is evident above all in the vicinity of arboreally embedded temples and wooden houses. The golden color of the leaves is reflected in the windows, in the *tatami*, in the dark boards, in the copper and bronze fittings and is caught by the bamboo structures. Even the air acquires a tinge that is somewhere between lacquered gray and pale gold, floating between buildings, enveloped in a foliage of a radiant green, red and gold.

This glow is most intensive in the twilight when nature again explodes in colors before it fades into a soft gray. At the transitional moment of the day, like the year, the colors smoulder in a peculiarly passionate and simultaneously mat way, the gold appears unpolished, the red as copper and orange like flickering ashes, but always the shadows project the impression of a fire that is slowly dying. The autumnal colors are accompanied by a virtually burnt aroma, a certain impotence of being, a slowness and a coolness which crawls around the corners; overall a peculiarly archaic atmosphere prevails. Twilight and autumn – the color of the buildings embodies the ultimate metamorphosis between fertility and death, between the final moments of a cycle that is reaching its end and the interlude between the end and a new beginning.

Hidden in the majestic rebellion of the colors is a breath of melancholy and the last beautiful warming days are accompanied by a degree of nostalgia. The mood reflects an existential condition at its peak, such as the late afternoon or early autumn. Full of vitality and equally faintly morbid, this last moment of the glowing colors in the smokelike atmosphere of composting leaves. These competing feelings are the purest expression of *wabi* and *sabi* and can be experienced in full in the

Above
Choju-kan
The golden color of the leaves is reflected in the windows, in the *tatami*, in the dark boards, in the copper and bronze fittings and is caught by the bamboo structures. Even the air acquires a tinge that is somewhere between lacquered gray and pale gold, floating between buildings, enveloped in a foliage of a radiant green, red and gold.

Opposite
Choju-kan
Like the cherry blossom in spring, the golden autumn in Japan expresses a mood and a state of existence far beyond any seasonal importance, being also a spiritual experience.

old mountain temples such as Nanzen-ji by Kyōto. The light oscillates between the fire of autumn and the winter frost. In this quintessential Japanese season, the antagonistic elements of this country live side-by-side, the luxuriantly bizarre and the direct, the eloquent and the calm, the end and the beginning of time. The golden red opulence against a weathered gray background is a scene pervading autumnal Japan and envelops its artistic products in unattainable variety.

Living tradition in Choju-kan

The owner of Choju-kan believes in the power of the past and will not tolerate even the smallest piece of plastic in his house. And the past is not only alive in tangible forms in the different buildings that make up the ryokan, which was largely constructed during the last century, but also when the sound of two sticks clapped together is heard as the sun goes down as a reminder of the danger posed by open fires, a sound that was once heard throughout Japan when evening fell.

The nostalgic rural cuisine consists of the freshest products from the mountain rivers and streams such as the legendary *ayu* and numerous other freshwater fish and large carp; the thick forests provide the most magnificent types of mushrooms and are a fantastic reservoir of herbs and edible plants. In some guest rooms, a stew of vegetables and game simmers above the *irori*, and a particular speciality is *konnyaku*, a jelly produced from the tubers of the *konnyaku* root, also called "devil's tongue root jelly." The old Japanese "family and guest meeting place," the *irori* room, where one gathers in the evening around the soot-blackened fire place is also a well visited and popular place in the Choju-kan ryokan. The *irori* is used both for heating and cooking, and here in the fresh mountain air one can investigate the traditional Japanese methods of heating the dwelling houses and guest rooms at Choju-kan.

Right
Choju-kan
Japan's ubiquitous "natural art"; maple leaves on a moss covered ground.

Opposite
***Byōbu*, folding panel, "Autumn on the River Tatsu in Yoshino"**
Part of the pair of folding panels "Spring and Autumn on the River Tatsu in Yoshino" (see Chikurin-in Gunpou-en p. 46/47)
Edo period (1615–1868). Painting on gilded paper,
6 panels each approx. 70 x 165 in. (177.3 x 418.5 cm), detail,
Nezu Institute of Fine Arts, Tokyo

Above left
Choju-kan
Mossy stepped roof on one of the guest houses in the garden of the ryokan. In the foreground a stone lantern, *ishi-doro*, and a "sculptured erratic boulder," a traditional attribute in a tea-house garden.

Above right
Choju-kan
Detail elevation of a half-timbered house at the ryokan. The autumnal colors are an inimitable backdrop for the black and white buildings and hardly experienceable more regally than at Hōshi Onsen.

Opposite
Choju-kan
The *irori* room at the ryokan, a place for relaxed conversation among guests late in the evening. Protected against the cold of the mountains, one drinks the tea or sake warmed above the open fireplace. During the day also a welcome refuge, the picture here allows the viewer to experience the interaction of light and shadow, of the rays of sunshine which penetrate the *shōji* and evaporate on the dark wood of the room.

A traditional Japanese house does not have glass windows and the paper sliding door, the *shōji* is located next to the wooden sliding door, the *amado*, the "rain door." It functions in the same way as shutters in the West, the sole artificial manipulation to keep the cold outside. The space above the frame of the *shōji* is covered with Japanese paper, keeping the room warmer than the guest would imagine as it retains the heat in the room and simultaneously aids ventilation.

The close links the Japanese maintain to nature are possibly expressed in their quasi-resistance to wind and weather. One often hears complaints from Westerners that a place is too hot or too cold although a Japanese person there feels perfectly comfortable.

Irori, hibachi, tabako-bon and *kotatsu* – Japanese "sources of warmth"

While in other countries the rooms are fitted with stoves or heating systems, the Japanese hardly seem to worry about heating their dwellings, simply: there are no heating systems. The sole source of warmth in a Japanese house is the transportable coal brazier, the *hibachi* or "fire holder," which is more for warming one's hands than heating the room. It is square, round, rectangular or of highly imaginative design. The braziers are usually 12 to 20 inches in height and between 12 and 28 inches in length. Charcoal is burnt in the *hibachi* and is one of the most important fuels for heating in Japan.

The *ayu*

"Of all fresh-water fish in Japan *ayu* (*plecoglossus altevelis*) is perhaps the most prized in season on account of its special flavor, though the eel may be said to be among the most popular. *Ayu*, according to some scholars, means 'small-white-fish,' but others are of the opinion that the word *ayu* is derived from the verb *ayuru* meaning 'coming down,' the fish being so called because it comes down the river. Its name is written by two ideograms meaning 'year-fish,' because, according to the Wamyosho [an old textbook from the Heian period, 794–1185, N.C.], *ayu* is born in spring, grows up in summer, weakens in autumn and dies in winter." [56]

I joined "the queue, right at the back, which moved slowly, slowly to the fire and the wooden table where I would be given my fish. 'Name, name,' I asked, as I held it in my hand, and I was told: '*Ayu*, fish *ayu*.' Only later did I realize [...] that people from a wide radius make a pilgrimage to the *kaiseki* restaurants at Arashiyama and pay vast sums for an ayu meal." [57]

"It is traditionally said that in the fourth month of the year 200 A.D., while the Empress Jingo was staying at the village of Tamashima, Kyushu, on her expedition to Shiragi, a kingdom in Korea, she caught some 'fine-scaled fish' by using as bait boiled rice tied to the end of a thread taken from her dress. The fish, it is now known, was *ayu*. Because of this the place was named *Mezura* ('unusual'), which later on changed into *Matsuura*, as the place is now known. The *Nihonshoki* [Japanese chronicle from 720, N.C.] mentions this custom of fishing *ayu* with boiled rice.

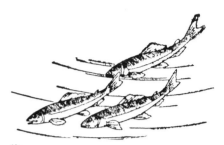

Above
The legendary *ayu* fish
Line drawing from: *We Japanese*, Fujiya Hotel Ltd. (publisher), Miyanoshita, Hakone 1949, p. 369

Ayu has fine scales and a wide mouth with rows of fine teeth. When grown up, it is black-backed, yellowish white on the belly, and reddish about its head. It is born in the river and goes down to the sea, to return up the river, in April or May. When young, it lives on animal food in the river, till it is 3 or 4 inches long and after that it eats only moss. It measures over a foot when fully grown, though a special kind found in Lake Biwa does not grow larger

Above
Choju-kan
A rural evening meal at Choju-kan with fresh vegetables and wild mushrooms and the *ayu*, the most prized freshwater fish in Japan.

Left
An *ayu* angler on the River Kamo (Kamogawa) in Kyōto.

on a moonlight night. The boat, lighted with torches, has a cormorant handler, an assistant and two rowers. The chief handler generally manipulates twelve cormorants i.e. six by each hand, while his assistant handles four or five. Each cormorant is tethered, and a hook is put round its neck in order to prevent it from swallowing the *ayu* it catches. Great skill is required to manipulate the cormorants, which, swimming in zig-zag fashion, and in great disorder, in their wild chase after *ayu* in the water, would cause an endless entanglement of the cords in less skillful hands. Then from time to time the fisherman pulls the cormorants one after another to the prow of the boat to take out of their mouth all the fish they catch. *Ayu* fishing by means of trained cormorants shows the typically clever and ingenious way of the Japanese cormorant fishers."[58]

than 2 or 3 inches, and it does not go down into the sea. The fish lays its eggs in October, when many of them die through fatigue from their long swim. Some *ayu*, however, survive the winter in a deep river. The close season for the fishing of *ayu* is from the first of October, when its spawning season begins, till the end of May.

Ayu is found nearly all over the country, but the following rivers are specially known for *ayu* and *ayu*-fishing in Japan: namely the River Nagara, Mino province; the River Tama, Musashi province; the River Chikuma, Kyushu; the River Gokase, Hiuga province; the River Niyodo, Tosa province; the River Iwakuni, Suwo province; the River Ohta, Aki province.

There are four principal ways of fishing *ayu*: They are (1) with rod and line; (2) with what is called the 'cormorant-rope' and a net; (3) by means of a trained cormorant, (4) by what is called *tomozuri* (literally, catching by means of a friend).

In catching *ayu* with rod and line, we generally use false hooks because it is hard to catch it with bait.

In the second way of catching *ayu*, the *unawa* or 'cormorant-rope' with black feathers put on it at intervals, is used to chase the fish. *Ayu* takes this rope for

cormorants, and few dare swim out of the range of the rope. When they are encircled by the rope, a net is thrown over them for a catch at a single cast.

In *tomozuri* we use an *ayu* as a decoy. It is tied fast with a few hooks about it and other *ayu* are caught of their own accord.

The fishing of *ayu* by means of trained cormorants is a most clever and ingenious method. The cormorant is employed usually at night, after the moon has set, for it does not work well

Top
Cormorant fishing at night in Gifu

Right
Cormorant fishing
Line drawing from: *We Japanese*, Fujiya Hotel Ltd. (publisher), Miyanoshita, Hakone 1949, p. 370

Above
Choju-kan
View of the window of a guest room at the ryokan. The maple tree spreading out in front of the façade can be seen on the opposite page as a "natural picture" in a *shōji* frame.

Opposite
Choju-kan
A natural painting with glowing colors, framed by the black and white of the *shōji* rice paper doors. In the foreground the *kotatsu*, the traditional Japanese multipurpose item of furniture, source of warmth, dining table and footwarmer at night.

There are also glowing charcoals in the *tabako-bon*. This "tobacco box" is also a portable receptacle which is not only used to warm one's hands but also to light cigars, pipes and cigarettes. Thus its name. Like the *hibachi*, tobacco boxes are available in large range of designs.

The source of heat in Japanese houses is determined by the architecture; installing radiators would eliminate the wall materials and the flexible room structure: tiled stoves are very difficult to imagine on the *tatami* mats.

"A Japanese house has hardly any furniture to speak of. Stoves, fireplaces, and stair-rails are conspicuous by their absence. Doors do not open, they slide in grooves. Doors inside the house are never locked, the rooms being inter-communicating, more or less.

Japanese pack away their pictures, curios, and ornaments and have as little as possible in their rooms, in contrast to the Western custom." [59]

This special aesthetic of not cluttering the room also facilitates the use of furniture for multiple purposes. This includes the source of warmth, the *kotatsu*, which covered by a board placed on the wadded cover serves as a dining table and

in the night as a "hot-water bottle" if the ends of the *futon* are pushed underneath the wadded cover in a star-shaped arrangement.

"The *kotatsu* is the popular foot warmer. A square container of charcoals is put into the *tatami* (mat-floor) with a wooden frame-work, over which a wadded cover is put to keep the *kotatsu* warm. The Japanese put their feet and sometimes their hands under the wadded cover to keep them warm. Children like to sit around a *kotatsu* and to listen to a nursery tale told by their father or mother. The *kotatsu* is a cozy warmer." [60]

The *onsen* – An illustrative visit to the bathhouse

Before one withdraws to one's room to sit on the *tatami* mats, warm one's feet on the *kotatsu* and enjoy the delicacies of the regional rural cuisine in informal privacy, one pays a visit to the bathhouse. Visiting Choju-kan means above all visiting the *onsen* to regenerate and relax in the famous thermal waters.

The ryokan is built in immediate proximity to the river bed so that the water bubbles from the source, without piping, directly from the rocks into the bathhouse. The healing water contains calcium and magnesium sulphate and thus healthy ingredients for broken bones, arterial sclerosis, burns, rashes, states of agitation and other nervous ailments.

The parts of the guest house grouped around the hot spring are interconnected and linked to the bathhouse via covered passages and corridors. Freed of workaday clothing, one saunters here or in the picturesque environs wearing the kimono, the traditional garment on the way to the *onsen*. In his or her room the guest will find a simple variant made of cotton, although in traditional guest houses one may be able to admire considerably more lavish "private kimonos."

The bathing ritual in a "bathing church"

Before entering the actual bathing room, one disrobes in an anteroom and places the kimono in a basket provided there for every guest for this purpose (fig. Shoro-tei p. 138). After washing oneself thoroughly sitting on a small wooden stool with soap and after carefully rinsing off the soap, one douses oneself with the hot water which is filled into the wooden pail at hand. Absolutely "clean," one now enters the unforgettable experience of the *onsen* wearing solely the small towel called the *tenugui* that one will find in one's room, usually laid out together with the toothbrush.

The actual procedure for bathing is highly ritualized; with its almost religious character, the bath represents a holy act. In his book *Common-sense Architecture*, John Taylor defines the

act of bathing as one of the most exemplary art forms of Japanese culture.

The extraordinary bathhouse at Choju-kan resembles a church with its soaring open timber roof comprising solid wooden beams and the high bow windows, a "divine" place. Built before the turn of the 19th century, this place of "bathing meditation" was largely unequalled in Japan. One glides into the chestnut wood pool, divided by round logs into eight basins and one floats in the 43°C warm thermal water in divine relaxation. The healing spring bubbles directly from the large-grained pebble floor of the pool, and while one rests one's head on the wooden log, the smooth round stones massage the feet. There cannot be a more exquisite form of casual relaxation. For Westerners it is perhaps unusual that the pool is a so-called mixed bath, *kon-yoku* – men and women bath naked side by side – but even persons of a shy nature will enjoy themselves.

The steam from the hot water, the filtered light and the solemn atmosphere provide a befitting private sphere. On the contrary, the uninhibited mutuality of the sexes per se yields a casual and relaxed atmosphere. While the men drink sake and possibly discuss business matters, the women giggle at the latest gossip – or vice versa. One is reminded of medieval bathhouses in Europe, which were also places of communication and social life before the prudery of the church forced their closure. By the late evening, the jointly sung songs echo around the high cupola, almost begging for a song contest, the *uta-awase*. After a cup of sake and three multiple stanza songs it is often wise, even though one may be reluctant to do so, to take in the fresh air again.

Furo – The bath

"The Japanese are extremely fond of a hot-water bath, which they take irregularly or regularly, once a day, or once, twice or three times a week, and so on, sometimes in the morning, but generally in the evening after a day's work is done. The cold ablutions are taken for a religious purpose, and a cold-water bath seems to be early introduction.

When we take a bath, we first wash our face, and then get into the bath-tub after pouring a pailful or two of hot water over our body. Our bath-tub [*sic*], which is made as a rule of zelkova or some other hard wood, may be round, oval or square in shape, and it is full of hot water, which is deep enough to cover your shoulders when you bend down in the tub. While a foreigner can hardly stand the heat of 25° C, the Japanese will get in water 45° to 50° C hot. After we stay in the hot water for a few minutes to get warm, we get out and wash and soap ourselves on the sink [*sic*]. Soap is never used in a bath-tub, but everybody washes or soaps his body clean outside the tub and rinses soap off before he gets into the tub again [...] because all the members of a family take a bath in the same water one after another, instead of throwing the water away every time one has taken a bath. Nor is it proper to use a towel in the water. This process we repeat two or three times by getting in and out of the

Preceding double page
Choju-kan
In the covered passages, which interconnect the individual buildings of the ryokan, one never tires of taking in the autumnal colors and moods at different times of the day and especially in the evening, and of forgetting time altogether.

Left
Choju-kan
The bathhouse at the ryokan, like hardly any other place in Japan it allows the almost scared ritual of bathing to be discovered and experienced personally.

Opposite
Choju-kan
Already thrilled in anticipation of the heavenly bath ahead, one nevertheless stops to absorb the light evening sky, the pale gold from the reflection of the foliage. Under heavy wooden beams, the way to the bath in the *yukata* and *tanzen* is an experience in itself.

tub and washing ourselves on the sink [*sic*], and then we wipe the water off with the same wet towel that we use in washing the body, instead of a dry one, as most foreigners do. Our towel, by the way, is much smaller in size than a foreign one, being about 7 or 8" x 2.5' and it is commonly used for various other purposes.

Public bath-house: For those who cannot afford to have a bath tub at home, we have a public bath-house, where the charge for a bath is very cheap. While in feudal days, mixed bathing was allowed or overlooked of both sexes, each public bath-house has a bath-tub in a separate compartment for either sex. Each compartment has a large bath-tub [*sic*] that will accommodate a dozen or more people at one time in it while others will wash their bodies on the sink [*sic*].

You will notice that a public bath-house is [...] sort of an information office, where one can have the first-hand news, and all the customers of a public bath will talk with one another either in the tub or on the sink [*sic*]. At rural places they are served with a cup of tea, after they have taken a bath, and they have chats before they go home. A public bath-house [*sic*] is open from early in the morning till late in the evening.

Shobu-yū (lit. iris-bath): On May 5th, when the Boys' Festival is observed in Japan, many orthodox Japanese will take *shobu-yū* or iris-bath. A few blades of the iris are put into a bath-tub when they take a bath. [*sic*]

Daidai-yū (lit. citrus-bath): On the day of the winter solstice [*sic*], *daidai-yū* or citrus-bath is prepared in many orthodox Japanese families. A few pieces of citrus-skins are put into a bath-tub when they take a bath. Even a public bath-house will put some citrus-pieces into its bath-tub. [*sic*] They seem to believe that this kind of bath has a medicinal value."[61]

Right
Choju-kan
The magical, spiritual atmosphere in the church of bathing is created by the solid timber structure used for the open beam ceiling and the large bow windows whose filtered light swathes the bathers floating in the steam. Mixed use – that means both sexes as God made them – in archaic familiarity and virtuous intimacy in the healing waters of the hot spring.

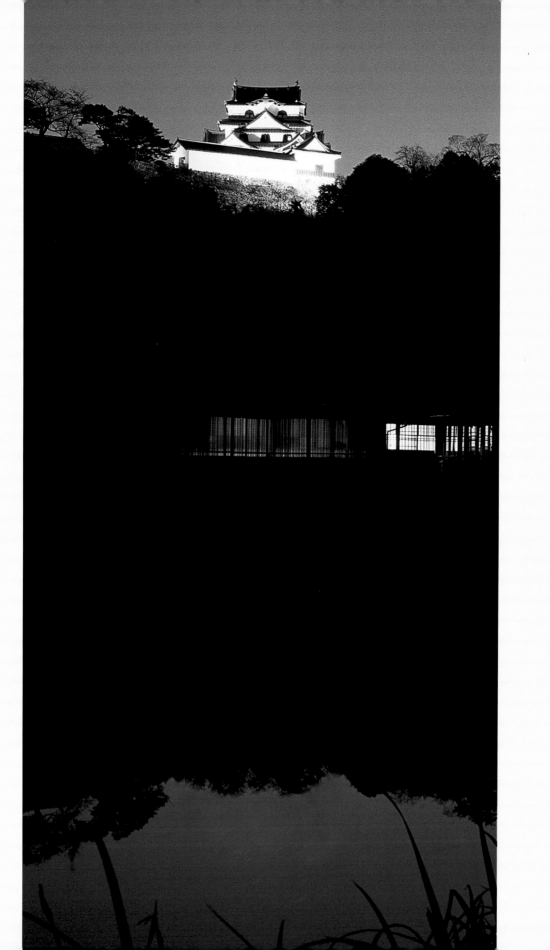

Hakkei-tei, Hikone

Hakkei-tei – a *sukiya* world filled with life

The Hakkei-tei ryokan is over three hundred years old and is situated in the middle of the famous Genkyu-en landscape gardens, which were laid out in the grounds of the Hikone castle in 1677. Hikone-jo is the chief attraction in Hikone, the provincial capital not far from Kyoto on Lake Biwa. A stroll through this town full of historical buildings takes the visitor on a voyage of discovery through Japan's Edo Period (1615–1868), which has been kept alive here more than in any other place in Japan. The fortified castle, which dates from 1603, was occupied by one of the most illustrious families of Japan, the Ii family, whose descendant Naosuke Ii (1815–1860), 13th Lord of the Hikone clan and minister to the last Togukawa Shōgun Iemochi (1846–1866), spoke out in favor of opening up towards the West. His progressive attitude made him many enemies and he fell victim to assassination by reactionary forces.

The castle – one of the most beautiful in Japan and declared a National Treasure – has largely been maintained in its original state and its three story structure can be seen from afar towering up on a hill in the heart of the town. In spring the slopes of the castle hill are bathed in a sea of cherry blossom, while later in the year they take on the glowing red color of the autumn foliage. At the foot of the extensive castle grounds lies the Gengkyu-en, laid out in the *chisen-kaiyu* style. This is a "landscape garden of walks," around a large pond. The complex, completed in 1677, was modelled on the palace gardens of the Chinese emperor Genso, of the Tang Dynasty (618–907). Fixed points in the garden, such as artificial hills, trees and cliffs imitate the Eight Views of the Omi region as well as the island of Chikubujima and the white cliffs of Oki, three of Japan's popular tourist attractions in West Honshu. Bordering onto the garden are the grounds of the feudal lord's private residence, the Keyaki-goten. The fourth lord of Hikone started to construct this residence in 1677 too. All the neighboring *daimyō* admired the beauty of this house, many parts of which are still in their original state today, and which was constructed in zelkova, a particularly durable and robust wood. Ii Naoki, the twelfth lord of Hikone, had an annex called Raku-raku-no-ma built around 1800. This name comes from a line of a poem, the gist of the meaning being: bold men take pleasure in the mountains, wise men in the water.

In addition to using this celebrated residence, the lords of the Hikone clan entertained their most eminent visitors in the Hōshō-dai guesthouse (1677), a pavilion constructed above a pond, its position offering an impressive view of the castle and the entire garden. The same family has held the lease of this marvel of Japanese architecture, elegance and aesthetics built in the *sukiya* style for three generations now and they have made it accessible to mere mortals too in the form of the Hakkei-tei ryokan. The Hakkei-tei is the oldest "inn" in Japan, being over 320 years old, and it offers its guests the unique experience of tasting the ultra refined, traditional lifestyle developed and lived over many centuries by the most distinguished families in Japan. The Hakkei-tei hovers on posts above the pond in magnificent gardens and provides the pleasures of an era long since disappeared. At evening, when the last visitors have left the park, a picture of elegiac beauty, unspoilt by intrusions from the modern world, is revealed to those on the *engawa*. This amounts to enjoying "understated luxury" to the full, without distractions, in a summer pavilion that has always been one of the most treasured of its kind and which became legendary as a place from which to observe the moon in the month of October. The trees are discreetly supported so that they allow an uninterrupted view of the October moon from the pavilion. The view, the atmosphere are pure magic, and when the guest leaves the Hakkei-tei with a heavy heart, he is not departing from a world that is unknown to him, but rather finds it difficult to cope in the world that is supposed to be his own.

The Hakkei-tei does not carry out any public relations work and is run by a young man and his family. This young man completed his studies in the USA and then returned to the home of his fathers to preserve his heirloom, this jewel, which enchants all who see it. The building is classified as a historical monument, and preserving it is a Herculean task as public funds are hard to come by and the restoration work necessary for conservation purposes is barely affordable.

The ryokan has two splendid guest rooms and two additional rooms for accommodation. Here the guest can experience and discover the unspoilt pure culture of the *sukiya* world. Following an old tradition friends of the host travel from all over the world to Hikone to indulge in moon gazing in what must be the most beautiful place in Japan for it, and to compose poems about this mysterious satellite of the earth.

Opposite
Hakkei-tei
View of the Hōshō-dai inn (1677–1679) of the lords of Hikone, constructed in the *sukiya* style. The former "summer pavilion" is today almost unaltered and houses the Hakkei-tei ryokan, sun house, so-called after Shōshō Hakkei, eight famous scenes of Lake Dong Ting in Hunan province, China, or rather Omi Hakkei, Omi's eight famous scenes. The buildings standing above the water are called *riuchi-kaku*, those on land on the southern man-made hill *Hōshō-dai*. *Hōshō-dai*, literally the hill of the Hōshō, is the place where Hōshō, an imaginary Chinese phoenix, flew heavenwards.

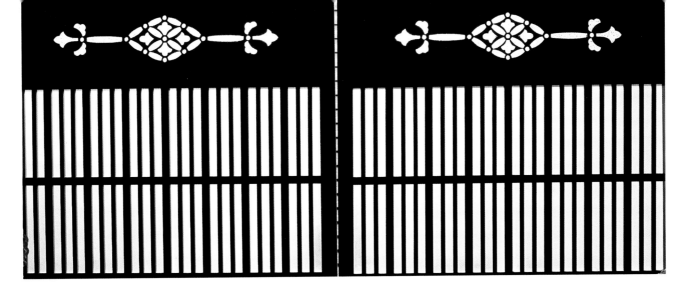

"Artistic, Aesthetic, and Poetic Tastes of the Japanese – Moon-Viewing.

An inherent love of nature is a strong national characteristic of the Japanese, shared by all classes, from the humblest person to the most exalted – and the yearning to express and perpetuate the impressions made on refined tastes by nature in her varied moods has resulted in producing the paintings and exquisite fine arts in metal, wood, clay, and other materials for which Japan is famous the world over. Japanese genius touches perfection in small things, for which the Japanese flexible, artistic hands are peculiarly adapted.

[...] The aesthetic tastes of the Japanese are evidenced in the *Cha-no-yū* or Tea Ceremony, in their annual moon-viewing parties, in flower arrangement, in their *bonsai* and *bonkei* creations, their insect-hearing and incense-smelling parties and in many other ways [...].

Moon-viewing: There are two moon-viewings, determined by the lunar calendar, the *jugoya* on Aug. 15, the *jusanya* on Sept. 13, and it is a superstition that if the *jugoya* is observed it is also necessary to observe the *jusanya* in order to avoid bad luck. By the Gregorian calendar these moon-viewings are about a month later, varying somewhat every year.

When the moon is in the full and at its best, thousands of families on the prescribed nights place tiny altars on the veranda where the moonlight falls and make offerings of food, fruits, flowers and the autumn grasses to the brilliant satellite. Poems are composed for the occasion and appropriate stories are told in the light of the moon." [62]

Sukiya décor – features of *sukiya*

The concept *sukiya* originally meant "seat of ennoblement," and the most successful and best examples of the *sukiya* style combine the elegance and culture of the formal *shoin* with a nonchalant atmosphere and artistic idiosyncrasy, suitable to a personality with exquisite taste and a cultivated lifestyle. Every *sukiya* design is unique for this reason, and yet the form shows striking common features, the most important of which are probably understatement and irregularity. For the purpose of greater understanding it should be mentioned that the *sukiya* style unfolded as an antithesis in an age when a type of rusticity was in favor, stemming from the aesthetics of tea drinking with its preference for roughly hewn supports and simple ink paintings, in so far as paintings were used at all as decoration. The best of *sukiya* was created by a social elite, whose discreetly understated lifestyle went hand in hand with aesthetically noble details of the most luxurious style of all.

Numerous *sukiya* rooms have windows with s-shaped fluting, *katōmado*, and suggestions of latticework in the lintels, complicated open-work on the shelving, even the metal nail heads have ornamentation. "The metal clasps moulded into the sliding-doors, as well as the metal mountings fastened to the fillets above were as exquisitely worked as the sole piece of jewellery worn by a lovely woman who otherwise is but simply dressed." [63]

Sukiya prefers to put itself to the test with an eccentric reinterpretation of the classical *shoin* concept. Formal *shoin*

Above left
Hakkei-tei
View into the canopy of the *engawa* of the guest room shown on page 242. The thatched wooden roof is supported by a bamboo structure made of pieces of bamboo crossways and lengthways, tied together with cords of brushwood. The beautiful texture of the bamboo is left in its original state as a feature to supplement nature.

Above right
Hakkei-tei
Tatami covered *engawa* of the guest room shown on page 242.

Opposite
Hakkei-tei
On the *engawa*, which also serves all year round as a seat for viewing the moon, one of the ladies who looks after the guests keeps a lookout for the swans making their way across the pond.

rooms usually have the decorated niche and the shelving side by side against the rear wall of the *jōdan* and the writing platform against the veranda wall opposite the decorative doors. *Sukiya* rooms on the other hand almost never have decorative doors – just one example of how the traditional organization of all *shoin* fixed points is constantly being reconsidered. So reflection on and recreation of the traditional *shoin* features is the touchstone of the *sukiya* style.

In the *sukiya* estate of Manshuin (completed in 1656) in the north-east of Kyōto many of the features described here are, as it were, "carried to the extreme." The ingenious *jōdan*, which is only the size of two *tatami* mats contains no shelving and is cleverly reflected in the canopy-like ceiling, itself irregularly coffered to suggest the pattern of the crossbeams. The compartment with the writing platform has as s-shaped arched window and there are three shelves, as in the *futon* cupboards. In another room there are crossbeams with unconventional ornamentation, including bas-relief carving and some open-work of chrysanthemums, the emblem of the Imperial family. Every detail of this room called "Fuji" has been properly thought out, even the nail heads of the circumferential

Previous double page
**Katsura Rikyu, Kyōto,
1616/1641/1660**
The bamboo fence surrounding the
Imperial villa in the summer month of
August.
"Driving up the gravelled path amidst
the bright green foliage of the trees,
we stopped in front of the entrance
portal. We stood a long time gazing at
that portal. It seemed quite new,
made of bamboo; the fence shut off
something beautiful from the outer
world but, in spite of its height, it did
not seem to do so with an imperious
gesture." (Bruno Taut)

Opposite
Genkyu-en, 1677
"Relief of roots" in the Genkyu-en.
The Hakkei-tei ryokan is situated in the
landscape garden of the Hikone fortified
castle. It is open to visitors and is one
of Japan's most well-known gardens,
providing a classic example of the
mastery with which the Japanese can
reproduce nature in an artificial yet
seemingly natural way.

Left
**Katsura Rikyu, Kyōto,
1616/1641/1660**
Irregular stepping-stones in a bed of moss.
The path from the *shōka-tei* teahouse,
"Pavilion of the Admired Blossoms" to the
shōka-tei teahouse, "Pavilion of the Lute
and the Pine Trees" in the Katsura garden.

crossbeams bear the silhouette of the sacred mountain. Next to the Fuji room is a tiny "spiritual" room, a minimised "tea corner" only standard size plus half a *tatami* mat, called *daime*.

A relaxed version of *shoin*

The formal *shoin* style can be seen in the Ninomaru Palace, which is open to the public, in the grounds of the Nijō Castle (1603) in Kyōto. This style was suitable for grand ceremonies, being fitted out with brilliantly painted sliding walls, curved, coffered ceilings, square-edged, carved supporting posts and heavy circumferential crossbeams or *nageshi*. The grand scale of this was, however, far too imposing for daily life and everyday activities, even for the upper strata of society. Consequently a different type of *shoin* style developed in harmony with the formal type: supporting posts with rough, unbevelled corners, *menkawabashira*, exquisitely structured sections and "understatement decoration" for the more dignified fittings of official *shoin* rooms. Intimacy and intuition were the maxims of this *shoin* type, which is frequently called the *sukiya* or *sukiya-shoin* style. In this too can be seen much of the flair that is typical of the essence of

sukiya and is borrowed from the ideas of the architecture of the tea ceremony. The art of making and drinking tea is inextricably associated with mental discipline, physical control and aesthetic sensibility. The bare tea cottage with its rough walls, open ceilings and surrounding garden contributed greatly to a precept of rustic simplicity, which is found again in a different form in *sukiya* houses. Tea ceremony architecture, though, takes from much older traditions, such as for example anchorite hermitages and medieval scholars' retreats, as well as from the simple homes of the Kyōto aristocracy – these did not take on a more exalted style until later.

The Katsura – "The neighboring palace"

The Katsura, a country villa belonging to the Katsuranomiya, a line of Japanese princes beginning with Hachijōnomiya Toshito (1579–1629) and his son Toshidata (1619–1662), is often referred to by both Japanese and Western reviewers as the quintessence of Japanese aesthetics. A comparison with the Hōshō-dai inn (1677), now the Hakkei-tei ryokan, is obvious as the same artistic and cultural form is inherent in both.

The Katsura villa complex is situated in south-west Kyōto near the Katsuragawa river and includes the Old *shoin*, the Middle *shoin*, a music room and the New Palace. In the garden stand the five teahouses: *gepparō*, "The Tower of Waves Illuminated by the Moon," *shōkatei*, "The Pavilion of the Lute and the Pine Trees," *shōiken*, "The Lodgings of the Laughing Thoughts," *shōkintei*, "The Pavilion of the Admired Blossoms" and *enrindō*, "The Hall of the Garden Grove."

The Old *shoin* and parts of the garden were built by Toshihito and date approximately from the year 1616. The commission for the Middle *shoin* (1641) is ascribed to Toshihito's son and the music room and the New Palace are presumed to have been added by Yasuhito, the third descendant in the Katsuranomiya line. He initiated the building plan in anticipation of the advancement in the Imperial hierarchy of his father, the tonsured Emperor Gomizunoo, the latter having some time previously withdrawn from official duties. The relevant date, 1660, was discovered in a braid trimming on the *fusuma* in the appropriate section of the residence; it is assumed that the music room and the New Palace were completed or renovated at this time. According to this information the Katsura complex was built in several stages, but it was without doubt intended from the beginning not merely as a pavilion for outings, but also to provide accommodation for several days or even weeks. A kitchen, bathroom and toilet were without question originally annexed to the rear of the section of the building known today as the "Old *shoin*." Bathrooms and toilets can be seen today in the area of the music room and the New Palace.

The symbiosis of palace and garden

The exquisite Katsura Villa is the private Xanadu of a nobleman and was constructed in rural surroundings so that the occupants could enjoy relaxing informally in the midst of nature. At their feudal retreat Toshihito and Toshidata and their select guests would admire the cherry blossom in springtime and the crimson leaves in autumn, while they prepared tea and enjoyed delicious cuisine or drifted to and fro in a boat on the large pond making the most of the "flowing, transitory world."

The gardens and buildings of the Katsura estate make up a unified whole. The cliffs placed with the utmost taste, the artistically supported trees and the bushes are not intended as objects of fleeting glances or reasons for a brief digression, they are trusty and active confidants to the residents.

The Katsura Teahouse

In the chronicles of the Hachijōnomiya family the villa is discreetly referred to as "the Katsura Teahouse." The family had other teahouses in Misasagimura, close to Uji towards the Southeast and the Kaidemmura, close to the old Nagaoka capital. The Kaidemmura was situated not far from the Nagaoka-Temmangū shrine, formerly called Kaiden Temmangū, and was a popular place to stay for occasional visits to the shrine or for hunting expeditions. It also provided the opportunity to collect the rare and delicious *matsutake* mushrooms. It should be mentioned that the Hachijōnomiya family did not have the monopoly of places of refuge such as this, but rather the majority of the nobility had residential refuges such as this, places for relaxation and rest, for recovery and restoration. The occupants took pleasure in the tea ceremony, devoted themselves to peaceful studying or to the beauties of nature.

The *sukiya* atmosphere

The Katsura villa is traditional Japan's most impressive and perfect legacy in respect of the homogenous blend of architecture and natural surroundings. The rustic teahouses, set idyllically in secluded corners of the garden, the stones that lead from the pond to the *shoin* complex, the open verandas and the moveable outside screens are details of this interaction. Without intending any disparagement, it should be noted that today's image of the Katsura *sukiya* world differs without doubt from the ambience that delighted Gomizunoo, Yasuhito and *Yōshō*. A later (mid-Edo Period around 1700–1750) owner of the Katsura, Prince Yakahito, seventh head of the

Preceding double page
Hakkei-tei
Part of the gardens of the Genkyu-en
with the large pond and a bridge. In the
background one of the tall maple trees,
its autumnal red leaves providing a
carefully considered splash of color
against the evergreen pine trees behind.

Opposite
Hakkei-tei
Inner room of the tea pavilion, which
was added to the Hōshō-dai inn (1677)
of the lords of Hikone, now the Hakkei-tei
in more recent times. Visitors to the
garden here may pay to take part in a
tea ceremony.

Left
Hakkei-tei
The thatched roofs of the Hakkei-tei,
with their harmonious wealth of crafted
shapes, fit into the natural garden
landscape of the Genkyu-en like a
sculpture, creating a prototype for the
symbiosis of scenery and architecture.

Katsuranomiya line, was particularly taken with the villa and certainly had much of it altered and extended according to his own personal taste. In addition the Katsuragawa River had, and still does have, the tendency to burst its banks and this repeatedly has an effect on the shape of the garden and the pond. The spirit of the old Katsura is nevertheless ever present and will live on through the ages, so that today's visitor too may experience and enjoy the *sukiya* atmosphere.

It should come as no surprise that the well proportioned right-angles and the contrasts between white and dark gray seem strikingly modern even in the eyes of the 21st century, for the Katsura is one of the models and sources of inspiration for the Bauhaus movement and influenced an entire generation of architects and artists in the West – from Charles Rennie Mackintosh through Piet Mondrian right up to Frank Lloyd Wright, who understood better than any one else that the site as well as the building are equally important components.

"From time to time in the past I had argued that the most important basis for the further development of modern architecture lay in its function. My words 'everything that functions well looks good' had sometimes been misunderstood;

they had been taken as referring exclusively to utilitarian usefulness and function. Here in Katsura, on an old building, I found full confirmation of my theory that I thought I had discovered as a valid basis for modern architecture." [64] [freely translated by J.B.]

Shūgakuin – An imperial residence

In contrast to the Katsura villa, the equally imperial Shūgakuin residence, like the Hōshō-dai inn (1677), is situated in a location provided with a background of "borrowed scenery."

"However, by far the finest and most complete examples of noble architecture that are to be seen date from the much later 17th century: the Shūgakuin palace located on the slopes of Mount Hie to the north-east of the city; and the Katsura palace, which is on flat land next to a river in the southwest. Although many of the refinements in these buildings came about as a result of tea aesthetics, they probably resemble the kind of noble residence that had also been enjoyed in earlier centuries.

Cha-dō – The Way of Tea, *cha-no-yū* – The Tea Ceremony

Dō = way; *cha* = tea; *no* = a particle; *yū* = hot water

Japanese monks returning from studying in China in the 12th century did not just bring back home with them a new meditation method, Zen Buddhism, but also seedlings from the tea plant. Legend has it that Boddhidharma, the Indian monk who made Zen Buddhism known in China, often became tired with the effort of concentration when meditating and one day tore off his drooping eyelids in a rage, throwing them to the ground. From them grew the tea plant, the leaves of which drive away weariness, and not just for meditating monks. Sleepiness was not tolerated among the samurai either, and so

tea drinking immediately became one of their favorite pastimes. Strict rules were established for using the noble tea utensils, deeply imbued with an elitist tea philosophy and tea aesthetics. Only selected pupils were initiated into the solemn tea ritual by the tea master.

When tea drinking became popularised in the 15th and 16th centuries, this fitted in especially with the idea that more people could discover inner calm and peace through the tea ceremony and would therefore train themselves to become better human beings. The Way of Tea was made complete by Senno Rikyū (1520–

1591), when he defined what "tea people" had to learn in the course of their practice: *wa*, *ka*, *sei* and *jaku* – harmony, respect for everything that exists, purity and tranquility. These principles should be experienced inwardly and not be enforced through rigid rules.

Senno Rikyū favored teahouses that were only the size of two *tatami*, the perfect expression of *wabi*, an aesthetic ideal of noble sparseness, which can, however, perfectly well conceal great wealth within itself. The nobility and the feudal lords, on the other hand, built themselves magnificent teahouses, in which the

Opposite
Wooden ladles, used when cleansing the mouth and hands before entering the teahouse, are placed ready on the *uchi-roji*, a stone washbasin.

Left
Chikutei Yagyu-no-sho
Nijiriguchi (28 x 32 in.), "crawling entrance" of a teahouse in the bamboo grove of the Chikutei Yagyu-no-sho ryokan near Shuzenji on the Izu peninsula.

tea ceremony promoted communication and intellectual exchange in an elegant and cheerful atmosphere.

In order to experience a traditional tea ritual the visitor must enter the *roji*, a small tea garden, through the outside door on the path to the middle door, called the *amigasa-mon*, or gate of the woven umbrella. Here he leaves the outside world behind him and then cleanses his mouth and hands with a wooden ladle at the *uchi-roji*, a stone washbasin. Even the handling of the simple wooden ladle has to be practised, as all the actions linked with the tea ceremony require the utmost concentration. Guests have to bend down to slip through the tiny opening to the tea-room, *nijiriguchi* (28 x 32 in.), as a measure that they have finally left behind the everyday world. They sit up straight, facing the *tokonoma* in order to admire the picture

scroll, selected according to the season, that hangs there. This is the beginning of the *cha-ji*, the tea ceremony. The visitors then give their thanks for the careful preparation of the tea, and thereafter conversation is confined to what is happening in the tea-room.

The man of the house heats water in an iron kettle, cleans the tea bowls and the other utensils, places some powdered tea into a bowl with a bamboo spoon and then pours hot water on it. Next he whisks the infusion with a bamboo whisk until the top layer is thick and hands the bowl to the guests. The ceremonial brew is a creamy, bitter tea, *koi-cha;* less formal is the thin, mild *usu-cha*, served later on in personal bowls. The choice of tea bowls also depends on the time of year: in summer they are flat and wide, so that the tea cools down more quickly, while bowls for winter

are taller, and thicker too, to retain the heat. The host's own personal taste is also a deciding factor in the choice of bowls. However, the tea bowl, *raku,* is always the "chief work of art" of the tea ceremony and is frequently priceless.

"Overseas visitors to Japan usually desire to witness at least one *cha-no-yū*, an ancient observance which has come down through the ages and which is a development by certain priests of the Buddhist Zen sect of simple tea drinking into what is now an aethetic [*sic*] cult, its outstanding tea-master being Rikyū, once a close friend of the great Taiko-Hideyoshi. From its inception the *Cha-no-yū* ceremony has been regarded as a promoter of mental composure. In the mere handling of the utensils employed there must be the utmost exactness, and not a single error must occur in the performance of the

function itself. It is declared by its devotees that the accurate and delicate performance of each act teaches precision, poise and tranquility, courtesy, sincerity, unselfishness and daintiness, and produces harmony in every sense.

Situated in every large garden and in some small gardens is a tea-ceremony house, constructed on prescribed lines, and in the homes of many wealthy families a room is set aside for the *cha-no-yū.* These rooms are only 9 feet square, their floors being covered with 4 mats (*tatami*), each mat being about 6x3 feet in size.

Space does not permit a description of the ceremony itself, or of the 'Don'ts' in connection with it, or of the utensils employed – but it may be said that while to Occidental eyes some of these utensils may appear crude crockery ware, many of them are valued at thousands of yen. The tea itself is made of powdered green tea-leaves and when made has the consistency of thick pea soup. This thick-tea ceremony is called *Koi-cha.* There is another style of tea ceremony, the *Usu-cha,* which differs from the *Koi-cha* in some respects. It is less ceremonious, and the tea, of good quality, is drunk like ordinary tea and is made with lukewarm water, and the bowl is filled afresh for each guest, being rinsed out with water each time. The tea used in both these ceremonies comes from Uji, near Kyōto, the most noted tea district of Japan. [...]

The tea ceremony with its long formalities cannot be fully appreciated by the casual Westerner, but when he witnesses it he cannot fail to be impressed by the sincere enjoyment evidenced by the Japanese participants in the function – which for them still carries a trace of its religious element." [65]

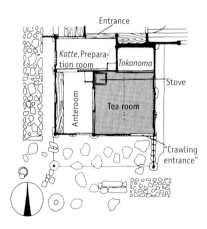

Opposite

Nonomura Ninsei (active around 1600/1666)
Tea ceremony bowl with decoration of autumn grasses
About 1660.
Stoneware painted and glazed.
Height approx. 3¹/₂ in.,
Nezu Institute of Fine Arts, Tokyo
Ninsei was born in the town of Nonomura to the
north of Kyōto. He founded a pottery in Kyōto opposite
the Ninnaji temple and derived his name from the
characters nin and *sei* (an alternative version of *kyo*).
The exact dates of his birth and death are not known,
but he was most honored around the year 1659.
Ninsei mainly created vessels with cream-colored
sections for the tea ceremony, painting them with
soft colors in enamel glaze. In his later years his
decorations became more lavish and colorful. The
factory continued to operate successfully in the 17th
and 18th centuries and was famous for its splendid
decoration and delicate crackle.

Left

***Cha-gama*, tea ceremony kettle**
Iron tea kettle with the impression of a hand as a motif,
probably North Honshu, 18 C,
Height 14 in., width 12¹/₂ in.,
Mingeikan, The Japan Folk Crafts Museum, Tokyo
The tea ceremony requires beautiful, top quality iron
kettles. A fine kettle is looked after and treasured over
generations of tea masters.

Above left and right
Hakkei-tei
The entrance to the ryokan adorned with chrysanthemums on both sides.

The imperial flower blooms in autumn. Separate exhibitions are held to celebrate the numerous varieties and award prizes.

Opposite
Hakkei-tei
Room divider made of bamboo sticks and woven bamboo.

Detail of the sublime interior decoration in the *sukiya* style, characterised by delicately structured segments and "understatement decoration."

'Palace' is not perhaps the most appropriate word to use, conjuring up as it does European images of heavy stone, glazed windows, and expansive parklands. These two Japanese buildings would be better described as villas or princely country retreats. Both are famous for their simple and elegant architectural lines and superb gardens; the most refined merging of nature and building that at first appears to be totally artless, but which could only have been achieved by the most painstaking attention to detail and absolutely sure taste. Both types were built for the use of Imperial family members and courtiers: a place where they could escape from the tedium of everyday rituals and relax in a rustic setting, to practice the tea ceremony, compose poetry, and enjoy the beauty of nature as it progressed through its seasonal changes.

The Shūgakuin was built on a site that was chosen for its natural beauty and the extensive views it offered of the city and distant mountains. On the lower slope, a long embankment was constructed, at great effort and expense, to contain a large pond with one or two islands, a pond that was kept supplied with water from a diverted stream. Although the garden has been organised with great care and skill, the topographical features and surrounding scenery have been ingeniously utilized as part of the total design. The forested hillside behind the buildings acts as backdrop to the garden, giving the impression that it is much larger than it in fact is – an excellent example of the previously mentioned *shakkei* ('borrowed scenery'), where available natural features and scenery have been incorporated for maximum effect in the planning of the villa.

The buildings are in the style known as *sukiya*, in which construction is kept simple and the natural textures of wood and plaster are left bare so that their own beauty will complement that of the natural world all around. Decoration is minimal and restricted mainly to paintings on the sliding doors. One door in Shūgakuin is of plain, honey-colored cedar wood and has the design of two painted carp swimming behind

a torn net (a gold tracery that covers the whole surface); the eye of the larger fish peers out through the mesh to complete a composition that is quite startlingly modern in its conception. Another pair of doors have paintings of two wheeled floats that were used in the annual *Gion* festival – filled with flowers, exquisitely costumed dolls, and decorations – and again the lavish design is toned down but made more elegant by the plain cedar wood background. The only other adornments in the villa consist of discreetly patterned paper in the shelved *tokonoma*, and the intricately worked details on metal fittings such as nail-head covers and door-pulls." [66]

The chrysanthemum – Nature's ornament and mythology

Nature, in other words the materials borrowed from it and their texture, is transformed into a "decorative whole" in the *sukiya* style. "Artificially" created nature and "natural" art should not be experienced and considered as separate entities. Furthermore, in a transcendental sense everything is as if belonging to a higher order, determined by religion, ritual and elemental forces. The progress of the seasons has far-reaching effects on the appearance of all architecture, both in the garden and in internal fittings and decoration. For example, the natural event of autumn finds its expression in the glowing colors of the autumn foliage, appearing as a decorative feature all over screens, ceramics, kimonos and everyday equipment. The imperial chrysanthemumkiku or *kusan*, is also a symbol of autumn. Its many types adorn gardens, entrances to houses and objects, and are even used in food recipes.

The name "chrysanthemum" comes from the Ancient Greek – literally translated "golden flower" – and in many countries of the world legends have been woven around this Delphic flower. On the other hand, however, the story has been handed down that the chrysanthemum had its origins in China; hence to this day it is predominantly associated with Japan.

For a thousand years now a golden chrysanthemum with 16 petals has been the imperial emblem of Japan. During the dynastic wars, which began in 1357 and lasted for over 55 years, every warrior belonging to the Southern Court wore a golden yellow chrysanthemum as a mark of his heroism. Japanese mythology has its own detailed variation on the origin of the imperial flower, which without question differs considerably from the Chinese version.

The traditional Japanese story relates that in the dim and distant past the Nipponese heaven was so overpopulated with gods that some of them, including the god Izanagi and the goddess Izanami, were ordered to descend to earth on a bridge of clouds.

Above
Hakkei-tei
The formal 30-mat guest room of the ryokan with open-work ramma made of the simplest bamboo sticks arranged in an irregular pattern.

In the *tokonoma* of the room is a wall-cupboard, in which the lord's bodyguard would hide, so that he could protect his master even in the presence of guests, without detracting from the elegant, relaxed atmosphere.

Opposite
Hakkei-tei
Part of the *byōbu*, the decorative folding screen, in the official guest room. Rather than being adorned with impressive paintings, this moveable screen has fan pictures, ink drawings and pages from albums mounted on it (and therefore preserved), in the discreet, poetic *sukiya* manner.

Once down on earth the goddess was extremely diligent towards Izanagi, creating the gods of the wind, the mountains, the lakes and, after creating further gods, the god of fire, whereupon she died exhausted. However Izanagi missed Izanami so much that he followed her to the Place of Eternal Night, where, although he experienced many abominable things and moreover had a spell cast on him by the Old Witch of the Dark Night, he never saw his beloved again.

Having just escaped back to earth, the god Izanagi hurried forthwith to a river to cleanse himself in it. When he removed his clothing it came into contact with the ground and as it did so it became transformed into twelve gods in an instant, while his jewellery produced flowers – a bangle became an iris, another a lotus and his necklace a chrysanthemum.

Numerous festivities pay homage to the legendary flower in the months of October and November. Extremely popular competitions take place – who can grow the most voluptuous bloom? – and there is barely a park in Japan that cannot offer a chrysanthemum show at this time. Crowds of rapt admirers file past the long row of flower heads that have been trained, or tied up straight with wire. Politicians and other illustrious personalities hold chrysanthemum parties and all the other "children of the nation" arrange convivial gatherings in the name of the chrysanthemum. All these events go back to a

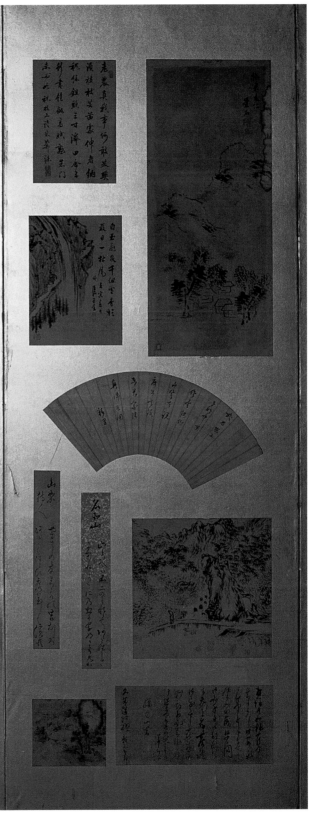

Opposite
Hakkei-tei
Shōji screen made of woven bamboo in the connecting corridor of the ryokan. Moveable screens and dividing walls with open or covered window openings were a type of decorative "coup," as when they were elaborately adorned they fulfilled a functional purpose effectively: they served as a source of light and fresh air and made intimacy possible, while at the same time being a purely aesthetic component in the arrangement of the room.

Right
Katsura Rikyu, Kyōto, 1616/1641/1660
View into the rooms of the *shōiken*, "Lodgings of the Laughing Thoughts," teahouse; open *shōji*; roughly plastered crossbeams in the rustic teahouse style with round, woven bamboo open-work *shōji* windows.

centuries old national tradition, which was passed on from China before that. There, as the chronicles would have it, the first celebration of the chrysanthemum was held on the ninth day of the ninth month in the year 200 B.C. The host was the Han emperor Kao-tsu, who held an event for the contemplation of chrysanthemums in memory of his favorite lady Ch'i. Likewise on the ninth day of the ninth month, but not until A.D. 685 the first chrysanthemum party was held in Japan at the behest of the Emperor Temmu (the 40th).

Byobu as decorative room dividers and "poetry books"

Moveable screens were not used just as temporary room dividers in *sukiya* rooms, but also served architecturally, alongside the calculatedly discreet embellishments in natural materials, as decorative backgrounds to lend the room a prestigious appearance on special occasions. Particularly exquisite examples of an individual genre of moveable screen can be seen in the Hakkei-tei ryokan. These folding screens are not provided with striking, large-scale paintings, but instead have mounted on them (and therefore preserved) fan pictures, ink drawings, pages from albums and fragments of paintings in unmistakably *sukiya* style irregular arrangements. The preferred activity indulged in by those in a *sukiya* rooms finds its parallel here, spontaneous ink drawings and poetry composition.

"Every Japanese has a poetic nature and is, so to speak, a poet by nature, possibly because, born in a country of scenic and artistic beauty, he is naturally charmed to express himself in verse [...]." [67]

The aesthetic circle of the *sukiya* world is brought to completion with the lines quoted above. Scenery and art are inextricably tied to one another and inspire one another in a singular – Japanese – way.

Above
Niki Club
Partial view of the spacious water pool in the inner court of the main building from 1985.
Much has been written about the meeting of arts from East and West. The Niki Club
delivers the corresponding full contemporary interpretation from the Japanese
perspective. The resort was built between 1985 and 1997 by the architects and designers
Akira Watanabe and Takashi Sugimoto.

二期倶楽部

Niki Club, Nasu

East and West – Tradition and contemporary building materials

The Niki Club, as the name of this "inn" suggests, is not an authentic ryokan in the traditional sense and the word "Club" when interpreted faithfully is a more fitting expression than the term "hotel" used in the Western sense for overnight lodging possibilities for paying guests. A "Club" is also understood in the West to be a place for board and lodging which is reserved for a select clientele and which has certain rules. Synonyms for "Club" are, for example, "community of interests," "guild" or "alliance." In spite of all Western adaptations, the Niki Club remains a ryokan as regards the guest's behavior, the traditional rules such as those for arrival and departure times, the bathing ritual, etc. Excluded from this regime are the dress regulations and the meals. Food is also served after the bath, but not in one's private rooms. Rather in the restaurant and in evening dress, instead of in a kimono and a *yūkata* – more or less a homage to the Eastern-inspired, tantalising cuisine offered by the French chef de cuisine.

Above
Niki Club
View of a cottage in the annex from 1997. The wall extending crosswise into the shallow water pool adopts the function of a traditional Japanese standing screen or a *fusuma* by separating the dwelling area from the publicly accessible space of the lobby and the restaurant while at the same time allowing detail-like vistas.

Opposite
Niki Club
Bridge to the reception area of the annex with a glowing red maple whose intensive colors, like in "old times," are also able to demonstrate perfectly within the frame of modernity the desired contrast between the "gray" Japanese architecture and natural autumnal tones.

"East meets West." This sometimes overused phrase only holds for the Niki Club at the first appearance. Although some of the rooms – above all those in the annex - are appointed in a Western style, however, if a closer look is taken the resort and the architecture are pure Japanese. The Niki Club is not a hotel in the Western sense and does not present a typical Western construction style, even if the buildings, the main house with the spacious inner court from 1985 and the cottage annex from July 1997, were constructed using "Western" building materials. These materials include glass and concrete, that is, not specifically Western rather simply contemporary, modern materials which are used world-wide.

The particularly striking thing about the Niki Club is the traditional Japanese construction style with in part new building materials. Japan's most famous contemporary architect, Tadao Ando, remarked that for him concrete is the equivalent of timber and that concrete in his buildings virtually replaces timber as a traditional material. Structures that conventionally were made of timber have been replaced in the Niki Club by concrete or glass. Parallel thereto a broad range of traditional natural materials is used and it is fascinating to see how timber and concrete, natural stone, gravel, loam rendering and glass, *tatami*, bamboo, rice paper *shōji* and brick complement one another in a symbiosis because they are used in a "Japanese" way. In the spirit championed by Tadao Ando, the timber panel wall is replaced by concrete, forming a tight joint with the *fusuma*, the sliding wood door, likewise the glass window against the *shōji*. The ingenious feature of this construction style is that traditional functions are retained: "screening" on the one hand and the intentional use of vistas and apertures on the other. The "wall" is not conceived as a constructional enclosure in the Western sense, that is as impediment and fortification. A further Japanese characteristic is leaving the material in its original state; for instance, concrete is not rendered but is allowed to keep its irregular texture. The concrete is poured in timber shells and the concrete walls at the Niki Club carry the grain of the timber, a "cast stone wall" with wood grain. The "natural" beauty of the concrete is utilized and it is not modestly faced with wood as in the West. In the same way as in a traditional Japanese inn, preference is given to local materials – and thus an economical and ecological construction. A prominent feature of the Niki Club buildings are partition walls, passages and paths comprising *oya-ishi*, stone from Oya, which is quarried locally. The granular, porous nature of this distinctively colored stone signifies the surrounding countryside.

The space in the main houses and in the cottages is organized strictly in a traditional Japanese way. The main

house has nothing but *tatami* rooms with the open ceiling structure that is found in rural Japanese houses. The cottages combine interlinked Western style rooms and *tatami* rooms, but also the rooms with Western furnishings are strictly traditional in the way space is partitioned and as regards the principle of *shakkei*, of borrowed scenery. Logical consistency is provided by the bathroom and its customs: cedar wood tubs with water from the hot spring for relaxation and recreation and also a "cleaning area" with a stool, shower and wooden pail. The toilet is entirely separate. In Japan, no matter how humble the dwelling, one will never find a bathing area and a toilet in the

Left
Niki Club
Views from one of the cottages in the annex across to the restaurant.
Like a traditional Japanese inn, the Niki Club was also built largely using local materials in an economical and ecological construction style. A prominent feature of the buildings of the Niki Club are the partition walls, the passages and the paths which are made of *oya-ishi*, stone from Oya, a porous, speckled stone which is quarried locally.

same room as is often the case in West. Because bathing is a strictly ritualized act of almost religious character, this questionable Western practice is basically forbidden. A further criterion of Japanese tradition is illustrated by the embodiment of the cottages. The immediate entrance area is visually separate from the living space and also in respect of the "dignity levels." Here there is also the so-called *dōma*, the ground floor level, with a clay, earth or stone floor in front of the higher wooden floor. The *dōma* is where one removes outside shoes. The Niki Club imparts impressively the realization that traditional construction is not solely material-dependent but that it revolves around the organization of space, on seeing the room as space and a place, on its spiritual presence, on the materials used and their optical effect.

The lobby, the bar, and the restaurant appear to be Western, but only at first glance. Changing views between slots in the towering walls, sudden vistas of the "wild" landscape or calm water pools also signify that this part of the complex is Japanese. This impression is rounded off when the more than 33-foot high glass façade facing the mountain stream is pushed aside and the restaurant is suddenly located in the midst of the untamed landscape.

Moreover, what happens on the tables – not just at the table – is sensational. The best French cuisine has adapted the noble cultivation of *kaiseki* food. The plate is not dominated by cream sauces and primary herbs but by local products, regionally savored and arranged. The meals, however, remain French in composition and essence. A "bouquet des legumes," for example, consists of classic vegetables such as carrots and asparagus, complemented by local herbs and mushrooms.

The close relationship between the room and the landscape and the flowing transition from nature to room are also integral to the resort, to the building principles and to Japan, as are, of course, the "open air baths." Embedded in the rather rugged scenery, a short walk from the Club, the *onsen* for men and women are situated on a hill in the spacious natural garden of the ryokan hotel. The design of the baths is unadulteratedly traditional with natural stone pools, bamboo fences, wooden boards, and as a special attraction, relaxing in the water one has a magnificent view across the plain of the mountain silhouettes, with the exciting aspect of having one's sights on an active volcano.

The eleven hot springs at Nasu are situated in the north-east of Tochigi prefecture. According to legend, the probably most famous and most popular hot spring was discovered by a hunter in hot pursuit of a deer. The animal fled its persecutor into the mountains and finally to the spring to find protection. Like the hunted creature, the hunter found the hot water pleasant and healing, and thus began the human use of the hot spring at Nasu Yumoto. One of the public baths in the region bears testimony to this tale – *shika-no-yū*, the deer bath. During the Edo period (1615-1868), Nasu Yumoto was extremely popular, more than one hundred ryokan and six public bathhouses invited guests for relaxation. The famous *haiku* poet Matsuo Bashō (1644-1694) praised the spa which is particularly helpful for ailments such as gastric complaints, rheumatism and female disorders.

Nasu's altitude makes a sojourn there ideal to escape the oppressive heat of summer or to enjoy the spectacular color of the foliage in autumn. The Imperial family also maintains its summer residence in Nasu.

Japanese adaptation

The Niki Club is thus overall an extremely successful symbiosis between East and West which, however, could not be repeated successfully were it switched and were it in the manner of this experiment, namely the selection of Japanese architectural elements for Western buildings. Western houses –

All illustrations on this double page
Niki Club
An exciting feature in the architecture of the Niki Club is the unusual synthesis of timber and concrete, gravel, loam rendering and glass, *tatami*, bamboo, rice paper *shōji* and brick. In the spirit championed by the Japanese architect Tadao Ando, the timber panel wall is replaced by concrete, forming a tight joint with the fusuma, the sliding wood door, likewise the glass window against the *shōji*.

The *tatami*

The *tatami* is a rush mat and the traditional floor covering inside a Japanese building. In a conventional Japanese house there are only so-called *tatami* rooms, but also in houses that are Western influenced in large cities there is usually one classic *tatami* room, the other rooms are termed "Western-style" rooms. The clear basic difference is that in the *tatami* room one sits on the floor, directly upon the *tatami* or upon a seating cushion and no chairs or other seats are used. This also requires among other things the custom of removing one's shoes before entering the room.

A *tatami* room consists of a number of *tatami* mats. The size of the individual mats is not the same in all regions of the country. A *tatami* mat in Tokyo, for example, measures 3 x 6 feet, in Kyōto 3.1 x 6.2 feet, and there is often a smaller size, 2.6 x 5.2 feet, called *danchi*. Because, however, one side of the *tatami* mat is always exactly half the length of the other side, a square or a rectangular room is easily created.

This is done as follows: 3 *jyou*, a room with 3 *tatami* mats, is the smallest room, which is usually used as a storage room; 4.5 *jyou*, a room with 4 and a half *tatami* mats is a square room and the minimum needed for one person; 6 *jyou* is the most popular size; 8 *jyou*, a room with 8 *tatami* mats is the second most frequent variant and also a square room.

Of course, there are much larger *tatami* rooms, above all in elegant ryokan. Usually these rooms have an adjoining space, the

oshiire, a type of closet, which measures 1 or 2 jyou.

A tatami room epitomizes the "multi-functional room," used as a living room, a study, a dining room, a bedroom, and as a guest room. Depending on the number of guests, one or more futons, which are taken from a cupboard, are laid out on the tatami floor. This way of using space – although centuries old – is doubtlessly modern and contemporary. With an increasing shortage of dwelling space, this lifestyle optimizes the use of space.

Jyou is the popular room measurement in Japan, even Western style rooms without tatami floors are calculated in jyou. Land surfaces are also measured used the tatami mat as a basis: 1 tsubo is 2 tatami mats, or approximately 35½ sq. feet.

The tatami mat is made of rush on top of a rice straw base. The woven rush has to be replaced every couple of years, while the base is more durable. To protect the mat against moisture newspaper or cardboard is used as an underlay when the flooring is installed. New tatami flooring is light green and has a fresh natural smell. However, it is also highly flammable and subject to insect attack. A mat is approximately 1½ x 2½ inches thick and has a cloth border on the sides to prevent fraying and simultaneously to allow various possibilities for patterns and designs.

Tatami floors fully replaced the wooden floors of earlier shinden palaces of the Heian period (794–1185) over the centuries and were one of the most important innovative elements of shoin architecture,

whereby in the shoin architectural style wooden floorboards and tatami mats were still combined.

In shoin architecture the border edging was a type of status symbol; the exquisiteness of the embroidered, frequently valuable brocade borders reflected the societal position and wealth of the house. A further sign of the rank of a person was whether this person sat on the tatami mat or had to sit on the wooden or earthen floor of the house, the difference in height being somewhat less than 2 inches.

During the Muromachi period (1392–1573) the tatami mat developed into the full tatami floor. This also led to the gradual covering of the floors with tatami to express differences in rank through seating heights.

Above
Niki Club
The autumnal red foliage provides formal, conscious colorful impulses amid the minimalist concrete walls of the cottages which are interconnected by a traditional "tea path."

Opposite
Niki Club
Zen in concrete, glass and *tatami*. The irregular stepping stones, essential attributes to every tea house garden, lead between "timber and concrete" walls to the autumnal mountain stream. In the foreground, the traditional seating cushions, the *zabuton*.

Wright, Adolf Loos, down to Mies van der Rohe, Egon Eiermann and David Chipperfield, who adapted Japan at a completely different level. They integrated the functionality, the clarity, the interplay of light and shadow, and the irregularity of Japanese architect in the traditional Western construction style, in a quasi Western modification. Above and beyond all architectural and design elements, these artists, quite rightly called the "heroes of architecture," tapped the spiritual level of the Japanese house. Bruno Taut, the great Expressionist architect (1880–1938), writes about the "high philosophical spirituality" of Japanese architecture as exemplified in Katsura. He too "decoded" the inner most essence of Japanese spatial organization where the invisible is to be recognized behind the principle of utilitarianism. "The entire arrangement [Katsura], from whichever side one might care to look at it, followed always elasticaly in all its divisions the purpose which each one of the parts as well as the whole had to accomplish, the aim being that of common and normal utility, or the necessity of dignfied representation, or that of lofty, philosophical spirituality. And the great mystery was that all three purposes had been united into a whole and that their boundaries had been effaced." [68]

East and West - Japanese customs in "modern" Japan

It is appropriate in a chapter that is dedicated to the exchange between East and West to speak about the Japanese mentality, Japanese superstitions, and Japanese emotions. The doubtlessly significant problems that Western visitors have in Japan are the result of fully incorrect expectations. Modern Japanese in large cities and cities per se wear Western clothing, conduct themselves outwardly in a Western manner and business-wise appear to be optimized Westerners. Not least, Japan is a leading technological nation, therefore we expect the Japanese to have the same feelings and behave in the same way as Westerners. Because, however, this is effectively not the case, visitors are gripped by a degree of mistrust, are uncertain of themselves, and as a consequence rejection may well up inside them. We are much more likely to accept exoticism – a person in a grass skirt is naturally "strange" – than otherness in someone wearing the same clothes.

Everyday Japanese life is still heavily ritualized, drawing on thousands of years of tradition. Superstition is a permanent part of everyday life and is based on a deeply rooted animistic attitude. A class and caste system which developed in isolation (until almost 150 years ago) still has a decisive impact. A country constantly faced with a shortage of living

usually private residences – which attempt to absorb Japanese stylistic features remain strangely sterile, or in the worst case have an ethnological aftertaste. It is not just that the natural surroundings do not fit – the seasons in Japan are largely similar to those in Europe and thus also the appearance of the landscape, although less rugged and cultivated in a different way. Basically, however, the entirely different lifestyle makes a transposition impossible; in Europe or America, everyday Japanese culture remains a decorative backdrop.

A fully different category are the buildings by inspired architects such as Charles Rennie Mackintosh, Frank Lloyd

Opposite
Niki Club
The Western bed in the Japanese room. Bedroom of a cottage with a traditional inner court, bath and a *tatami* room.

Above left
Niki Club
Bathroom in a cottage dedicated to Japanese tradition: cedar wood tub with thermal water, also a "cleaning area" with stool, shower and a wooden pail.

Above right
Niki Club
A criterion of Japanese tradition is shown in the construction style of the cottages. The immediate entrance area is visually separate from the living area and as regards the "dignity levels": *do̅ma*, the ground floor level, comprising a clay or earth floor, also stone, in front of the higher wooden floor. One, of course, removes outside shoes on the *do̅ma* before entering the inside room and one wears the traditional *geta* on the way to the *onsen*.

space and a large population has learned to exercise great courtesy. Full employment has a been basic element of social harmony, whereby no one was able to leave the country to work elsewhere. Thus today a Westerner is amazed that numerous activities are carried out by so many "middlemen," a relict from the period of isolation. The survival mechanisms that were developed also resulted in fundamental differences in the way the Japanese and Westerners express emotions.

"[...] During this long period of isolation – 1639 until 1854, after all 15 generations – the Japanese lived on their island chain like in a spaceship which had freed itself from the earth's gravity. Taken in retrospect, this was perhaps the greatest sociological experiment of modern human history: thirty million people had to live herded closely together 15 generations long – on productive land which if yielding normal harvests would barely be sufficient to nourish thirty million people.

In spite of this extremely precarious situation, the Japanese were able to live with one another extraordinarily peacefully for more than two-hundred [*sic*] years. This certainly would not have been possible if they had not ensured that the social conflicts, which smoulder in every society, were defused in an uncomplicated way and manner. There was no extreme divide between poor and rich. [...] Only if one looks more closely at Japanese society at that time can one understand today's Japan because much of what is valid in Japan and what concerns the Japanese – both in good and evil – derives in a direct line from that period of time. The way that Japanese society is still structured today – vertically and horizontally, how people treat one another, how they tackle problems and solve or shelve conflicts – everything is still almost as it was in the Japan of the spaceship age. [...] This analogy, so I believe, means the Japanese spaceship experience will suddenly acquire global importance for the 21st century and the time afterwards." [69]

"There is a countless number of superstitions in Japan [*sic*] – those peculiar to certain localities, to certain professional groups, and those common to all classes throughout the country. [...]

There are superstitions concerning direction (*hogaku*), Physiognomy, (*ninso*), House Structure (*kaso*), Omens (*engi*), Dates (*higara*), Fortune Telling (*bokuzai*), Exorcism (*majinai*), etc. [...]

[...] When the owner of a newly built house dies from accident or illness, people attribute the cause of death to certain defects in the *kaso*. If each person has his physio (*ninso*), each house has its house fortune, *kaso*. Some houses have good *kaso* while others have bad *kaso*.

"Many a house cannot be sold or rented because it is built in an unlucky *hogaku* or has a protruding part in the direction of *kimon* [north-east, in Japanese, 'devil's gate.']. When a house burns or burglars break into it or the family living in it decline [*sic*] in fortune, the house is more often blamed than the carelessness or indolence of its occupants.

[As a construction material] pine is used because its other name is *chitose*, which means "a thousand years;" bamboo is employed because it is a symbol in Japan for 10,000 years (*yorozuyo*). [...]

One often sees the Chinese character (　) for 'water' written on a roof-tile as a charm against fire. Most Japanese houses were thatched with straw or reeds in former days, and their roof could easily catch fire from the sparks flying from a burning house. So the character was used on a roof-tile as a preventative charm against fire. [...]

When Japanese are annoyed by visitors who outstay their welcome and wish to get rid of them, they usually set a broom upside down and tie a towel (*tenugui*) around it in the same way that a scarf or other wrap is sometimes tied around the face, and the caller's footgear or *geta* are warmed up and placed

Japanese never drink tea which has been kept overnight. It is considered an insult if one is served such tea. In feudal days, every criminal condemned to death was served with overnight tea [*sic*] before he was beheaded – which explains the Japanese aversion to stale tea. [...]

Japanese mostly drink hot, nt iced tea. t is made with boiling water, but is drunk lukewarm. "However, most Japanese take tea every morning since they believe that they may meet with some accident if they leave home without taking tea in the morning. [...]

A Westerner stirs his tea in the way the hands of a watch move, a Japanese does it in the reverse way. [...]

By 'reverse water' is meant hot water poured into cold water. When a dead person is finally washed before the remains are put into the coffin, water is poured into the tub in this way. 'Reverse water' is considered unlucky and it is never used on an ordinary occasion. [...]

A Japanese set of cups, plates, etc., is 5 or 10, not 6 or 12 [pieces as is usual in the West]." [70]

"Topsy-turvydom"

Aside from the very many superstitions the Japanese have, the frequently incomprehensible expressions of emotion and actions in everyday life of the Japanese make life difficult for the Westerner because often reactions and habits appear to be "topsy-turvy." Respect, for example, is expressed by drawing in the breath and is not a sign of displeasure as in the West. In Japan the wife has control of the purse and is the financial manager of family expenditure. It is still customary for the man's salary to be paid directly to the spouse by the employer, as the consensus is that a woman budgets the money in a more "family friendly way."

Whereas Western women's wear is sealed right over left, women's clothing in Japan is closed left over right. Right over left is only used to seal the "shroud," the clothing for the deceased on their last journey. It is therefore understandably considered sacrilegious to seal a kimono right over left.

next to the handle in order to speed the visitor's departure. In case this charm fails to produce results, they cauterize the footgear of the visitors with the *moxa*, believing that the burning treatment will set the objects into action."

Special attention is paid to the meals and the observation of particular prescriptions concerning the food and beverages. "Another food indispensable not only at wedding and birthday dinners, but on all other happy occasions is lobster. The crustacean is served because its body is bent, which to Japanese means old age.

When invited to a dinner Japanese never eat one bowl of rice only; they eat at least two because one bowl of rice means an offering to the spirit of a dead person (*hotoke*). [...]

The Japanese bow when they introduce themselves. Westerners shake hands and look at one another. When the Japanese beckon someone over, the palm of the hand is turned outwards whereas the Westerner beckons somebody with the palm turned inwards.

The Japanese say "yes" when Westerners would say "no." For example: "You don't have any relatives in Japan, do you?" The answer would be : "Yes, we don't." There are no words in the Japanese language which correspond exactly to the meaning of "yes" or "no" as they exist concisely in Western languages.

"When telling about the death of a parent, wife, child, or some near relative a Japanese will often smile, his face in no way evidencing the grief he feels, which is in direct contrast to a Westerner's expression under similar circumstances. This custom comes through [*sic*] a desire to suppress all signs of deep emotion, and not to inflict a personal grief on another person." [71]

Japanese emotion and its suppression

"The Japanese are highly emotional but early acquire the habit of suppressing evidences of their deep-seated emotion, and encase themselves in an armor of inscrutability impossible of penetration [*sic*] by the Westerner. But occasionally emotion cannot be suppressed and it breaks out violently even in high places, as revealed in the scenes which sometimes occur during the sittings of the Diet. [...] There is one place, however, where emotion cannot be

Above
Niki Club
Guest room in one of the cottages.
A traditional Japanese room as regards
the room structure and the architecture,
nonetheless furnished in a Western style.

Opposite
Niki Club
Multiple reflections of the French-
Japanese restaurant of the "ryokan club"
on the still surface of a water pool, a
concrete wall and the glass façade. The
"mirror image" of East-West architecture.

Right and opposite page
Niki Club
The Japanese Provence restaurant "La Brise" tempting guests during the day and for dinner.
The behavioral patterns required in the Niki Club are traditional Japanese, with the exception of meals. Although food is also served after the bath, it is not profered in one's private rooms but in the restaurant, and in evening dress instead of in a kimono or a *yūkata*. However, Japanese by nature are the unexpected views from an orderly architecture of the "wild" landscape.

Below
Niki Club
The Japanese inspired cuisine offered by the chef de cuisine, Marc Bonard, is the culinary high point of the East-West encounter. "Millefeuille de legumes d'automne à la vinaigrette de Miso" or "Filet de boef de Nasu" are impressive evidence of the perfect rendezvous of cultures "on the plate."

wholly suppressed, and that is at a theater where, during pathetic scenes, men and women weep with little restraint but this does not alter the fact that suppression and not expression is a characteristic of the Japanese. When telling about some misfortune or about the death of a parent, wife, child, or near relative, a Japanese will smile in a way which a Westerner considers heartless, although the teller, because of grief, may be near the breaking-down point [*sic*].

One reason for this attitude is the characteristic consideration for the feelings of others in that one's personal grief should not be inflicted upon others. However, though a rigid repression of emotions is exercised, the emotion of grief is sometimes so strong that in spite of self-control tears will glisten in the eyes.

The English language has many expletives – and they fill a useful function, but in Japanese swear words are practically non-existent, which would indicate that in that language no provision is made for the expression of the emotions of anger [*sic*].

This suppression leads to a poise seldom found among the people of other countries; and even the children have this poise. Tranquility and absence of haste are the outward manifestations of Japanese life except, of course, in the major activities in the great cities.

Japanese regard self-control as the highest of the virtues, and from time immemorial self-control has emanated from the Zen Sect [*sic*] of Buddhism down through the masses. Their ascetic practice of the tea ceremony, and of flower arrangements, are methods of training Japanese in self-control and poise which long have been practised." [72]

In the frame of all these possible misjudgements and thus "sources of errors" in the encounter between Japan and the West, the explanations by Andreas Meckel in "Germany Japan – 100 views" are extremely illuminating. Germans and Europeans, Westerners as a whole, have an egocentric view of life. They consider themselves to be individualists and thus, as it were, the center point of the world, which in end effect derives from the traditions of Christian culture. The Westerner – whether consciously or unconsciously – is shaped by the Christian idea that he can influence fate through his actions. A higher instance (god) will then assign him a place in heaven or hell depending on how his moral performance is evaluated.

The Westerner sees himself as a autonomous creation and the ego thus is of enormous importance. This egocentric view of the world contradicts the Zen-Shinto view diametrically. In the everyday life of Japanese and Westerners this means that "we," because we assume ourselves to be responsible, give more free reign to our emotions than the Japanese would ever do being obligated to the group and the general harmony of the universe. Therefore, the behavior of the Westerner is often considered to be obtrusive and highly emotionally driven and conversely that of the Japanese as closed and cold. Where this is one of the most fundamental misunderstandings because the Japanese approach everyday life with much greater feeling than they approach the "world order," act more strongly on "gut" feelings than their Western counterparts who think in abstract and logical terms.

This differing "emotional basis" also deeply defines the relationship to nature. The Westerner is usually unable to become immersed in nature with the same devotion as a Japanese person and to entrust himself to its rhythms. Nature, the sequence of the seasons have a determining influence upon people and in Japan one not only respects the seasons one also pays homage to them in everyday life and in art, literature and philosophy. Certain acts, foods and artworks are bound solely by the seasons and a Japanese person would never hit upon the idea of disrupting this canon. A once likewise living tradition that has long been lost in the West.

On the other hand, the West often complains about the destruction of the natural world by Japan. The Japanese can still feel a unity with nature even if it necessarily has to change owing to new conditions. A strength that the West does not possess where one suffers from the fact that nature does not act in the way that humans want, compounded by the fact that in the West people do not see themselves as part of a whole but as "creation's crowning glory."

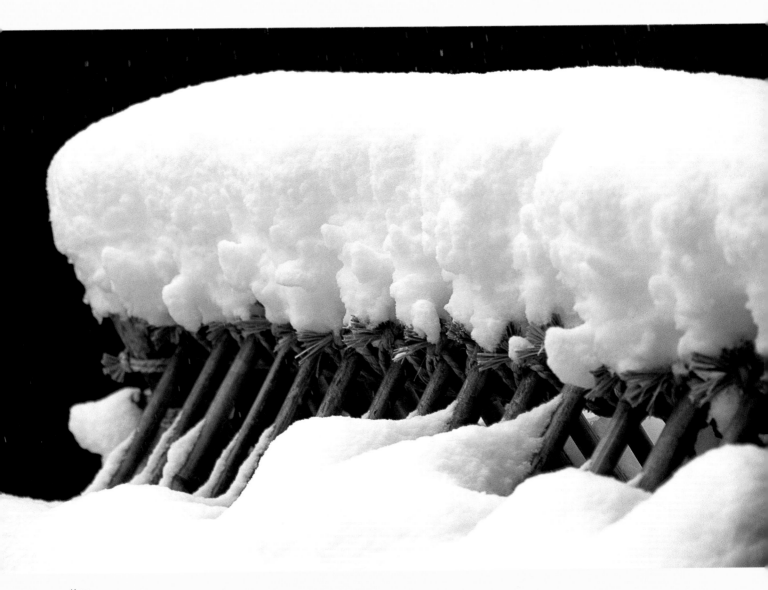

Above
Ryugon
The time-honored pine trees, bushes and carefully trimmed shrubs are protected from
the weight of the snow by a lovingly tied "bamboo installation."

龍言

Ryugon, Muikamachi

The Japanese year has turned full circle – the symbiosis of art and nature has perfected itself in the changing plant life. The harsh, cold winter experienced over much of Japan is bare of plants, and yet not lacking in "the art of nature." The scenery is buried under a thick blanket of snow lending a new shape to the thatched roofs, the *torii*, the strange pine trees and the dry garden. A Japanese Zen monk once defined absolute beauty as "pure white snow in a silver dish." So the snow, with its colorlessness, its crystalline consistency and its ephemeral quality, is another aesthetic ideal and a refinement of natural creation in the same way as are cherry blossom or rays of sunshine, the iris or rain, autumn leaves or mist.

The shadows inherent in Japanese art and architecture as a creative medium take on a unique, refined, picturesque quality in the cool transparent light of the low sun: the "shapes" cast by the shadows are not gray and diffuse, but a pale, icy blue.

The preservation of buildings and ways of life – The *chūmon-zukuri* style

The spacious Ryugon estate consists of a collection of traditional houses that were taken down in Northern Japan and carefully reconstructed in their new home in the grounds of the ryokan of today. The main building, *kura-zashiki*, with its entrance and reception area, as well as the imposing gatehouse from the Edo Period (1614–1868), come from Shiozawa; the dayrooms, *shin-zashiki*, come from Takayanagi; the outbuildings from Muikamachi.

The Ryugon was brought into being as a "inn" in 1964, the year of the Tokyo Olympic Games, so strictly speaking it cannot be called a historic ryokan. Nonetheless, all of the seven traditional houses making up the ryokan originated during the Bunka-Bunsai Period (1804–1829), and are built in a specific style characteristic of the residential houses of the high-ranking liegemen of Uesugi Kenshin, a famous16th century feudal lord from Echigo (traditional name of Niigata). These houses were conscientiously restored and erected again in their original form on the Ryugon site. They are without exception designed

Opposite
Ryugon
This group of old buildings was taken down, restored and erected again as the ryokan. The houses came from various locations in Niigata and were put together again on the Ryugon site to make a lively traditional place. The architecture of all the buildings is in the *chūmon-zukuri* style.

in the *chūmon-zukuri* style, which constitutes a characteristic *minka* architectural style of Northern Japan. *chūmon-zukuri* architecture was named after the *chūmon* projecting part of the building, which was commonly added to the original living area, *shuya*, in homes in the Akita, Yamagata and Fukushima provinces. The *chūmon* had developed out of the *chūmon-ro*, the projecting corridor of the *shoin* style. This projection usually contains an entrance area on the front façade, a *dōma* ground floor area, a storeroom and often a toilet, thus guaranteeing sheltered access to these rooms in the cold and snowy winter months. All the "original houses" have interconnecting passages.

"National heritage" rather than modern comfort

In 1964, when the Ryugon came into existence, Japan was just experiencing a phenomenal economic boom. Unfortunately the growing affluence of the population went hand in hand with the attitude that old things are of no value and should be replaced by new ones. Consequently one old village after another was demolished and replaced by faceless housing developments. Everything, not just the buildings, but also the interiors and the traditional utensils were "modernized," frequently without any taste or instinct. Mr. Utsugi, the founder of the ryokan, was deeply hurt by this development and decided to preserve the old buildings and their atmosphere, which he treasured and loved exceedingly. Not wanting to see the old *minka* kept as a purely nostalgic artefact, and realizing what is more that its restoration and maintenance would involve considerable costs, he opened a ryokan.

To his sorrow, the appeal he had made previously to the population of Niigata to preserve their houses as precious Japanese cultural assets had been unsuccessful, for the occupants were happy to be able to exchange their labor-intensive dwellings for comfortable modern buildings. In winter they had suffered from the cold in their poorly heated *minka* and had fought against the snow on their thatched roofs, which then regularly had to be repaired in spring. Mr. Utsugi was even blamed for standing in the way of progress, as the buildings identified as national heritages were not many in number and so little money was to be expected from the state. Furthermore, the owners incurred considerable costs, in particular because the accommodations were not habitable during the repair work. So, logically, Mr. Utsugi decided to take action himself.

In centuries past it was a quite common practice to "transplant" old buildings; however, in the 1960s it was more

Opposite
Ryugon
Wood, bamboo, straw and rice paper are the building materials of the "northern" *minka*. In the foreground of the room is the *kokatsu*, behind it the Japanese dressing table *kyodai* with its covered mirror.

Above, 3 illustrations
Ryugon
Some-tsuke, blue underglazed porcelain and lacquer work.
The founder and owner of the Ryugon did not just restore traditional houses, he also preserved the traditional Japanese way of life by collecting crafted objects that had been handed down through the generations at a time when to large sections of the population a "Tupperware" item seemed much more practical and also more desirable than these conventional porcelain, ceramic and lacquered receptacles.

Next double page
Ryugon
Guest room in the ryokan with view of the frozen winter scenery across the veranda.
The strong construction of wooden beams gives the room a clear outline. In this authentic ambience of former times there is one concession to the "modern era" in the shape of a television set.

than unusual to collect old houses, restore them and convert them into an inn. The challenge the owner had set himself turned into a Herculean task, for suitable craftsmen had to found, who would preserve the original beauty of the individual buildings and protect them from wrong intervention. The experiment succeeded, the incomparable quality and the spirit of traditional Japanese craftsmanship are visible and alive everywhere in the Ryugon.

All of the ryokan buildings have one story, for Mr. Utsugi heeded the words of Sekiryus, a priest in the historic temple of Unto (founded around 1200): "It is not good to be sitting on top of another's head."

The Ryugon was subsequently expanded by the addition of neighboring paddy fields and rice storehouses, but never with buildings of more than one story. So even the entrance hall with its two-story high ceiling construction has no intermediate floor, but is a high, wide room with heavy, solid wooden structures in dim light, which capture the guest and take him back to the atmosphere of former times as soon as he arrives. On entering the *yucho-no-ma*, the room next to the entrance area, the guest finds the *iori*, the central place for communication in each and every traditional Japanese house. Next to the *iori* room are the two oldest rooms in the ryokan,

keisetsu-no-ma and *koshoin-no-ma*. They are exquisitely furnished with regard to the combination of colors, the materials used, the delicate woodcarvings of the *ramma* and the artistic design of the *shōji* doors.

In the *mushin-no-ma* in the annex the guest welcomed by the amazing massive zelkova wood pillars, which date from an age when wood was respected and held in high regard, and time and careful craftsmanship were employed to work and shape it as befits its stature.

In another, very intimate *tatami* room, *kogetsu-no-ma*, there is a "private" *irori*. Each room has its own individual character and fits in harmoniously with the overall picture of the building. The rooms are simple, yet never "flat," as the power and strength of old buildings is dynamically expressed in the structure.

Above
Ryugon
The Ryugon has both an indoor and an open-air *onsen*, the two being interconnected. In the cold winter months when the temperature outside is low it is particularly pleasing to enjoy the hot spring, to float in the steam, which lends all shapes a soft outline.

Opposite
Ryugon
"Winter sculpture" on the pond in the garden of the ryokan. The harsh, cold winter experienced in much of Japan is bare of plants, yet not lacking in "the art of nature." The scenery is buried under a thick blanket of snow lending a new shape to the thatched roofs, the *torii*, the strange pine trees and the dry garden.

Japanese carpenters and the art of woodworking

No other nation has adopted traditional values and skills into modern life to such an extent as Japan. This is also particularly true of the woodworking methods that have been handed down through the ages.

An extremely complicated jointing system for wood, *tsugi*, forms the basis of Japanese woodwork and architectural construction. In fundamental contrast to European jointing systems for wood, Japanese dovetails in architecture as well as in interior fittings and furniture making are pliant rather than rigid. They stay in place without nails or adhesives, acting almost as "shock absorbers," thus guaranteeing both strength and durability. The endless variations of possible joints depend on the wood itself and on its function. Japanese joint types were developed out of practical and aesthetic experience gained over many centuries.

Wooden joints are of such great importance for the art of the joiner that a Japanese term for furniture *sashimono* means: placing things together. The refined marquetry of Japanese cabinet makers closely mirrors Zen philosophy and has surpassed the art of the French in this field. The pattern of the inlay work is not achieved through the use of different woods, differing color values and complex shapes as is common in Europe, but by means of a combination of different shades from just one "material source." One type of wood alone is examined carefully in order to discover its "natural design," which it is then a matter of using and enhancing artistically. A certain grain or intensification of color, already carrying within itself an "organic portrayal," is selected and then modelled to create a new aesthetic expression. A creative act that only makes a minimal intervention in the "work of art by nature" and treats it with the greatest respect. This restrained, understated type of decoration met with the best of responses from Western artists, and still does.

Kumi-te and *tsugi-te* – The "art of making joints"

The traditional Japanese method of architectural construction is a system of posts and beams with dovetail joints. Two types of basic joints are used: *kumi-te*, connecting joints, and extending joints, *tsugi-te*. As both furniture making and architecture are based on the use of wooden joints, the two are very similar.

Japanese woodwork is put together with the greatest of care, but regardless of whether it is a piece of furniture or a house that is being constructed, the end product is always of the highest quality, strength and durability.

After the timber has been cut to the appropriate length, the craftsman marks all the pieces in the places where they must be cut to shape for the joints with a carved strip of bamboo dipped in black or red ink. The joint is then variously chiselled and sawn to shape and the surface smoothed with a hand plane. This last process also gives the wood a warm glow.

After all the individual parts have been carefully prepared they are lined up in the workshop, the joints are fitted together, the surfaces coated and wrapped in paper so that the surface is not damaged during transport or assembly. The craftsmen who assemble the parts wear white socks and no shoes so that the wood stays clean. This might seem excessive to a Westerner, but it is absolutely essential because in the traditional Japanese house the structural woodwork is not concealed and there is no ceiling to prevent anyone looking up into the roof truss. The building time is kept very short so that the joint parts can be fitted together without the accuracy of fit being affected by any work carried out on the timber.

One type of wood frequently used for fittings is *hinoki*, Japanese cypress, a soft wood which does not splinter, does not warp even in a damp climate and is totally resistant to pests. As this wood is very light the Japanese also like to use it for items of furniture. Hiba wood has similar qualities to that of *hinoki*. Another popular local wood is *suginoki*, Japanese cryptomeria.

Keyaki, or zelkova is a frequently used hardwood. Other hardwoods of the elm family are paulownia, mulberry, chestnut and woods imported from South East Asia such as *karaki*. Deciduous wood lends itself especially well to precise working due to its short fibrous structure. Pine is of course extremely robust, but has the tendency to warp when exposed to sunshine. All joints in oak and maple are inlaid with other materials. Bamboo, *take*, is used for rafters, slats, latticework and fences. In comparison with this wealth of types of timber the selection used in European house construction looks very modest.

The different woodworking tools in Japan, the *daikudogu*, are just as numerous as the types of timber used.

Opposite
Ryugon
The entrance and reception hall with its two-story high ceiling construction has no intermediate floor, but is a high, wide room with heavy, solid wooden structures in dim light. The guest is captured by the atmosphere of former times as soon as he arrives. In the foreground is a table made from a tree trunk with inset fireplace and "tone in tone" wood inlay work. Behind it is the *irori*. Left a traditional *shoin* room with graduated shelving, *chigaidana*, *fusuma* with calligraphy and *shō* picture scrolls.

Above
Ryugon
Detail of the ceiling construction, wooden beams and bamboo. The dovetail joint *hozo-tsugi*, worked to fit exactly, makes the use of nails or glue superfluous and can bear the greatest of tensions and loads.

The "basic tools" tried and tested over many generations are *nomi* (chisels), *kanna* (hand planes), *toishi* (polishing stones), *genno* (hammers), and *nokogiri* (saws). In Japan the production of woodworking tools is an art in itself. Each tool serves as an extension of the hand's actions and must be designed to be the best for the task it has to perform. The Japanese carpenters' precise mastery of their materials leads to an artistic virtuosity that has its beginnings in the tools. It is the artistic handling of exclusively produced tools that really makes the unsurpassed quality of Japanese woodworking possible.

Various types of joint have become established in different countries. In Japan it is mostly highly sophisticated longitudinal joints that are found, as the Japanese have tried to avoid transverse or diagonal joints, which do not provide sufficient pliability in earthquakes. However, to provide the buildings with the necessary stability, long structural beams must be used. The joints with the posts have to be resistant to both tensile strength and pressure.

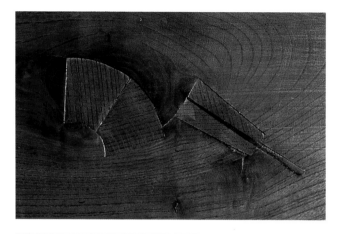

Illustrations above
Ryugon
Marquetry, wood inlay work, *Sensu* design (fan pattern) in a supporting beam in the entrance/reception hall and a fish motif in the "tree trunk table" of the reception hall.
The Japanese cabinet maker selects a piece of wood after a long search for one that already contains a natural "design" in its grain and coloring and then gives it a freshly created inherent artistic coherence.

Illustrations opposite
Ryugon
Details of the *ramma*, decorative crossbeams, from the oldest rooms in the ryokan, *keisetsu-no-ma* and *koshoin-no-ma*.
There appear to be no limits set to the artistic creation of the *ramma*. The sculptural open-work, showing a host of subjects in lively relief carvings contrasts with the straight lines of the room layout in Japanese houses.

a wealth of different joints that can be used in masterly designs, so that the shapes of the joints per se look like modern wood sculptures.

Ramma – "Architectural *objets d'art*"

Open-work wooden beams, *ramma*, are an essential feature of rooms in Japanese residences. On the one hand *ramma* serve the practical purposes of ventilation and a source of daylight between the various sections of the room, and on the other hand they are decorative features of the internal space. The *ramma* are situated horizontally between the ceiling and the upper guide-rail *kamoi* of the *shōji* or the *fusuma*, the sliding doors. They are mostly embellished with latticework or with open-work carvings of animals, birds, flowers and clouds, as well as religious and mythological motifs.

Sculptural design in wood or metal has in every respect been an essential part of Japanese architecture since early times, whether in houses, shrines or temples. In contrast to Western architecture, where religious buildings differ considerably from houses, private residences and temples in Japan are alike.

During the Nara Period (645–794) architectural ornaments and accessories were kept extremely simple - cloud shapes, latticework patterns and linear engravings on beams and consoles. From the Muromachi Period (1333–1573) sculptural work was common as part of the design of the building, and this new taste culminated in the Momoyama style (1573–1614) with sculptural design in glowing colors, colored paintings on sliding walls and doors and gold-plated metal fittings. As there is hardly any furniture in a Japanese house, architectural decoration was the only means of demonstrating prosperity and grand interiors. So the *ramma* developed into attractive, three-dimensional *objets d'art*.

Sensible "multi-purpose aesthetics"

The counterpart of the striking, yet practical and functional *ramma* is found in the decorative *shōji* windows, which on the one hand serve to admit light into the room and have a protective function, but are at the same time an essential decorative feature of the room. Japanese rooms naturally have no "hanging" pictures, as the flexible arrangement for dividing up the room with sliding walls does not permit this. The only means of decoration are the "ornamental alcoves"

The Japanese carpenter works with approximately 120 shapes of wooden joints, and his Western colleague with about 10. In the West there is a rule for wood construction work, in contrast to in Japan, that as far as possible only one or two different types of wood should be used in any one work piece or construction piece, so that differing amounts of distortion due to shrinkage do not lead to stresses within the construction. The Japanese artist or carpenter uses many different woods in his structure, the choice being dependent on which part of the building is involved, the desired appearance and intended decorative effect. Working in this way it is absolutely necessary to have

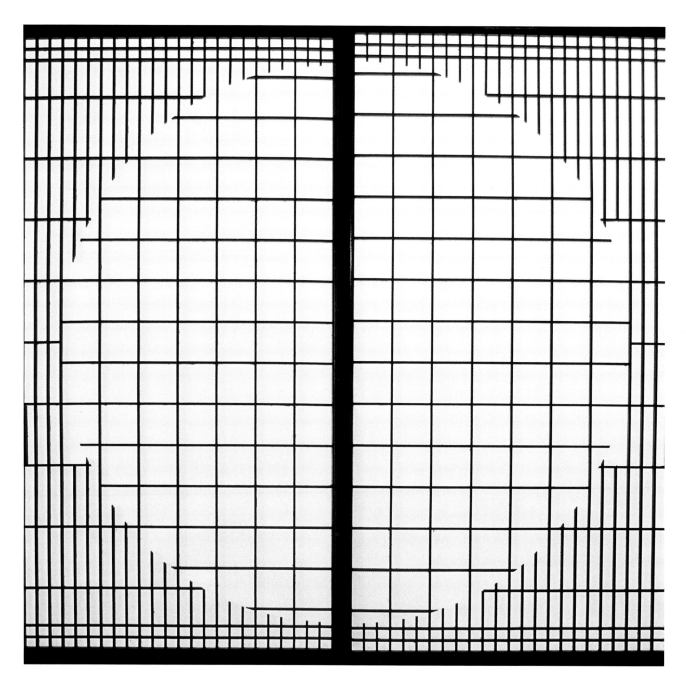

Above
Ryugon
Decorative *shōji* window in a guest room of the ryokan.
Irregular patterns are created using fragile wooden sticks with a rice paper covering, so one can look through the window, but intimacy is also ensured. The result is decorative masterpieces such as this.

Opposite, 4 illustrations
Ryugon
The *futon* is the bed in the traditional Japanese room. After the evening banquet the table and cushions are removed and the *futon* is spread out on the *tatami*. In the last picture the *andon*, or Japanese lamp, and some water to quench the guest's nighttime thirst are placed ready. Here one can see why the *shōji* has open sections at floor level.

Too idle to be ambitious,
I let the world take care of itself.
With enough rice in my bag for ten days,
and a bundle of sticks by the fireplace.
Why prattle about disappointment and enlightenment?
Listening to the night rain pattering on my roof,
I sit contentedly, my legs stretched out before me.

Ryokan, Zen master   *[freely translated by J.B.]*

or *tokonoma*, and the artistic embellishment of individual parts of the architecture and of the room; the resulting creation is harmonious and restrained in its avoidance of excess and distraction. Furthermore, rooms designated for one particular use as in the West, and therefore furnished and decorated only for specific purposes such as eating, living and sleeping, would be totally unsuitable. In the Japanese house people live, eat, work and sleep in just one room, and the same is true of the ryokan.

After the epicurean evening meal, the guest goes for a stroll in the garden or a walk in the neighborhood of the ryokan wearing a kimono-like *yūkata*, with a *tanzen*, a quilted coat-like jacket, over it if the weather is cool, and *geta*. If too large a quantity of sake has been enjoyed for this, then the guest will at least step out onto the *engawa*, veranda of the room.

In any case, the guest must leave the room. Here, where just a short while ago he was sitting on a *zabuton* indulging his palate, the *futon*, his bed for the night, is now being prepared. The dining table disappears into the neighboring wall cupboard or into a small side-room, and the *futon* is brought out of the *oshiire*, a narrow wall-cupboard, to replace it.

The *futon*

The belief is that the *futon* developed from some sort of nightwear, and the concept is also closely connected to the development of materials made of cotton. The first known use of the word *futon* in the modern sense is from the year 1592, and even then it is not clear whether bedding or nightwear is referred to. Prior to that, in the Kamakura Period (1185–1333) and the Muromachi Period (1338–1573) *futon* always clearly referred to the *zabuto*, or cushion for sitting on. The increasing use of cotton was accompanied by the increasing use of the word *yagi*, nightwear, and *futon*, quilt. Even in the Tokugawa Period (1600–1868) the *futon* cover was cut like a *kosode* (forerunner of the kimono) with a collar and sleeves. The sleeper would wrap himself in the *kosode* with his hands free, which was particularly important for survival in the case of the samurai. Then in the 19th century the Japanese bedding of today came about, this being what those in the West also understand by the term *futon*. The growth in cotton textiles was considerable, as hitherto the bedding of simple folk had consisted of raffia, bark, or straw, and the form of the modern *futon* requires the use of cotton.

In the ryokan the *futon* is most often laid out for the guests by a male servant, as a considerable amount of physical effort

Opposite
Ryugon
A guest room.
Winter impressions of light and color in
dark wood, opaque white *shōji* and pale
green *tatami*.

Right
Ryugon
A winter day filled with ancient
Japanese poetry draws to its close, a
seido-toro, or Japanese bronze lantern,
casts its soft light into the night-blue
winter scenery.

is required to move the futons. Especially in a larger ryokan, the tasks of setting up and putting away tables and beds are carried out by men.

The Japanese mattress, *shikibuton*, is laid directly on the pliable, warm, and slightly perfumed *tatami*, which makes an ideal base. A sheet is placed on this mattress just as it would be in the West. The rest of the procedure depends on the room temperature. If the room has no heating and the outside temperature is frosty, then one or two additional, thinner mattresses are placed on the bottom mattress. The number of quilt-like top blankets, *kakebuton,* also depends on how cold it is. Then comes a *makura*, or pillow, not a neck support as in the old days in Japan, when elaborate hairstyles had to be preserved at the expense of comfort. The pillow is most often filled with rice husks, in true Japanese style, heavenly for the neck; in fact, sleeping on a *futon* is altogether divine experience.

The guests are spoiled by their attentive hosts until bedtime, which is normally quite early. On the matter of how the guest expresses his thanks, here is a comment from *We Japanese*.

Chadai – Tea money

"With few exceptions, in addition to the rates quoted at Japanese inns, the custom of giving a sum of money, known as *chadai* ('tea money'), upon the guest's departure, still prevails. [...] To foreign visitors tea money appears to be a gift to the innkeeper for his good will, general care of the guest, and possibly for sundry cups of tea of welcome upon arrival. In view of the fair rate made for lodging and meals, Japanese regard it as part of the regular charge, based largely upon the location, size and furnishings of the room occupied, bedding, food supplied, grade of inn, etc. [...].

This custom, it is said, originated long ago when inns were not so numerous as they are today. In those olden days, when devotees made their pilgrimages, the only accommodation available was in the temples visited — which is still the case today in many places. The temple authorities made no charge for lodging or meals, but it became the custom for guests to offer a sum of money, carefully wrapped up, a sum in accordance with the guest's circumstances, upon their departure. This custom spread to the inns.

[...] Upon the guest's departure it is customary for the innkeeper to present some small gift: a towel, a cup, or some article made or produced in the vicinity. [...]

Shugi-bukuro: Japanese etiquette requires that in presenting a tip, the money shall be wrapped in white paper or placed in a *shugi-bukuro*, a special envelope made for that purpose. In no case should the money be handed uncovered, although in these days modern people do not always conform to this old custom.

The practice probably originated through *bushido*, the moving spirit of the country. In days gone by, money was rather despised, especially by the samurai, and its possession was looked down upon, and, consequently, the crude presentation of naked money offended the Japanese sense of politeness and consideration."[73]

Left page

Wano-sato

Detail of the *mizuya-dansu*, the kitchen chest in the drawing room and the *irori* room of the ryokan.

In the foreground a flower arrangement in the *atebana* style (standing flowers). Toward the mid-15th century the art of arranging plants and flowers literally "blossomed." The large elegant rooms of the castles and fortresses in the *shoin-zukuri* style of the Muromachi period (1392–1573) were made less severe and simultaneously refined aesthetically by the dynamic and natural arrangements.

Wano-sato, Hida

The Wano-sato ryokan is situated in a spacious natural garden measuring 10,000 *tsubo* in cloister-like seclusion against the backdrop of the Hida Mountains. From the main house and the thatched cottages, the *hanare*, through the *shōji* frame one has exquisite views of the changing "landscape painting" with game birds and a torrential mountain stream. Nature is simply omnipresent. The Hida region with the hot springs at Gero, the historic city of Takayama and the Shin Hodake mountain resort is considered one of Japan's best areas for admiring and enjoying the four seasons. Wano-sato, constructed in an authentic Japanese style, refines the seasons in a nostalgic way in the furnishings, the delicate seasonal meals, the tableware, in every aspect of the dwelling and in the tremendous hospitality. Like in past ages, one relaxes in the evening with the hosts around the *irori*, where the sake proffered by the house is warmed in hollow bamboo canes in the embers. In Wano-sato the pulse drops and the spirit is refreshed. Nothing disturbs the perfection, the subliminal simplicity of Japanese aesthetics and the Japanese way of life.

Japanese aesthetics

For many years "Japanese aesthetics" has been a kind of cult concept in the West, a metaphor for a direction in taste that is often a counterpoint to the West. Contrary because the Japanese aesthetic sensibility operates in virtual contradistinction to the Western ideal of art. In the Western interpretation, "style" on the one hand is true to the term "stylistic," which means assigned to a defined school of style, and on the other hand the term style is always associated with a specific type of preciousness and elaborated form. Stylistic features derive from the association with a certain epoch of art and cultural history or with an explicit category of objects or works. These are criteria that do not have a role in the Japanese understanding of style. A further, now deeply rooted misunderstanding is the association of "Japanese" with linearity, purism and frugality. Japanese art is always "unostentatious," simple, but only in terms of the Western understanding, for what we conceive to be simple may be received as noble and lavish by the Japanese sensibility.

Moreover the term "linearity" would have to be replaced by "clarity." Although Japanese architecture and Japanese art forms are always clearly defined and functional, irregularity and haphazardness are evident features of Japanese art. "I would suggest that the character of Japanese aesthetics can be summed up in two points: economy in the use of space, and asymmetry. An essential aspect of Japanese aesthetics is asymmetry. [...] Symmetry is static in character, whereas asymmetry suggests dynamic and mobility. The aesthetic of dynamics in Japan has been strongly influenced by Zen Buddhism. The central idea of Buddhism is "emptiness," insubstantiality. In this philosophy things have no substance, everything is in flux. Each thing is only a combination of elements which will dissolve in course to form something new." [74]

The creative consequence of the Zen way of thinking are the ultimate reality of emptiness and an asymmetry suggesting mobility in the organisation of space in rooms, gardens, flower and food arrangements. In fact even numbers are treated with suspicion and avoided, above all four, which signifies death. The attempt to order things, says the great French poet and philosopher Paul Valéry (1871–1945), is a colossal, unnatural project. This fundamental realisation proposed by an after all European thinker is easily recognizable in the Japanese organisation and structuring of space: in urban planning, landscaping, architecture and in various art forms such as painting, calligraphy and ceramics. The Japanese artist is in direct contact with the things of the cosmos. The world is nothing more than a world of illusions. If the subject does not have a central, independent point of reference, aesthetic sensibility is more intuitive and the product of the efforts is not planned and thought-out.

A striking divergence to the Western art sensibility lies in the use and evaluation of the material. Especially costly Western art products are usually also characterised by their material value; for objects these materials may be, for example, silver, gold, fine woods, porcelain and precious stones and in the fine arts oil paints or bronze, in architecture expensive stone such as marble or ornamental plasterwork. In Shinto-influenced Japanese art the value of the materials is measured by their naturalness, the unspoiled evidence provided by the material. Rough stoneware, the scarred grain of the wood, obdurate straw and bamboo, dull lacquer is of high quality. Whereas the West restores its traditional *objects d'art* at great expense, the Japanese admire "beauty born by use." In fact these visible signs of use, which create their own unmistakable pattern and their own "style," are highly valued. On the other hand, age does not play a role. The question most usually asked in conjunction with the evaluation of an art object – "Which period is it?", assigning it to an epoch – is irrelevant in Japan. Because Japanese art has a tradition now of almost 2000 years, in a final evaluation the quality, the sublimation of a specific form, and a certain aesthetic is decisive.

A chain of misinterpretations arises. We have as it were picked out from Japanese art and culture that which can be integrated into our appreciation of art. The Japanese ideal of "beauty," which is so difficult for us to define, is most purely formulated in the *wabi-sabi* force of an object or of a state. *Wabi* means more or less faded, abstinent, impermanent; and *sabi* a spiritual path, an intellectual attitude and perspective – however all attempts at translation are ultimately doomed to fail.

A concrete example from the autumnal Wanosato ryokan helps to illuminate somewhat the Japanese ideal of beauty and the term "Japanese aesthetics."

Early in the morning on the way to the *onsen*, walking alongside the racing mountain stream, one sees on the winding path an employee of the ryokan in the traditional indigo blue garments of the rural population. Carrying a simply woven, flat basket he walks slowly along the forest path leading to the main house, a natural path which is not intended to be an approach road and which is reserved solely for pedestrians. Situated in thick deciduous woods, the path is covered by gloriously colored autumn leaves. While one observes the harmonious picture of the landscape with delight, one becomes aware of what the man is doing with the basket – and one can hardly believe one's eyes. From the basket he scatters, quite systematically, colorful leaves in red,

Opposite
Wano-sato
View of the interior rooms of a guest cottage; a prime example of clear lines and the asymmetry in the partition of space in Japanese rooms that suggests mobility. In the *irori* room a *mizuya-dansu*, in the room with "teahouse entrance" (see tea ceremony inset) a *kotatsu* and in the rear room a *ryobiraki-isho-dansu*, a two-door wardrobe.

yellow, brown and polychrome patterns that had previously been carefully selected from the adjacent woods onto the path already strewn with the autumn foliage. Nature exalted by nature, where the human hand lends it transcending form and refined perfection – ultimate sophistication – Japanese aesthetics.

The Japanese arts such as the tea ceremony, flower arranging, archery, and poetry, which cannot be compared to the "free arts" of the West, have the same objective as the seated meditation of Zen Buddhism. They require of the body a specific composure. This training is simultaneously training for the mind as the mind must follow the composure learned by the body. The aim is the unity of body and mind, of subject and object. This also leads to full devotion to the seasons, the cherry blossom, the change in color of the leaves, the element of transitoriness present in the festivals, which always celebrate impermanence.

Ike-bana – The ordered art of flower arranging

Once the famous Hideyoshi (1536–1598), ruler of all Japan, heard that Rikyū (1520–1591), his tea master, had a mass of beautiful bindweed flowers in his garden. He wanted to visit him and admire them, but when he came into the garden Hideyoshi saw none of the celebrated blooms. Rikyū,

however, received him into the teahouse, which was decorated with a single, glorious bindweed flower in the picture alcove. Just before Hideyoshi's arrival he had had all the flowers in the garden picked. Hideyoshi, who loved magnificence and opulence, was deeply impressed by Rikyūs courageous act.

This tradition explains the basic aesthetic principle of *ike-bana* extremely poignantly; abbreviated and in simple terms: less is more.

The expression *ike-bana*, which is meanwhile also common in the West, outlines the Japanese art of arranging flowers. The term comprises two parts: the first, *ike,* means to "breath and live;" the second, *bana*, "flowers." Whereas a painting, for example, represents a creative process of oil painting on canvas, *ike-bana* is a three dimensional artistic form of expression which arranges "plant materials" in a vase. Basically, the perfection of a flower, a plant or a tree in its natural environment is very difficult to better. If one therefore seizes the branch or flower by "snatching" it from nature to imitate the original beauty in a vase in a foreign milieu this effort must fail. The original vegetative beauty is not reproducible. The aim therefore is to select, with reverent aesthetic attentiveness, the most beautiful aspects of the plant, to create with it a new order, and to provide it with an artistic value which exceeds that of nature. *Ike-bana* thus commences with the careful observation of natural

Left
Wano-sato
Bowl with lid for preparing food. The exterior is unglazed clay with a relief leaf application, the black interior surface is glazed: beauty in everyday utensils.

Opposite, top right
Wano-sato
Suzuri-bako, a box for writing accessories, lacquer on wood and gold *maki-e*, relief decoration with gold grains on a black lacquer.
The *suzuri-bako* contains the ink stone, the *suzuri*, the ink stick, *sumi*, a water container, *mizuire*, and the ink brush, the *fude*. The *ryoshi-bako* is a larger box which also contains a paper drawer. Frequently, the writing box is placed on a small writing desk, *bundai*, which is also adorned with a lacquer decoration.

Opposite, left
Wano-sato
Panel of a standing partitioner (detail), water color on paper in the style of the bamboo paintings by the monk Obaku Taihō (1691–1774).

elements for only with the help of nature can beauty be newly created by human hand. In contrast to Western flower arrangements, which strive more for luxuriant wealth, *ike-bana* searches for the harmonious structure of rhythm, line and color. Moreover, aside leaves, branches and flowers, the art of plant composition also includes the vessel and follows three prime linear aspects which symbolise the sky, the earth and human beings.

The origins of *kado*, today *ike-bana*, begin with the ritual flower offerings in Buddhist temples and date from the 6th century. Thus *ike-bana*, like all Japanese arts, has its origins in Japanese religion.

The maxims of *ike-bana*, which still have currency today, have their origins, like any number of Japanese arts, in the Momoyama period (1573–1614), during which Ikebono Senko I (early 16th century) developed and made popular the *rikka* form. A family of priests with the name Ikebono, which means "living close to a pond," act as "trustees" of the *kado* style and personify at the same time the central and guiding spirit of the *ike-bana* world. The *rikka* art, which evolved from the *tatebana* compositions (standing flowers) of the Muromachi period (1392–1573), is the most sophisticated style under the different kinds of Japanese flower arrangements and its expression has little to do with the always somewhat artificial arrangements known in the West. The *rikka* form projects the Sumeru Mountain, a mythical mountain from Buddhist cosmology and a metaphor for the universe. Thus this style is rich with symbolism, for example, pine branches signify rocks or stones and white chrysanthemums flowing water. *Rikka* art reached its peak in the 17th century; however, over time it was adapted to the rather limited space of the *tokonoma*. Nonetheless the

traditional guiding principle still holds of maintaining the beauty of nature and to add refinement through our own wit. *Ike-bana* should moreover reflect the harmony between the plants and the other forces of nature: branches bent by the winter wind or leaves gnawed at by insects. In unison with the plant world humans are a vital component of nature and the arrangement of *ike-bana* discloses this conviction.

Besides *rikka*, the basic forms of *ike-bana* are: *shoka* or *seika*, live flowers in vases, *nageire*, to throw flowers in a bowl and *moribana*, piled-up flowers in plate-like containers.

"While there are different methods of arranging flowers according to various schools, the fundamental principles underlying the first steps are the same in that every arrangement must be made to symbolize 'Heaven,' 'Man,' and 'Earth.' If a single plant or tree branch is used, the main part that shoots upward represents 'Heaven,' a twig on the right, bent sideways, denotes 'Man,' and the lowest twig or branch on the left, the end slightly bent so that it points upward, signifies 'Earth.' This is the *yo*, or male style. The female style is [*iu* which has a "man" branch bent to the left.] Three separate plants or branches placed closely together, not necessarily of the same kind, are often used to represent these three elements; for instance, a bamboo may be used to symbolize 'Heaven,' with a pine and plum-blossom branch as 'Man' and 'Earth' respectively, and sometimes grasses are used to signify 'Earth.'

Invariably, there is an odd number of stalks or branches in an *ike-bana* for the reason that odd numbers are considered lucky; even numbers are unlucky and are never used in flower arrangements. Flower arrangement is an important factor in the decoration of a Japanese room. The word

'flower,' in Japan, is used in a broad sense and covers not only the flowers of plants but also blossoms of fruit and other trees, and even flowerless trees and shrubs: the pine, willow, bamboo, maple, etc.

The receptacles for *ike-bana*, and the relative height of the vases and flowers are important essentials in the art. [...] The following quotation is a translation of a Japanese saying [...]: 'Heaven and earth are flowers – Gods as well as Buddha are flowers. The heart of man is also the soul of flowers.' " [75]

Japanese ceramics

When we speak of Japanese art, we are not talking about art as it is understood in the West. When evaluating art, different historically determined measures specific to particular societies, epochs, and cultural areas are used to assess the value, quality, and connotation of works of art. Art works require a cognitive and virtually sensorial appropriation of the world; this happens in that the world is perceived and interpreted, however, always in a meaningful sensory context for the respective society. The hubris of the West consists in the presumption of transporting the art sensibility evolved from local determinants, in an unreflected manner, and applying it to other cultural groups. What is considered a utensil with a decorative touch in the West, for example, has the status of art in Japan and is respected in the same way as our free arts of painting and sculpture. In accordance with Japanese sensibilities, ceramic works are the pinnacle of artistic achievement. For us they are considered sub-

Above and opposite
Wano-sato
Light and shadow in the reflection of the winter sun: a *hinoki* (cypress) floor, natural silhouettes in front of the *shōji* and a ceramic vase on a *tansu*. "The aesthetic of dynamics in Japan has been strongly influenced by Zen Buddhism.

The central idea of Buddhism is "emptiness," insubstantiality. In this philosophy things have no substance, everything is in flux. Each thing is only a combination of elements which will dissolve in course to form something new." (Aisaku Suzuki; freely translated by N.C.)

ordinate, a view that is as offensive in Japan as the statement that the Sistine Chapel is simply a pleasant fresco would be in the West.

"Then the aesthetic of the fine deformation and the material inaccuracy, also the stylistic defect – a poor country declared neediness an artistic virtue. And then there is always beauty at second glance, which is modest and unobtrusive, which does not overwhelm, which endures longer and blasphemes the gods less than striving for perfection. There are potters who scratch perfect vessels to lend them beauty and character. Their wares are among the most expensive. [...] That there is essence to water without flowing and an essence of the trees without wilting is a heretical opinion, found the Zen philosopher Dōgen in the 10th century. Who would contradict him?" [76]

Thanks to the tea ceremony, which used different ceramic vessels, Japanese ceramics developed into a separate art form. The *cha-dō*, The Way of Tea, prescribes summer and winter bowls. The summer tea bowl has an open form so that the tea can cool quickly, while the winter tea bowl with its closed form retains the warmth of the tea longer. The tea caddy, the water pot and the flower vase are usually also pottery. The tea master, the host of the tea ceremony, must therefore be a collector and connoisseur of tea ceramics in order to have available the correct choice of vessels for the occasion and the season. The perspective of the way of tea has also entered everyday meals: one eats in summer from a different service than that used in winter.

If one observes tea bowls, one sometimes sees that the form of the tea bowl has been intentionally distorted in the production process. The foot of the bowl is also an object of particular attention as it should reveal the motion involved in its creation. For this reason two photos are usually made to show a particularly fine tea bowl: one from the side and one of the foot. It can be seen from this that the Japanese value dynamism and spontaneity in the forming of a tea bowl. Thus an art connoisseur and ceramics collector, before

From top left to bottom right / opposite
Wano-sato
Freely modelled bowl with overglazed painting in the style of Kutani ceramics; curved bowl with lipped edge in the style of Echizen ceramics; plate-like bowl with an scratched leaf decoration in the *raku* style of ceramics; bowl with lid, black lacquer on wood with gold *maki-e* decoration; square narrow-necked vase with drawn bamboo and finger decoration, reddish body.

praising an object, would not solely consider the form, design and the texture of the surface, but would trace the "spirit" of the potter at a metaphysical level who with his hands has mastered the impressive transition from a "lump of clay" to an art object.

Even today, the Japanese potter learns his trade in the traditional way and manner through years of apprenticeship with an established master. This means constant repetition and imitation of the same movements and performing elementary chores such as collecting wood, raking the fire in the kiln and kneading the clay. The apprentice has to master this basic work to perfection before he has permission to work on his first vessel. Now, in turn, many years pass during which he has to create the same object time and time again until the individual movements become intuitive and are automatically optimised. Only

when the apprentice has attained this level of training is he considered worthy enough to put to the test his own forms and designs which arise from his intuition. Japan's best potters, whether in the past or in contemporary times, enjoy in their country the status of heroes and the same admiration as in the West a Michelangelo or a Van Gogh. In contrast to other traditional skilled trades which are disappearing with time, Japanese pottery and ceramics have such an inherent artistic relevance for the country that their futures are assured.

The Western observer who has Meissen porcelain or French Sèvres in mind as a measure will not find pleasure in the most highly valued ceramic vessels in Japan. For the Western artistic sensibility they appear asymmetrical and unstructured with a rough surface, are bland in color and overall very plain. But precisely such vessels "reveal" the Japanese appreciation of beauty, although not completely until they assume their designated use, provided with a *rikka* flower arrangement or filled with the frothed green tea for the tea ceremony. In the diffuse velvet light which falls through the *shōji* Japanese ceramics reveal their nuanced beauty and allow us to recognize and possibly comprehend such a different culture.

The production of ceramics in Japan has a very long tradition, perhaps the oldest in the world. Fragments of pottery excavated from a cave on the island of Kyushu, which forms the south-western tip of the country, have been dated to the *Jōmon* period (about 12,000 years ago). Basically, Japanese pottery can be divided into two main categories: extremely fine porcelain following the models of the wares imported from China and simple native stoneware vessels with a natural ash glazing. It is surprising that both wares are the perfect complement, above all if the objects are selected with care for serving food. Genuine Japanese ceramics, whether for everyday use or ceremonial purposes, in contrast to the porcelains, are characterised first and foremost by simple beauty which arises in the discreet combination of clay and natural glazings. And their colors always harmonize with the colors found in nature and the seasons. Imperfections of any kind are considered interesting special features. Damaged or shattered items, quite often using lacquer mixed with gold dust, are put back together and do not lose any of their value – a fundamental contradiction of the traditional aesthetic values we attach to art. The visible "injury" suffered by an outstanding art work adds to its worthiness and tends to increase its quality rather than reduce it.

Opposite and above
Wano-sato
Kaiseki meal at Wano-sato with rural, regional ingredients in various lavishly decorated vessels on placemats with winter motifs.

Tansu – Japanese furniture

In our time, *tansu* has become a collective term for Japanese furniture per se, but the word describes insufficiently the great range of chests, caskets and trunks, plain and lavish cabinets, cupboards and boxes that exists. Japan is probably home to the largest variety of cupboards, in keeping with the motto: a place for everything and everything in its place.

The first mention of furniture dates from the Nara period (710–784). This refers to *tana*, the first form of free standing cabinets with shelves, furthermore *hitsu*, boxes for stowing away garments; these were further divided into *kara-bitsu* (on legs) and *wa-bitsu* (without legs). These items are largely replicas of furniture from the Chinese Tang Dynasty (618–907). This is when, with few exceptions, the special form of Japanese furniture begins: including the *tansu*, it does not have legs, the furnishing objects stand flat on the floor, adapted to the lifestyle of the times, giving perfect access to the boxes when sitting on the *tatami* mats.

Tansu, storage and depository chests with a clear functionality and restrained design, are almost always made of

wood with metal fittings; only the most costly pieces are adorned with *maki* lacquer work. Often the pieces consist of stacked individual units, *kasane*, in order to transport them more easily during earthquakes. Frequently used types of wood include *kiri* (paulownia), zelkova, mulberry and plum tree wood, and cypress. The *tansu* are also designed according to the *wabi* principle. The wood remains undecorated and obtains its discreet pattern from careful implementation of the wood grain alone. The hand pulls are unadorned and utilitarian. The sole exception are occasionally flamboyant fittings.

There are two categories of *tansu*, one for "domestic use" and one for shops and workshops. The main types of "domestic furniture" are *isho-dansu*, a portable chest of drawers for storing kimonos and other garments, and a special variation of this chest called the *ryobiraki-isho-dansu*, a two-door clothing chest. "Business furniture" are the *cho-dansu* (also *choba-dansu*), literally the merchant's ledger chest; *cha-dansu*, a tea chest; and *kusuri-dansu*, the medicine chest. These are the most common categories, in addition to which numerous special types can also be found. The largest *tansu* are the *mizuya-dansu*, the kitchen chests, and the *kaidan-tansu*, the "step chest." The *katana-dansu*, sword chests, are samurai furniture. A further speciality are the *funa-dansu*, ship's or sea chests, which in turn are subdivided into *hangai*, clothing boxes with a front flap, and *kakesuzuri-bako*, writing cabinets with hinged tops. *Kuruma-dansu* are shop chests on wheels for valuable objects. Owing to the frequent "flowers from Edo" – a poetic formulation for the scourge of conflagrations – this type of chest was developed to facilitate rapid escape. Especially elaborate examples are the *yome-iri-dansu*, the bride's chest.

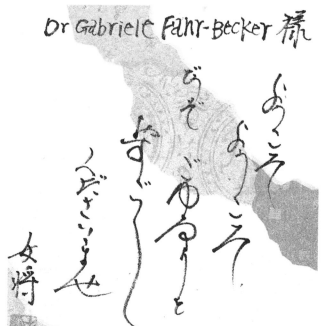

Dr Gabriele Fahr-Becker

Above
Wano-sato
Detail view of the drawing room and the *irori* room.
The *noren* decorated with an *enso* circle, hiding the corridor to the *onsen*. *Enso* are the simple brushed ink circles that Zen monks draw in a single brush movement. Strictly speaking the circle represents "emptiness" upon which the mind is to be concentrated during meditation.

Above
Wano-sato
Welcoming greeting for the guest. A personal ink calligraphy on handmade paper with a watermark.

Below
Wano-sato
The drawing room and the *irori* room of the ryokan. As in earlier times, one relaxes here during the evening with the hosts sitting around the fireplace where the house sake is warmed in the embers.

Annotations

1 Saul Bellow, Entry in the Tawaraya ryokan guest book, Kyoto, in: The Tarawaya of Kyoto, Brochure, Kyoto before 1996

2 We Japanese, Fujiya Hotel, Ltd. (ed.), Miyanoshita, Hakone 1949, p 525

3 Ibid, p 22

4 Ibid, p 542

5 Ibid, pp 135, 74, 148 f.

6 Ibid, p 72

7 Asoi Ryoi, Tales from the Fleeting World of Pleasure, Kyoto 1661, quoted from Franz Winzinger, Shunga, Exhibition Catalogue, Nurmberg 1975, p 11

8 Leonard Koren, Wabi-sabi for Artists, Architects and Designers, Japan's Philosophy of Modesty, Matthias Dietz (ed.), Tübingen 1995, p 82

9 We Japanese, 1949, p 89

10 Michael Dunn, Japan, Painting and the Art of Wood Carving, in: Gabriele Fahr-Becker (ed.), East Asian Art, 2 vols. Cologne 1998, Vol. 2, p 166 ff.

11 Bruno Taut, Houses and People of Japan, Manfried Speidel (ed.), Berlin 1997, p 143

12 We Japanese, 1949, p 197 f.

13 Quoted from: Henry Plummer, Architecture and Urbanism, June 1995, Extra Edition, Tokyo 1995, p 110

14 Yasushi Inoue, The Mountain Azaleas on the Summit of Mount Hira, Frankfurt am Main 1980, p 204 f.

15 We Japanese, 1949, p 20 f.

16 Jun'ichirô Tanizaki, In Praise of Shadows, New Haven, 1971, p 18

17 We Japanese, 1949, pp 188, 146

18 Ibid, p 142

19 Kaii Higashiyama, Beauty in Japanese Art, in: Constantin von Barloewen/Kai Werhahn-Mees (ed.), Japan and the West, 3 vols., Frankfurt am Main 1986, Vol. 3, p 79

20 We Japanese, 1949, pp 90, 393

21 Tanizaki, 1977, p 21 f.

22 Dunn, 1998, Vol. 2, pp 212, 166

23 Julius Lessing, Reports from the 1878 World Exhibition in Paris, without indication of place of publication, 1878, no indication of page

24 Quoted from: Atsushi Tanigawa, Art Nouveau as a Phenomenon of the Arabesque, in: Gabriele Fahr-Becker (ed.), Art Nouveau, Exhibition Catalogue, Tokyo 1990, p 37

25 Quoted from: Thomas Zacharias, Japanism or Clapping with One Hand, in: Gabriele Fahr-Becker (ed.), Art Nouveau, Exhibition Catalogue, Tokyo 1990, p 24

26 Joseph Hoffmann, Programm of Work of the Viennese Workshop, Vienna 1905, no indication of page

27 Zacharias, 1990, p 25

28 Higashiyama, 1986, Vol. 3, p 79

29 Lessing, 1878, no indication of page

30 We Japanese, 1949, p 46

31 Ibid, p 150

32 Ibid, p 91

33 Taut,1997, pp 70, 71

34 We Japanese, 1949, p 144

35 Ibid, p 316

36 Ibid, p 15

37 Ibid, p 125

38 Sabine Hesemann, China, Song and the aesthetics of Simplicity, in: Gabriele Fahr-Becker (ed.), East Asian Art, 2 vols. Cologne 1998, Vol. 1, p 168

39 http://www.freiepresse.de/home/yvsc/Dojo.htm, quoted from: Werner Lind (ed.), East Asian Martial Arts, The Encyclopaedia, Berlin 1996

40 We Japanese, 1949, p 245

41 Taut,1997, pp 224 f., 185

42 Source: http://www.rc.kyushu-u.ac.jp/~michel/serv/ek/

43 Mitsunobu Satô, Utagawa Hiroshige - 53 Stations of the Tôkaidô, in: Gabriele Fahr-Becker (ed.), Clapping with One Hand, Three Centuries of Japanese Color Woodcuts from the Riccar Art Museum Tokyo in the Neuen Pinakothek, Munich, Exhibition Catalogue Munich 1992, p 341

44 Source: Toshihiko and Toyo Izutsu/Franziska Ehmcke (ed.), The Theory of Beauty in Japan, Articles on Classical Japanese Aesthetics, Cologne 1998, pp 203 ff.

45 Dunn, 1998, Vol. 2, pp 307 f., 315

46 We Japanese, 1949, p 257

47 General German Conversational Encyclopaedia for Educated People of all Classes, 10 vols. Leipzig 1840, Vol. 9, pp 571 f.

48 Alessandro Baricco, Silk, Munich 1997, p 22

49 Taut,1997, p 202

50 We Japanese, 1949, p 7

51 Taut,1997, p 303

52 Source: Tsuentomo Yamamoto, Hagakure, The Book of the Samurai, trans. William S. Wilson, Tokyo 1979, pp 17 f., 20 f, 33 f., 66 f.

53 We Japanese, 1949, pp 465 f.

54 Cf. Nold Egenter, The Japanese House. Or Why Western Architects have difficulty Understanding It – Comparative Reflections from the Point of View of Cultural Anthropology on the Traditional Japanese House and the Western Concept of "universal human needs." In: http://home.worldcom.ch/~negenter/410JapHouseTxD1; http://home.worldcom.ch/~negenter/410JapHouseTxD2, http://home.worldcom.ch/~negenter/410JapHouseTxD3

55 Dunn, 1998, Vol. 2, p 236

56 We Japanese, 1949, p 369

57 Cees Nooteboom, In Japan II, in: In Spring the Dew, Travels in the East, Frankfurt am Main 1995, p 199

58 We Japanese, 1949, p 369 f.

59 Ibid, p 46

60 Ibid, p 257

61 Ibid, p 536

62 Ibid, p 16

63 Taut,1997, p 289 f.

64 Ibid, p 291

65 We Japanese, 1949, p 17 f.

66 Dunn, 1998, Vol. 2, p 318 f.

67 We Japanese, 1949, p 461

68 Taut,1997, p 291

69 Hisako Matsubara, Spaceship Japan, Reality and Provocation, Munich and Hamburg 1989, p 20 f.

70 Cf. We Japanese, 1949, p 26 ff., 36, 47, 292

71 Cf. ibid. p 41 ff.

72 Ibid, p 24

73 Ibid, p 37 f.

74 Aisaku Suzuki, http://home.t-online.de/home/keramik.suzuki/

75 We Japanese, 1949, p 18

76 Uwe Schmitt, Tokyo Tango, Frankfurt am Main 1999, p 143

Periods of Japanese History

Period	Date	Period	Date
Jōmon Period	ca. 12,000–250 B.C.	Heian Period	794–1185 A.D.
Start of Jōmon Period	ca. 12,000–5000 B.C.	Fujiwara Period	897–1185 A.D.
Early Jōmon Period	ca. 5,000–2500 B.C.	Kamakura Period	1185–1333 A.D.
Middle Jōmon Period	ca. 2,500–1500 B.C.	Nambokucho Period	1333–1392 A.D.
Close of Jōmon Period	ca. 1,500–300 B.C.	Muromachi Period	1392–1573 A.D.
Yayoi Period	250 B.C. to 250 A.D.	Momoyama Period	1573–1615 A.D.
		Edō (Tokugawa) Period	1615–1868 A.D.
Kofun (Tumulus) Period	250–552 A.D.	Meiji Period	1868–1912 A.D.
Asuka Period	552–645 A.D.	Taishō Period	1912–1926 A.D.
Nara Period	645–794 A.D.	Showa Period	1926–1989 A.D.
		Heisei Period	from 1989

Bibliographical Notes

Acker, William R. B./Joseph Acker: Kyudo. The Japanese Art of Archery. Rutland 1998

Addiss, Stephen/Audrey Yoshiko Seo: How to Look at Japanese Art. Amsterdam/New York 1996

Addiss, Stephen: The Art of Zen. Paintings and Calligraphy by Japanese Monks 1600–1925. Amsterdam/New York 1998

Aichele, Frieder/Renate Möller: East Asiatica, Munich 1997

Aichele, Frieder/Gert Nagel: Netsuke. Munich 1975

Audrey, Yoshiko Seo: Art of Twentieth-Century Zen. Paintings and Calligraphy by Japanese Masters. Boston/London 1999

Avitabile, Gunhild: The Art of Ancient Japan, Stuttgart 1990

Baricco, Alessandro: Silk, Munich 1997

Barth, Johannes: Japan's Visual Arts Throughout the Ages, Wiesbaden 1972

Bashō, Matsuo.: On Narrow Pathways Through the Hinterland. Translated by G.S. Dombrady. Mainz 1985

Benedict, Ruth: Chrysanthemums and the Sword. Japanese Culture, Frankfurt am Main 2000

Benz Willi: The Art of Suiseki. Classic Japanese Stone Gardening. New York 1999

Berndt, Jürgen (Hrsg.): Japanese Art, 2 volumes. Leipzig 1974

Bester, John: Japanese Art. The Great European Collections. Chester Beatty Library, Dublin, Vol. 5. Tokyo/New York/London 1996

Bester, John: Japanese Art. The Great European Collections. Rijksmuseum Voor Volkenkunde, Leiden, Vol. 9. Tokyo/New York/ London 1996

Blaser, Werner: Structure and Form in Japan. Zürich 1963

Bognar, Botond: The New Japanese Architecture. Stuttgart 1991

Bring, Mitchell/Josse Wayembergh: Japanese Gardens. Design and Meaning. New York 1981

Brower, Robert H./Earl Miner: Japanese Court Poetry. Stanford 1961

Brüll, Lydia: Japanese Philosophy. Darmstadt 1993

Buddhist Sculpture form Japan and China. Stock Catalogue of the Musuem of East Asian Art Cologne. Starnberg 1992

Cawthorne, Nigel: The Art of Japanese Prints. Vermont 1999

Coudenhove, Gerolf (broadcast): Japanese Seasons. Tanka and Haiku from Thirteen Centuries. Anthology. Stuttgart 1997.

Croissant, Doris/Lothar Lederrose (ed.): Japan and Europe 1543-1929. Exhibition Catalogue. Berlin 1993

Dambmann, Gerhard: Instructions for Use for Japan. Munich/Zurich 1988

Daniel, Charles: Kenjutsu. The Art of Japanese Swordsmanship. New York 1991

Delank, Claudia: Imaginary Japan in Art. "Pictures of Japan" from Art Nouveau to Bauhaus. Munich 1996

Drexler, Arthur: The Architecture of Japan. New York 1996

Dumoulin, Heinrich: History of Zen Buddhism, Volume 2, Japan. Tübingen 2000

Dunn, Michael: Japan. In: Gabriele Fahr-Becker (ed.), East Asian Art, 2 vols. Cologne 1998

Engel, Heinrich: The Japanese House. A Tradition for Contemporary Architecture. Tokyo/Rutland 1980

Eternos Tesouros do Japao (Eternal Treasures of Japan). Exhibition Catalogue Fuji Art Museum, Tokyo. Tokyo/Sao Paulo 1990

Fagioli, Marco: Shunga. Masterpieces of Erotic Art from Japan. Tübingen 1998

Fahr-Becker, Gabriele (ed.): Clapping with One Hand, Three Centuries of Japanese Color Woodcuts from the Riccar Art Museum Tokyo. with contributions from: Mitsunobu Satō and Thomas Zacharias, Exhibition Catalogue National Graphical Collection Munich in the Neuen Pinakothek, Munich. Munich 1992

Fahr-Becker, Gabriele (ed.): Japanese Color Woodcuts. Cologne 1993

Fahr-Becker, Gabriele (ed.): Art Nouveau, Cologne 1996

Feddersen, Martin: Japanese Arts and Crafts. Brunswick 1960

Fujioka, Michio: Kyōto Country Retreats. The Shugakuin and Katsura Palaces. Tokyo/ New York/San Francisco 1983

Fujioka, Ryouchi: Tea Ceremony Utensils. Tokyo 1973

Fujiya Hotel, Ltd. (Hrsg.): We Japanese. Miyanoshita, Hakone 1949

Goepper, Roger: Art and Craft of East Asia, Munich 1968

Graubner, Wolfgang: Wooden joints. Comparison of Japanese and European solutions. Stuttgart 1997

Gundert, Wilhelm (ed.): Lyric Poetry of the East. Munich 1978

Gustafson, Herb L.: The Art of Japanese Gardens. Designing & Making your own Peaceful Space. New York 1996

Hall, John Whitney: Das japanische Kaiserreich. Fischer Weltgeschichte, Band 20. Frankfurt am Main 1996

Hammitzsch, Horst: On the Concepts of "wabi" and "sabi" within the context of the Japanese Arts. In: News of the Society for the Natural History and Ethnology of East Asia 85/86, 1959

Hammitzsch, Horst: Cha-Do – The Tea Way. Munich-Planegg 1958

Hanley, Susan B.: Everyday Things in Premodern Japan. Berkeley/Los Angeles/London 1997

Harbin, Robert/Kingsley Mitchell: Secrets of Origami. The Japanese Art of Paper Folding. Dover 1997

Hashimoto, Fumio: Architecture in the Shoin Style. Tokyo/New York/San Francisco 1981

Hayashiya, Tatsusaburo/Masao Nakamura/ Seizo Hayashiya: Japanese Arts and the Tea Ceremony. New York/Tokyo 1974

Higashiyama, Kaii: Beauty in Japanese Art. In: Constantin von Barloewen/Kai Werhahn-Mees (ed.), Japan and the West, 3 vols., Frankfurt am Main 1986

Hirai, Kiyoshi: Feudal Architecture of Japan. New York/Tokyo 1974

Hirayama, Ikuo: Japanese Art. The Great European Collections. National Museum, Krakow, Vol. 10. Tokyo/New York/London 1996

Hirayama, Ikuo: Japanese Art. The Great European Collections. The British Library, the Ashmolean Museum, Oxford, Victoria & Albert Museum, Vol 4. Tokyo/New York/ London 1996

Hotta, Anne/Yoko Ishiguro: A Guide to Japanese Hot Springs. Tokyo 1986

How to Wrap 5 Eggs. Ausstellungskatalog Meguro Museum of Art, Tokyo. Tokyo 1988

Hufnagel, Florian (ed.)/Makio Araki/Yohji Yamamoto: Japan, Wrapping and Receptacle. Exhibition Catalogue. Munich 1992

Inoue, Yasushi: The Mountain Azaleas on the Summit of Mount Hira, Frankfurt am Main 1980

Ito, Teiji: The Elegant Japanese House. Traditional Sukiya Architecture. New York/Tokyo 1969

Ito, Teiji: The Gardens of Japan, Cologne 1999

Itzutsu, Toshihiko/Toyo Izutsu/Franziska Ehmcke (ed.), The Theory of Beauty in Japan, Articles on Classical Japanese Aesthetics, Cologne 1998

Jahss, Melvin/Betty Jahss: Inro and other miniature forms of Japanese Lacquer Art. Tokyo/Rutland 1971

Kageyama, Haruki: The Arts of Shintō. Arts of Japan 4. Tokyo/New York 1973

Kakuzo, Okakura: The Book of Tea. Rutland/Tokyo 1956

Katoh, Amy Sylvester/Shin Kimura: Japan. The Art of Living. A Sourcebook of Japanese Style for the Western Home. Rutland/Tokyo 1999

Kawakami, Kenji/ Dan Papia: 99 More Unuseless Japanese Inventions. The Art of Chindogu. London 1997

Keene, Donald: Nō. The Classical Theatre of Japan. Tokyo/Palo Alto 1973

Kennedy, Alan: Japanese Costume. History and Tradition. Paris 1990

Kirby, John B.: From Castle to Teahouse: Japanese Architecture of the Momoyama Period. Tokyo/Rutland 1962

Kobayashi, Tadashi: Japanese Art. The Great European Collections. Museum für Ostasiatische Kunst, Berlin, Vol 7. Tokyo/New York/London 1994

Kokichi, Matsuki: Masterpieces of Japanese Garden Art, Vol. 1. Kyōto 1992

Koren, Leonard/Matthias Dietz (ed.): Wabi-sabi for Artists, Architects and Designers, Japan's Philosophy of Modesty, Tübingen 1995

Kosaki, Takayuki: This is How Japan Cooks. Munich 1998

Kreiner, Josef (ed.): Japanese Collections in the Museums of Central Europe.

Kreiner, Josef (ed.): Engelbert Kämpfer. Exhibition Catalogue. Tokyo 1990

Kümmel, Otto: Art and Crafts in Japan. Berlin 1911

Kurokawa, Kisho: Rediscovering Japanese Space. New York/Tokyo 1988

Lee, Yu-kuan: Oriental Lacquer Art. Tokyo 1972

Lee, Sherman: A History of Far Eastern Art. London 1964

Lee, Sherman: Japanese Decorative Style. New York 1972

Lessing, Julius: Reports from the 1878 World Exhibition in Paris, without indication of place of publication 1878

Lind, Werner (ed.): East Asian Martial Arts, The Encyclopaedia, Berlin 1996

Lobell, John: Between Silence and Light. Boston 1979

Makoto, Ooka: The Splendour of the Dew, Dreams and This World. Poetry and Poetics of Ancient Japan

Mason, Penelope: History of Japanese Art. New York 1993

Matsubara, Hisako: Spaceship Japan, Reality and Provocation, Munich and Hamburg 1989

McCallum, Donald F.: Zenkoji and its Icon. A Study in Medieval JapaneseReligious Art. Boston 1994

Meckel, Andreas: Germany – Japan. 100 Views. Düsseldorf 1989

Mingei Works of Anonymous Craftsmen in Japanese Tradition. Exhibition Catalogue Mingei Museum Tokyo. Tokyo/Munich 1993

Miyeko, Murase: Autumn Wind in the Pine Trees. Japanese Art of the Langen Collection. Munich 1998

Morita, Kiyoko: The Book of Incense. Enjoying the Traditional Art of Japanese Scents. Tokyo/New York/London 1999

Morley, John David: Grammar of the Smile. Japanese Inner Views. Reinbeck 1989

Morsbach, Helmut: The simple Guide to Customs & Etiquette in Japan. Folkestone 1994

Morse, Edward: Japanese Homes and their Surroundings. Tokyo/Rutland 1972

Münsterberg, Oskar: History of Japanese Art, 3 volumes. Brunswick 1904/1907

Naito, Akira: Katsura: A Princely Retreat. Tokyo/New York/San Francisco 1977

Newland, Amy/Chris Uhlenbeck (Hrsg.): Ukiyo-E. The Art of Japanese Woodblock Prints. London 1999

Nishi, Kazuo/ Kazuo Hozumi: What Is Japanese Architecture? Tokyo 1996

Nitschke, Günter: From Shintō to Ando. London 1993

Nitschke, Günter: Japanese Gardens. The Right Angle and Natural Shape. Cologne 1999

Noever, Peter (ed.): Ancient Japan. Tracks and Objects of the Siebold Journeys. Exhibition Catalogue. Munich/New York 1997

Nooteboom, Cees In Japan III, in: In Spring the Dew, Travels in the East, Frankfurt am Main 1995

Nute, Kevin: Frank Lloyd Wright and Japan. The Role of Traditional Japanese Art and Architecture in the Work of Frank Lloyd Wright. New York 1994

Ota, Hirotarō (Hrsg.): Japanese Architecture and Gardens. Tokyo 1966

Paine, Robert Treat/Alexander Coburn Soper: The Art and Architecture of Japan. Middlesex/New York 1981

Paine, Robert Treat/Alexander Coburn Soper: The Art and Architecture of Japan. London 1992

Paireau, Françoise: Papiers japonais (Japanese Papers). Paris 1991

Plummer, Henry: Light in Japanese Architecture. a+u, Architecture and Urbanism. Extra Edition June 1995. Tokyo 1995

Pörtner, Peter: Japan. Art Guide. Cologne 1998

Pound, Ezra/Ernest Fenollosa/Sergej M. Eisenstein: No. On the Genius of Japan. Frankfurt am Main 1990

Price, Margaret: Classic Japanese Inns & Country Getaways. Tokyo 1999

Richie, Donald: The Japanese Inn – Ryokan. A Gateway to Traditional Japan. Tokyo 1985

Rivera, Felix G: Suiseki. The Japanese Art of Miniature Landscape Stones. London 1996

Rother-Nakaya, Suzue: Ikebana. An Introduction to the Art of Japanese Flower Arranging. Aarau 1995

Ryoi, Asoi Tales from the Fleeting World of Pleasure, Kyoto 1661

Sadler, Arthur L.: A Short History of Japanese Architecture. Tokyo/Rutland 1963

Salmon, Patricia: Japanese Antiques. With a Guide to Shops. Tokyo/Honolulu 1985

Sansom, George: A Short Cultural History of Japan. Stanford 1952

Sasamori, Junzo/Gordon Warner: This is Kendo. Japanese Fencing. Berlin 1994

Satterwhite, Rob: What's what in Japanese Restaurants. Tokyo/New York/London 1996

Schlombs, Adele: Masterpieces from China, Korea and Japan. Museum for East Asian Art Cologne. Munich 1995

Schmidt, Ulrich: Porcelain from China and Japan. The Porcelain Gallery of the Landgraves of Hessen-Kassel. Berlin 1990

Schmitt, Uwe: Tokyo Tango. A Japanese Adventure. Frankfurt am Main 1999

Shikibu, Murasaki/Translation Edward G. Seidensticker: The Tale of Genji. New York 1976

Shikibu, Murasaki/Übersetzung Edward G. Seidensticker: The Tale of Genji. New York 1976

Shikibu, Murasaki: The Most Beautiful Love Stories of Prince Genji. Translation by Herbert E. Herlitschka. Selection from same: The Story of Prince Genji. Munich 1963

Shōnagon, Sei/Ivan Morris (ed.): The Pillow Book of Sei Shōnagon. New York/Oxford 1991

Speidel, Manfred: Japanese Architecture. Past and Present. Stuttgart 1983

Stanley-Baker, Joan: Japanese Art. London 2000

Suzuki, Daisetz Teitaro: Zen and the Culture of Japan. Munich 1994

Suzuki, Kakichi: Early Buddhist Architecture in Japan. Tokyo/New York/San Francisco 1980

Suzuki, Kiichi/Kazuyoshi Miyamoto: Japanese Tradional Hotels (in Japanese). Tokyo 1998

Tamburello, Adolfo/Yasunari Kawabata: Japan. Monuments of Great Cultures. Erlangen 1987

Tanaka, Ichimatsu/Masao Ishizawa: Heritage of Japanese Art. Tokyo 1992

Tanigawa, Atsushi: Art Nouveau as a Phenomenon of the Arabesque. In: Gabriele Fahr-Becker (ed.), Art Nouveau. Tokyo 1990

Tanizaki, Jun'ichirō: In Praise of Shadows. New Haven, 1977

Taut, Bruno: Houses and People of Japan. Ed. Manfried Speidel Berlin 1997 (First published 1936)

Taylor, Chris: Japan. Melbourne 1997 (Dt. Ausgabe: Berlin 1988)

Taylor, John S.: Common Sense Architecture. New York 1983. (German Edition: Building with a healthy understanding of human beings. Natural and uncomplicated architectural details. Reliable solutions from all ages and cultures as a stimulus for building today. Wiesbaden 1985)

Terukazu, Akiyama: Japanese Painting. Tübingen 1990

Ulak, James T.: Japanese Prints. The Art Institute of Chicago. New York 1995

Varley, H. Paul: Japanese Culture. Honolulu 1984

Wada, Yoshiko: Shibori. The Inventive Art of Japanese Shaped Resist Dyeing Tradition Techniques Innovation. Tokyo 1999

Watanabe, Yasutada: Shintō Art. Ise and Izumo Shrines. New York/Tokyo 1974

Wichmann, Siegfried: Japonisme. The Japanese Influence on Western Art since 1858. London 1999

Williams, Dominic: Very Simple Japanese. Folkestone 1990

Winzinger, Franz: Shunga. Exhibition Catalogue. Nuremberg 1975

Wolf, Richard: The World of the Netsuke. Wiesbaden 1972

Yagi, Koji: A Japanese Touch for your Home. Tokyo/New York/London 1992

Yamamoto, Tsuentomo/Hagakure. The Book of the Samurai. Tokyo 1979

Yonemura, Ann: Twelve Centuries of Japanese Art from the Imperial Collections. Washington 1998

Yoshida, Tetsuro: The Japanese House and Garden. New York 1955

Zacharias, Thomas: Japanism or Clapping with One Hand, in: Gabriele Fahr-Becker (ed.), Art Nouveau. Tokyo 1990

Internet addresses:

Egenter, Nold The Japanese House. Or: Why Western Architects have difficulty Understanding It – Comparative Reflections from the Point of View of Cultural Anthropology on the Traditional Japanese House and the Western Concept of "universal human needs." In: http://home.worldcom.ch/~negenter/ 417JapHouseTxD1; http://home.world com.ch/~negenter/410JapHouseTxD2; http://home.worldcom.ch/~negenter/ 417JapHouseTxD3

http://rc.kyushu-u.ac.jp/~michel/serv/ck/

http://home.t-online.de/home/keramik.suzuki/

Glossary

Abuna-e Risqué picture, erotic depictions and scenes of lovers

Agesudo Gate with bamboo pales

Aka-chochin "Red lantern bar," bar

Amado "Rain door," wooden latched or sliding veranda and outside shutters

Amagasa *Kasa*, Japanese umbrella, used as protection from the rain

Amaterasu Japanese sun goddess and progenitor of the Japanese imperial family

Amigasa-mon "Gate of the woven umbrella," middle gate in the tea house garden

Andon Standard lamp covered with rice paper, wooden frame

Anka Container filled with glowing charcoal, like a "hot water bottle"

Arita china Glass-like body, mostly decorated in underglaze blue and with colored overglaze enamels

Arts and Crafts A movement of artists and craftsmen that started in the mid-nineteenth century in England

Audition colorée "Listening in color," a kind of synesthesia, sensation experienced by one of the senses when another is stimulated

Awase-ko A type of incense

Ayu Japanese freshwater fish caught with a rod or by using cormorants

Azumaya Type of roof that slopes in four directions from the mid-point of the ridgepole without forming gables

Bana flowers

Bancha Second grade Japanese tea

Bangasa *Kasa*, Japanese umbrellas, placed at the disposal of customers in shops and inns

Banto Originally a scribe or a secretary, today usually a male employee in a ryokan

Bashi Bridge

Beauty born by use "Chance decoration" of utensils or furniture etc. that comes about through use, and which is highly valued aesthetically

Bento Japanese lunchbox

Bi The slightest inner movement that is emitted from an element or a thing

Bijin-ga Japanese color woodblock prints and Japanese pictures of beautiful women

Binkake Coal pan made of china

Biwa Japanese lute, similar to a mandolin

Bizen pottery Mostly large vessels with a dark red body, decorated circumferentially in the shoulder section by wavy lines and spots or drops of wood ash glaze in contrasting colors

Bogu Protective clothing for kendo sword fighting

Bokuzai Oracle

Bon Tray

Bon-kei Imitations of natural landscapes in miniature

Bon-odori Circle dance on the Buddhist all souls' festival

Bon-sai The art of cultivating miniature trees by careful pruning

Bracket and cantilever system Support point projecting from the joint in the wall or wood for ledges, arches, roofs, etc.

Buddhism The Indo-East Asian religious teaching propagated by Buddha

Budō The "way of the samurai," to concentrate one's mind and body in practicing the way. Philosophy of life of the rulers of Japan from 1160 to 1868

Bundai "Writing table/desk," Japanese desk for books and reading

Bungaku Dance pieces performed by groups of court musicians in pre-modern Japan

Bunjin-ga Painting by men of letters

Bunraku Japanese puppet theatre for adults

Bushi Warrior class in pre-modern Japan. Leaders of the fighting forces belonging to big land owners, who employed their own armies

Bushi-dō "The Way of the Warriors"

Butsudan Buddhist family altar

Buyo Dance drama

Byōbu Folding moveable screen with two to eight panels, used not only as a temporary room divider, but also on special occasions as a decorative background

Calligraphy Art of handwriting

Cha Tea

Chabako Teabox

Chabin Teapot

Chadai "Tea money," a type of tip

Cha-dansu Tea chest

Cha-dō "Way of Tea" in the tea ceremony

Cha-gama Teakettle for the tea ceremony

Cha-ire Tea caddy

Cha-ji The part of the tea ceremony after entering the tearoom

Chaniwa Tea garden

Cha-no-yō "Hot water for tea" for the tea ceremony

Chashitsu Two-mat tearoom

Cha-ya Originally teahouse, today restaurant in entertainments districts

Chigaidana Graduated shelving in the *tokonoma*

Chisen-kaiyu style A Japanese landscape garden style, in which a "strolling garden" is laid out around a large pond

Chitose Name for the pine tree; second meaning: a thousand years

Chi turrets Sickle shaped gables with ornaments and window openings found on Japanese castles

Cho Row of houses

Chochin Portable outside lamp

Chōdai Closed off, secure sleeping area in the traditional *shoin*

Chōdaigamae Decorated sliding doors in the *shoin*

Cho-dansu (also *choba-dansu*) "ledger chest," an item of furniture used by a merchant

Choko Small cups or bowls made of various materials, in which the Japanese rice wine, sake, is served

Chome Quarter of town comprising several blocks of houses

Choshi Ceremonial sake pourer or decanter

Chozubashi Water basin

Chu Humility

Chūban Middle size of woodblock print

Chūmon "Inner gate," projecting part of a building through which the living complex is entered

Chūmon-rō "Inner corridor gates," covered entrance arcades and projecting corridors of the *shoin* architectural style

Chūmon-zukuri A characteristic *minka* architectural style from northern Japan.

Named after the projecting part of the building, the *chū*mon - added on to the original living area *shuya* - and which arose from the chūmon-rō, the projecting corridor of the *shoin* architectural style

Cormorant Pelican-like water bird

Daidai-yō Citrus bath

Daikudogu Woodworking and processing tools

Daime 3/4 *tatami* mat

Daimyō Local feudal lords during the Shogun rule in Japan

Daimyō-yashiki Daimyō residence

Daito Large block in Japanese bracket complex

Daiyokujo Large bath

Demitsudo The projecting triple block of the Japanese bracket complex

Deshi Student who immerses himself in "The Way"

Do Chest and stomach guard in protective clothing for kendo sword fighting

Dō The way

Do Hall

Dobin Teapot made of pottery

Dōjō The place where the way *dō* is practiced, *jō* the place, kendo practice halls

Dojoji Play about the evil spirits in the nō drama, who are always female, but are played by men

Dōma The ground floor room in a Japanese house

Dori Street or avenue

Dotaku Bronze bell

Earthenware Unglazed clay items, baked at a low temperature

Ebenist Cabinet maker who specializes in working with high-grade wood inlays

Ebiko Potpourri cushion

Eboshi kabuto Helmet with neck guard

Echigo Traditional name of the north Japanese province Niigata

Echizen pottery Body of brownish coloring, mostly without decoration with interesting surface texture

Edo Old name for the Tokyo of today, the capital situated in the east. At the start of the 18th century Edo was the largest city on earth with approx. 1.3 million inhabitants

E-hon "Picture book," picture albums with illustrations on a wide range of subjects

Eiga Monogatari "Tales about blossoms"

E-maki Hand scroll pictures

E-makimono Picture scrolls depicting stories

En Garden

Engawa Narrow wooden veranda overlooking the garden

Engi Omen

Enrindō "The hall of the garden grove," teahouse of the Katsura

Enryo Restraint

Ensō circles Simple ink circles drawn by Zen monks with a single brush stroke

Flamboyant Emotional, blazing, after an ornamental tree from the tropics that blossoms magnificently

Fu Prefecture

Fu-bako Box for letters

Fuchi Mounting on lower part of the hilt of a sword

Fujin yokushitsu Women's bath

Fude Writing brush

Fūga That which is "aesthetically creative"

Fugu Poisonous puffer or porcupine fish

Fugu-chochin Puffer fish lantern

Fujibakama Chinese agrimony, perennial flowering plant with feathery leaves

Fujishiro Iris

Fukibokashi style Printing technique for color woodblock prints. The background color is applied to the printing plate with a cloth

Fukinuki yatai "The roof that has blown away." Feature of painting in the Heian Period (794-1185), palace interiors are reproduced as a bird's eye view

Fuku-cha New Year's tea

Funa-dansu Ship or sea chests

Funahijiki Boat-shaped bracket arm of the Japanese bracket complex

Fundoshi Loin cloth

Furidashi Herbal medicine

Furigana Japanese phonetic transcription of *kanji*

Furisode Kimono with long sleeves reaching almost to the ankles, worn by young girls until they marry and at court

Furo Bath tub, also name for different types of bath such as the hot bath

Fusuma Sliding wall-doors made of wood or with a wooden frame covered on both sides with non-transparent paper or material

Futaai Double indigo

Futai Brocade ribbons

Futon Japanese bedding

Gagaku Court music

Gaijin "People from outside," foreigners

Geiko "The practice of the way"

Geisha *Gei*, art, *sha* person, girl trained in singing and dancing, who is responsible for entertaining men, not necessarily with labors of love

Gekū The outer shrine of the Ise temple

Genius loci The spiritual atmosphere of a place

Genkan "The entrance to the anteroom," formal reception area in a Japanese house where shoes are removed. Originally in Zen: "The gateway to the esoteric path"

Genkyu-en Landscape gardens laid out in 1677 in the grounds of Hikone castle

Genno Hammer

Gepparō "The tower of waves illuminated by the moon," teahouse of the Katsura

Geta Traditional Japanese footwear with a wooden sole

Gifu-chochin Box lantern made of silk with splendid motifs

Gin-maki-e Lacquerwork decorated with silver

Gion Kyoto's entertainment quarter

Gion festival *Shintō* summer festival in Kyoto

Giri The individual's obligations towards society

Go Board game

Gohan Boiled rice

Gohei *Shintō* ritual stave with zigzag shaped strips of paper, religious paper gifts

Gongen Buddha manifestations

Goshintai The "Divine" in *Shintō* is not present in a "holy picture" such as for example a statue of Buddha, but as a "real symbol," that is in material objects

Gōten In the architectural style of a court residence

Gu Shrine

Gyō Peaceful, free shape

Gyosho Japanese cursive or light writing

Hagi Japanese clover

Hahaka Branch from a cherry tree that serves as a divining rod

Hai-dai Sake cup stand, usually made of china or lacquerwork

Haiden Ritual hall of the *shintō* shrine

Haiga Improvised sketch that has been dashed off quickly, forms a whole with *haiku* poetry

Haikai Short poem

Haiku Japanese literary genre, short poem of 17 syllables

Haisen Washstand or bowl

Hakama Loose culotte trousers, a type of "trouser-skirt"

Hako Box, tin, container

Hako-chochin A cylindrical box lantern

Hako-netsuke *Netsuke* in the shape of a small container

Hako-niwa *Bon-kei*, in which artificial trees and flowers, small human and animal figures and models of houses or other objects are included in the overall composition

Hamaguri Japanese clam shell

Han Seal

Hana-awase Flower card game

Hana-mi Cherry blossom viewing

Hana-mi-ju "Picnic box" for viewing the cherry blossom

Hanare Cottage in a ryokan estate

Hanegi Cantilever girder

Hangai Ship's clothes box with front lid

Hangyoku Maturing geisha

Haniwa Japanese grave figures made of clay, Kofun Period (250-552)

Haori Wrap in the shape of a short kimono

Haribako Sewing box

Haribako-gin "Little sewing box – silver," secret box for women's private things

Hashi Chopsticks

Hashibako Boxes for chopsticks

Hashitate Square holder for chopsticks

Hata Flag, banner

Hatagoya Another name for ryokan

Heiankio The imperial residence Kyoto was founded in 794 under the name of Heiankio.

Heika *Ike-bana* in the *rikka* style

Hibachi Transportable "braziers" filled with charcoal, coal basins made of wood or lacquerwork

Higara Dates and numbers

Higasa Japanese sun umbrella, a *kasa* as protection from the sun, lighter than the *amagasa*

Hijiki Elbow timbers, bracket arm in the Japanese bracket complex. The shape calls to mind the human elbow, *hiji*

Hikite Decorative metal mountings on the pulls of sliding doors

Hikone-jo The castle of Hikone

Himotoshi Cord holes on the *netsuke*

Hinoki Japanese cypress

Hiragana Japanese syllabic script – phonetic transcription – to render grammatical declension and conjugation endings

Hirajiro Lowland fortress

Hiraya Single story building

Hirayamajiro Lowland-mountain fortresses

Hiroshiki The part of the *dōma* with floorboards

Hirugao Field bindweed

Hisashi Peripheral chamber of a *shinden* residence, the so-called "secondary area," used for day-to-day living. Also a baldachin or roof.

Hito Tips for personal behavior while visiting the thermal baths

Hitsu Chests and boxes for storing clothes

Hogaku Directions, points of the compass

Hogyo A type of pyramid-shaped roof

Hōjō Quarters of the superior monk in the Zen monastery

Hōjō Major-domo

Hokku *Haiku* were originally called *hokku*, which means the same as the first verse of a *renga*

Hōkōnin Servant or employee

Hon Book

Honden Main seat of the godhead of a *shintō* shrine

Honkan Main or old section of a ryokan building

Horror vacui Abhorrence of the void

Hortus conclusus "Closed garden," secret place

Hozo-tsugi Japanese dovetail joint without nails or glue, can support great stresses and loads

Hozuki-chochin "Dwarf cherry lantern"

Hyakuninisshu "One poem from each of a hundred poets," anthology

Ichi-go Square wooden receptacle for sake

Idashifuzukue In the *shoin* table "for taking writing things out of"

Ideogram A written sign or symbol that represents a whole concept

Idiosyncrasy Oversensitivity, unusual susceptibility

Ie House, Japanese family system

Igusa Rush

Ike Breathing and living

Ike-bana The Japanese art of flower arranging

Iki Style, good taste in choice of clothing, being up to date, feminine attribute

Iko Clothes or kimono stand

In Temple, also stamp or seal

Inari Shrine

Indigo Oldest organic coloring, blue

Ingeniousness Imaginativeness, cleverness

Ingyo Seal

Inro *In*, seal, *ro*, container. Small, hanging case for keeping things in, medicine container

Irimoya Roof with two parts, consisting of a *kiri-zuma* and a *shichu*

Irori Open fireplace in the living room of a *minka*

Ise-monogatari Tale of Ise

Ishi-doro Stone lantern

Isho-dansu Clothes box for storing kimonos and other items of clothing

Itakarato Swing doors

Iu The feminine style in *ike-bana*

Izumi-dono Fountain pavilion

Izutsu Stone surroundings of a spring

Jaku Peacefulness

Ji Temple

Jikata Choir with six singers

Jinja Shrine

Jizai-kagi Adjustable hearth hanger on the *iori*, constructed from wood, metal and bamboo

Jo Castle

Jochū-san Maid-servant

Jōdan Substructure of the *tokonoma*

Jubako Tiered lacquer or china picnic box

Jyou A *tatami*, the common unit of measurement for rooms in Japan. Even Western style rooms are measured in *jyou*

Kabuki Song-dance-art, traditional play, which developed into a specifically Japanese art form towards the end of the 17th century

Kado Today *ike-bana*

Kago Woven bamboo basket

Kago-chochin Basket lantern

Kagu Furniture

Kagura Ritual dances and games

Kai-awase Shell matching game

Kaidan-tansu "Step chest," a type of stepped cupboard

Kai-oke Lacquered container for the shells of the *kai-awase*

Kairo "Pocket or chest warmer," small metal container for crushed charcoal

Kaiseki Sophisticated Japanese cuisine with multiple courses

Kaisho A separate building for official receptions in *shoin* architecture

Kaisho Japanese longhand

Kakebuton A quilt-like overblanket for a *futon*

Kakemono Hanging picture scroll, that is hung in the *tokonoma*, size 30 x 18 ins.

Kakesuzuri-bako Ship's writing cabinet with hinged lid

Kaki tree Ebony tree that grows in the tropics, fruit tree with yellow or orange colored fruits

Kakiemon China from Arita with milky-white body and decorated with patterns in underglaze blue and/or overglaze enamels, often in the orangey-red color of the kaki fruit, hence the name *kakiemon*

Kama Pot or kettle

Kamado A traditional stone, earth or tiled hearth with a hollow for cooking pots

Kami "That which is above," divine beings and spirits of nature

Kamidana *Shintō* house altar

Kamikaze Wind of the gods

Kamoi Upper guide rails of the *shōji* or *fusuma*

Kamuro Pupil and maid to a Japanese courtesan

Kana The two Japanese syllabic scripts, katakana and hiragana

Kanban Signs for businesses and shops

Kanji Chinese script, name for the Chinese characters used in Japan

Kanna Hand plane

Kano One of the main schools of painting in Japan since the middle of the 15th century

Kanpai Cheers!

Kara-bitsu Boxes with feet for storing clothing. These are usually copies from the Chinese Tang dynasty (618-907)

Kara-hafu Curved *shoin* gable over the approach for coaches or the entrance for sedan chairs

Karaki Imported wood from Southeast Asia

Karaoke "Empty orchestra," singing over a prerecorded backing tape

Kare-sansui Japanese dry garden

Karyūkai Niigata's blossom and willow district, entertainment quarter

Kasa Japanese umbrella, made of wood and bamboo and covered with oil paper; originally a large, flat rush hat

Kasane Tansu in two separate stacking sections, easier to transport in the event of an earthquake or fire

Kashira Mounting on upper part of the hilt of a sword

Kaso "House destiny"

Kata Garment

Katakana Japanese syllabic script with angular characters for certain concepts such as foreign names, foreign words etc.

Katana Long sword

Katana-dansu Chest for swords

Katei Home, made up of the Japanese characters for house and garden, *ka*, house, *tei*, garden

Katōmado S-shaped fluted window

Katsura Hagoromo *Nō* drama, which describes the life of women

Katsura Country villa of the Katsuranomiya, a line of Japanese princes, in southwest Kyoto

Katte Anteroom for preparing tea

Kayamon Japanese silver grass gate

Kazoku-buro Small family bath

Ke House

Kei Respect for everything that exists

Ken Prefecture

Kendai Japanese desk for books from the Nara Period (645-794), once reserved for the members of the imperial household and the priesthood

Kendō Fencing with bamboo swords, "The Way of the Bamboo Sword"

Kenjutsu Schools of sword techniques

Kesho-bako Cosmetics box

Keshōdaruki The lower layer of rafters in the temple roof

Keyaki Broad-leaved Mongolian oak

Kiko Travel report

Kiku Chrysanthemum

Kikyoku Container for tea ceremony utensils

Kimon The point of the compass North East, in Japanese "devil's gate"

Kimono "Dressing thing," item of clothing. Coat-like garment, worn by men and women and tied with an *obi* at the waist (for women) or at the hips (for men)

Kinchaku Brocade or leather money purse

Kingyo "Honorable goldfish"

Kin-maki-e Lacquerwork decorated with gold

Kinome Tender leaves of a type of ash tree, used in the summer months as a garnish

Kinumo Silk dress

Kiri Japanese paulownia, imperial tree

Kirikane Gold leaf cut in a pattern or in thin strips

Kiriro Small transportable stove

Kiri-zuma Gable roof

Kiseru Traditional Japanese pipe

Kiseru-zutsu Japanese pipe box

Kisohiuoki Coffered ceiling

Kiwarijutsu Primer with instructions on the proportions for *shoin*

Kobako Incense container

Kōdo Temple hall

Kodo Incense appreciation

Koen Park

Kogen High plateau

Koi-cha Ceremonial tea

Kojiki "Record of ancient matters," oldest Japanese written work (712), which recounts myths and imperial history up until 628

Komo Roughly woven straw mat

Komori-gasa "Bat umbrella," common Japanese name for a western umbrella

Komuso Basket-shaped hat, *komo*, roughly woven straw mat, *so* priest

Kon-yoku "Mixed" bath

Konnyaku Gelatin from the root of the devil's tongue (solanum)

Koro Incense burner

Kosode Undergarment, "forerunner" of the kimono

Kosode-hakama Loose culotte trousers, *hakama*, which were worn over wrapped *kosode*

Kosode kimono Kimono in several layers for members of the upper classes

Kotatsu Low table with a heat source and a cover over it

Kote Gloves for kendo sword fighting

Koto Japanese stringed instrument

Kuge Court nobility in Kyoto

Kugikakushi Decorative metal nail covers

Kumimono The Japanese bracket complex

Kumi-te The joints fitting the parts together in the Japanese system of wooden joints

Kura-zashiki Main building with entrance and reception area

Kuroshoin Decorative wooden support timbers

Kuruma-dansu Chests on wheels for valuables

Kusan Chrysanthemum

Kusemai Dance with sung accompaniment

Kusuri-dansu Medicine chest

Kutani pottery China from Arita with enamel coloring

Kū-tei Empty garden

Kuwa Mulberry tree

Kuzu Arrowroot

Kyaku Guest, customer

Kyō Long trains on court costumes

Kyō-baku Sutra case

Kyōdai Japanese dressing table with covered mirror

Kyōgen Farcical interlude at kabuki performances

Kyōsoku Wooden armrest with fitted cushion

Kyōto The capital of Japan from 794 officially until 1869, founded under the name of Heiankio

Kyō-yaki These types of china are stoneware with enamel flash glazing from the kilns near to the Kiyomizu temple close to Kyoto, hence Kiyomizu-yaki, today also frequently a generic term for china from the Edo Period

Ma Character for the concept of "space"

Machiai Central geisha house

Maiko Young geisha who has not yet completed her training; dancer

Majinai Calling up of spirits

Maki-e Pictures sprinkled with the finest of gold or silver grains on lacquer

Makiri Dagger

Makito Small block in Japanese bracket complex

Makura Japanese pillow, which today is usually filled with rice husks, rather than consisting of a wooden block, or china or straw as in earlier times

Marquetry Inlay work in wood

Maruobi The *obi* material is folded double instead of being lined

Masu Load-bearing block in the Japanese bracket complex

Matcha Traditional frothy green tea

Matsu Pine tree

Matsuri Festival

Matsutake Type of mushroom

Meisho Edō hyakkei 100 views of famous places in Edo

Men Helmet used in kendo sword fighting that covers face, neck, the top and sides of the head

Menkawabashira Supporting posts in the tokonoma with rough, unworked, unbeveled edges

Menuki Decorations wound round the hilt of a sword

Meoto-iwa "Wedded rocks," the married rocks in a coastal bay near Ise

Midaré-bako An open case like a tray for storing kimonos

Miki Sacred sake

Mingei Naturalness of traditional art; term put together from the Japanese character for folk and art; today in general use to mean Japanese folk art

Minka Japanese farmhouse

Mino Straw raincoat

Minshuku A type of family pension, simple inn

Mise Japanese shop

Mise-hibachi Small stove handed to customers in a shop to warm themselves

Miso Salty paste made of fermented soya beans

Mi-tama-shiro Another term for *goshintai*

Miyako-odori Dance performed five times a day in April in Kyoto

Mizu Cold water

Mizuire Water container for dissolving ink

Mizusashi Water container

Mizuya-dansu Kitchen chests

Mochi Sticky rice cakes for New Year

Momiji Maple

Mon Gate, also coat of arms for a family or business

Monogatari Story

Moribana Flowers piled up in dish-like vessels, type of *ike-bana*

Moxa Mugwort wool used as a herb

Moya Central area of the *shinden* hall

Munemochi-bashira Free-standing ridge pillar

Mura Village

Murodoko *Tokonoma* in which the back pillars are under the plaster

Muromachi Southern part of the town of Kyoto, period in history

Mushiburo or **Mushiyū** Steam bath

Nabeshima The exquisite Arita china, reserved only for the highest levels of society

Nadeshiko Wild carnation

Naga-bakama Divided skirt with a train, part of the official court costume

Naga-hibachi "Fire container," square (char) coal bowl from the Edo Period (1614-1868)

Nagamochi-kuruma Large chest cupboard on wheels

Nagaya One room apartments in long buildings, the Japanese equivalent of tenement buildings

Nagaya-mon Gatehouse

Nageire "Thrown in," a style of flower arrangement in bowls

Nageshi Weighty circumferential crossbeams

Naikū Inner shrine of Ise

Nando Enclosed side room of the *dōma* for sleeping or storage

Nanzen-ji Temple near Kyoto

Natura naturans Creative nature

Nawa-noren The "rope curtain," indicates a bar or an inexpensive restaurant

Negoro Lacquer ware first produced by monks of the Negoro temple in the Wakayama prefecture (not far from Osaka)

Netsuke Toggle for belt cord, small wooden or ivory sculpture worn on the *obi* for fastening small objects to it

Nigite Strips of white paper or material on the *shimenawa*

Nihon "Origin of the sun," Japan

Nihonga Japanese painting

Nihongi Chronicle of Japan

Nihon-to The Japanese sword, a weapon more than six feet long

Nijiriguchi "Crawling entrance" (28 x 32 in) to a teahouse, an act that symbolizes that guests have finally left the everyday world behind them

Nikkō Temple complex in the northwest of Tokyo

Ningyo Dolls seen as bringers of good luck

Ninso Physiognomies

Nippon "Origin of the sun," Japan

Nishiki Brocade

Nishiki-e Color woodcut, multicolor print

Niwa Garden, courtyard, part of the building in a Japanese house that includes the domestic workroom and the kitchen

No A particle

Nō Skill, art: pre-modern Japanese dance and lyrical drama performed in masks and magnificent garments on an empty stage

Nodaruki Second layer of rafters supporting the temple roof

Nokogiri Saw

Nomi Chisel

Noren "Warm curtain," entrance curtain

Nori Dried seaweed

Nuihaku technique Gold leaf spun on silk, creating a shimmering effect

Nure-en Open veranda added on to the house

Nurimono Lacquerwork

Nusa Another term for *nigite*

Nyobo shozoku Court costume of the Heian Period (794-1185) with twelve or more layers of clothing

O Prefix as an expression of respect for the person or thing being addressed

Ōban Extra large size of woodblock print

Oba-san Grandmotherly woman

Obi Sash for fastening the kimono

Obi-dome Decorative front buckle of the *obi*

Obon Festival in memory of dead souls

Ocha Clear green Japanese tea

Odawara-chochin Cylindrical folding lantern

Odori Japanese dance

O-furo The traditional Japanese bath

Ogi Folding fan

Ogura hyakuninisshu Collection of poetry based on an anthology of 100 poems by 100 different poets

O-hana-mi Cherry blossom festival

O-hashi Set of wooden or bamboo chopsticks, sometimes lacquered

Ohineri Traditionally a way of wrapping the money that was thrown to actors on stage as a gesture of appreciation; nowadays also paper wrappings for candy

Ojime Small sliding bead on the *netsuke* and *inro* cords

O-jukko Incense mixture

Okagami Historical tale

Okaiko-sama "Honorable silkworms"

Okami-san Lady of the house in a ryokan or an elegant traditional restaurant

Okazu Occasional table

Okimono Ornamental object, art object to put up

Okuzashiki Inner dayroom, formal style of a *shoin* room

Ominaeshi Toadflax

Onito Demon block with complicated beveled carvings on the plinth, load bearing blocks in the Japanese bracket complex

Onnaburo or **Onnayū** Women's bath

Onnagata Actor who plays women. Since the mid-17th century only men appear on stage in the *kabuki*

Onsen Thermal bath or spring

Oribe pottery Made of light-colored clay and produced in a kiln with many chambers, large shapes and a variety of decorations

Origami The art of paper folding

O-saisen "Honorable monetary offering"

Oshi The theory of the way

O-shibori Warm cloth for freshening up with, usually toweling

Oshiire Built-in wall-cupboard or cabinet with sliding doors

Oshogatsu New Year

O-sonae "Honorable offering"

Otearai Toilet

Otokoburo or **Otokoyū** Men's bath

Otoso Spiced sake for New Year

Oya-ishi Stone from Oya

O-zen Tray for meals, often with feet

Pachinko Gaming machines

Pagoda Reliquary in a temple complex, usually multistory

Podium Raised part of the floor

Raku bowl Synonym for tea dish

Raku pottery Black *raku* pottery accentuates the color of the green tea and has insulating qualities, keeping the tea hot and at the same time protecting the hands from the heat.

Raku style Movement in art that concentrates on the world of the "tea aesthetes" and of the *cha-no-yu*.

Ramma The openwork supporting beam in a Japanese house that serves to let in light and air

Regalia "As befits the king"

Reigi Etiquette

Reisho Japanese official or curial script

Renga Chain poem

Renjimado Windows made of narrow horizontal strips of wood

Reservage A resisting agent applied according to the desired pattern when dyeing materials, to prevent the color being absorbed

Rikka A form of *ike-bana*. *Rikka* maps out the Sumeru mountain, a mythological mountain of Buddhist cosmology and an allegory for the universe

Ro A kind of fireplace where water boils for the tea ceremony

Rō Long corridor

Roji Small tea garden in the area between the outer and middle gates

Romaji Latin transcription of the Japanese

Ronin "Abandoned" samurai

Rotemburo Thermal bath in the open air

Ryobiraki-isho-dansu Wardrobe with two doors for the storage of kimonos and other items of clothing

Ryokan Traditional Japanese hotel

Ryōri Cuisine

Ryōri-kaiseki *Kaiseki* cuisine

Ryōri ryokan A ryokan specializing in excellent food

Ryoshi-bako Larger writing box, which also contains a paper shelf

Ryotei Geisha houses, today also "top restaurants" with private *tatami* rooms

Sabi A spiritual path, an intellectual attitude and way of viewing things in calm solitude

Sage-ju "Picnic box," portable *ju-bako*

Sagemono "Hanging things;" today this name refers to popular items for collecting, such as *inro, tabako ire, kiseru-zutsu, kinchaku, yatate,* which are worn on the *obi* and held by the *netsuke*

Sageo A silk cord on the hilt of a sword, used to tie the sword to the *obi*

Saisen-bako Sacrificial stave in the *shintō* shrine

Sakana Little delicacies handed round mainly with sake

Sakazuki Small cups or dishes for sake, made of various materials

Sake Wine made from fermented rice

Sake cup Drinking vessel for Japanese rice wine

Sakura Cherry, cherry blossom

Sakura mochi Small, sticky rice balls the color of cherry blossom wrapped in a cherry tree leaf

Sakura-no-hana Japan's cherry blossom

Samisen Japanese melodies

Samurai Warrior class in pre-modern Japan, who served the nobility

Samurai residence The variations on the samurai house range from palace-like buildings with richly ornamented tiled roofs down to simple, yet positively elegant estates with houses with thatched roofs

San Suffix as an expression of respect towards the person being spoken to

Sanbo Tray-like mats for sake and snacks

Saobuchi Bamboo framework for attaching ceilings of wooden planks or wood or bamboo weave

Sashimi Raw fish

Sashimono "Fitting things together," a Japanese term for furniture

Saya Sheath of the Japanese sword

Seafood Edible saltwater fish or shellfish

Sei Purity

Seido-toro Bronze lantern

Seika Living flowers in vases, form of *ike-bana*

Seimon Main gate

Senbei Rice cracker

Senryu Humorous short poem

Sensu Folding fan

Sentō Public bathing house

Setomono Pottery from Seto, Japan's biggest pottery center; today often synonymous with pottery products from anywhere in Japan

Setto Cover for breakfast

Sèvres French china of the highest quality

Shachi Mythical dolphin-like creature of nature

Shakkei principle Principle of "borrowed scenery." The topographical and natural features of the surroundings are included in the overall picture of the architectural complex

Shakuhachi Bamboo flute played like a clarinet

Shamisen Three-string guitar that was played by courtesans and geishas, and was also used as an accompanying instrument in, for example, the *kabuki*

Shi Town

Shibui A subliminal quality of things, which encourages the observer to seek hidden beauty

Shibui konomi An inherent appreciation of the clearly ordered and balanced elements involved in art, life and personality

Shibu-kawa "Astringent skin." For example the different shades of chestnuts are called *shibu-kawa*

Shibumi Contents which express a restrained and yet distinctively fine taste

Schichu Roof that runs in four directions, starting from the mid-point of the ridge, without forming gables

Shida *Hojo* (Major-domo) of the Kamakura shoguns, Kamakura Period (1192-1333)

Shigaraki ceramics Colorful body in shades of red to salmon pink produced from clay with a low iron content; with glassy green spots of a natural wood ash glaze

Shiki Village

Shikibuton Japanese mattress

Shikki Lacquerwork

Shima Island

Shimbashi Embujo Theater in Tokyo

Shimenawa The holy rice straw rope

Shimmei *Shintō* architectural style

Shin Honest and correct, *budō* thought

Shinai Bamboo fencing stave

Shinden Originally "hall for sleeping in," residences of the nobility in the Heian Period (794-1185)

Shinden-zukuri *Shinden* style of building with pavilions

Shinkansen "New line" super express train

Shino pottery With white, gray or red body, decoration applied by painting with iron oxide before glazing and firing

Shintō "The way of the gods." Japanese national religion strong in ancestor worship, honors the spirits and forces of nature

Shin-zashiki Day rooms

Shirikume-na-nawe "No return cord"

Shisei To understand and observe the correct composure in the *dōjō* relationship

Shitajimado Small, square or round *shōji* windows with fragile pattern

Shite Chief actor in the *nō* drama

Shitei *dōjō* relationship

Shitomi Hinged wall panels

Shitomi-do Wood and rice paper latticework shutters that can be hooked on or folded

Sho Wind instrument made of graded bamboo pipes

Shō Japanese calligraphy

Shobu-yū Iris bath

Shōdana Container for books

Shōden The chief place of worship of the inner shrine at Ise

Shō-dō "The way of writing"

Shōgun Hereditary title of military rulers in pre-modern imperial Japan

Shogunate The office of a shogun

Shōiken "The Lodgings of the Laughing Thoughts," Katsura teahouse

Shoin "Built-in table," reading room, study. During the Muromachi Period (1333-1573) a way of life and type of building that came from the *shinden* style of architecture

Shoin-zukuri style The large, elegant rooms of the castles and fortresses of the Muromachi Period (1333-1573)

Shōji Sliding doors and windows in wooden latticework covered with rice paper

Shōjin ryōri Vegetarian cookery

Shoka Living flowers in vases, form of *ikebana*

Shōka-tei , "The Pavilion of the Admired Blossoms," Katsura teahouse

Shōkin-tei "The Pavilion of the Lute and the Pine Trees," Katsura teahouse

Shokudai Candlestick

Shokudō Dining room

Shomei "Bible" of *shoin* construction, manual that appeared in 1608 and which contains the precise details of proportions, *kiwarijutsu*

Shosa Physical practice of the *dōjō* relationship

Shōyu Soy sauce

Shrine In Shintoism a sacred place that is the seat of the *kami*

Shūgakuin residence Imperial villa near Kyoto, built from 1629

Shugi-bukuro White paper or an envelope specifically for tips

Shukubo Temple accommodation

Shun Aesthetic concept, refers to the "seasonal taste" of Japanese seasonal/regional cuisine

Shunga "Spring pictures," collection of erotic pictures

Shuya Living area

So Priest

Sō In flowing, free form

Sōan teahouse Small teahouse, between two and four and a half mats

Soba Buckwheat noodles

Soba-choko Receptacle for the sauce served with Japanese noodles

Soh-metsuke Overseer of all the nation's daimyō who were not allied with the Shōgun

Soku Cushions used as an arm rests

Sokutai Court costumes with long trains

Somen Terrifying masks

Some-tsuke China with underglaze blue

Sophistication Experience in the ways of the world, refinement, intellect

Sophistry style Over-subtle intellectual style

Sosho Japanese grass script, a type of cursive style

Stoneware Pottery with a light-colored, impermeable, non-transparent body

Stupa Buildings with a monumental or votive character. Originally half dome-shaped burial mounds with relics of the Buddha

Sugi Japanese cedar

Suginoki Japanese cryptomeria, a species of the red cedar

Suibokuga Water and ink pictures; applies to the majority of paintings that Zen artists created during the Muromachi Period

Suigara-ake Ashtray

Sukiya "Seat of ennoblement," residences with a nonchalant atmosphere and artistic idiosyncrasy, suitable for a personality of exquisite taste and a cultured lifestyle

Sukiya-shoin style Lifestyle and architectural style combining the features of *shoin* and *sukiya*

Sukiya style Simple, linear architectural style. The textures of wood and plaster are for the most part left in their original state of beauty to complement nature

Sumi Ink

Sumi-e Ink drawing

Sumi-tsubo Tool for drawing a straight line

Sumiyoshi *Shintō* architectural style

Sunoko-en "Barrier veranda" of a *shinden* residence

Sunoko-tenjō ceiling Ceiling consisting of wooden boards and woven bamboo leaves, asymmetrically subdivided with a bamboo framework

Suō Brown

Surimono Greetings prints

Sushi Japanese vinegared fish and rice dish

Susuki Silver grass

Sutras Collection of Buddhist dialogues and discourses

Suyehiro A folding fan

Suzuri Ink block

Suzuri-bako Box for writing things

Synesthesia Fusion of several sensual impressions, a sensation experienced by one of the senses when another is stimulated

Ta no kami / yama no kami Pre-Buddhist agrarian rituals

Tabako-bon Smoking set

Tabako-ire Tobacco pouch

Tabi Stocking/sock with separate toe

Typhoon Wet, tropical whirlwind. From *tai-fung* (Chinese: big wind) and *typhon* (ancient Greek: whirlwind)

Taiko Drumsticks

Tainoya Side rooms of the *shinden* halls

Taisha *Shintō* style of architecture

Taishi Crown prince

Takahari-chochin Lanterns for festive occasions, usually oval and suspended from the tip of a tall post or under the eaves of the house

Taka-maki-e Gold lacquer in relief

Take Bamboo, another meaning: mountain

Take-no-ko Baby bamboo or bamboo shoot

Takiyū "Cascade bath," bath with a type of artificial waterfall

Tana Originally a form of free-standing shelved cupboards, today built-in shelving

Tang The part of the sword not belonging to the blade, which is later covered by the hilt

Tanka Short poem of 5 lines, today also *waka*

Tansu Originally a chest or cupboard, today a kind of collective term for Japanese furniture per se

Tanzen A kind of over garment, worn with the *yūkata*, frequently quilted

Tare Waist protection worn in kendo sword fighting

Tatami Reed mat, the traditional floor covering inside a Japanese building. The size of living rooms is given in the number of *tatami*

Tatebana "Standing flowers" of the Muromachi Period (1333-1573), form of *ike-bana*

Tatebana-rikka style Composition made up of *tatebana* and *rikka*, popular today as *heika*. Style of *ike-bana*

Tea aesthetics Art form orientated towards the simple teahouse style

Tea ceremony architecture Architectural style which draws on ancient traditions, e.g.

anchorite hermitages and medieval scholars' retreats, as well as from the simple homes of the Kyoto aristocracy, which only later took on a more exalted style.

Tea money A kind of tip in recognition of good hospitality

Te-aburi hibachi "Hand warmer" stove

Te-bako "Hand box," cosmetics box

Tei Garden

Teishoku Midday cover

Temmyo-gama Iron teakettle with a rough surface used for the tea ceremony

Ten-chin-jin Principle concerning relationship between heaven, earth and mankind

Tenno Title of Japanese emperors

Tenshu "Watchman of the heavens." A building in the *honmaru* (castle keep) with several stories tapering towards the top

Tenugui Small hand towel

Tenugui-kake Stand for clothing accessories or hand towels

Terracotta Fired, unglazed objects made of colored (mostly red or yellow) firing clay

Tetsubin Iron or china teakettle

To Metropolis, capital city

Todai Candlestick or saucer

Tofu Soya-bean curd

Toishi Burnishing stone

Tojiri Plinth of the Japanese bracket complex

Tōkaidō "Eastern Sea Road," road linking the former capital Kyoto and Edo, now Tokyo

Tōkaidō gojūsanji The 53 stations of the Tōkaidō

Tokkuri Flacons and small bottles for sake

Tokobashira Main pillar in the *tokonoma*.

Tokoname pottery Made of relatively coarse clay, gray or reddish-brown body. Although never glazed artificially, the surface has an interesting texture made up of particles of charcoal, spots and drops

Tokonoma Traditional ornamental alcove

Tokugawa Name of the shogun family that took over the government in the name of the emperor in 1603 and transferred the seat of government to Edo. The period from 1603 to 1867 is called the Tokugawa Era or the Edo era as it corresponds to the period of rule of the Tokugawa shoguns

Tokyō The Japanese bracket complex

Tokyo Capital city of Japan. In 1868 Edo was declared the new capital and its name was changed to Tokyo (eastern capital city). Since 1869 residence of the tenno and seat of the government

Tonkotsu Small wooden tobacco holder

Torii Gateway into a Shinto shrine

Tōriniwa Side passage of a Japanese town house, leading to the rear

Tsū Savoir-faire, male attribute

Tsuba Guard on sword

Tsubo Unit of surface measurement corresponding to 3,954 sq. yds. A *tatami* is also the basic dimension used in surveying land, two *tatami* make a *tsubo*, which converts to about 3.95 sq.yds.

Tsubo-niwa Inner courtyard garden

Tsugi System of wooden joints, the basis for Japanese woodwork and construction

Tsugi-te Expanding wooden joints

Tsuitate Standing room dividers that do not fold up

Tsujibei Thick earth walls

Tsujikei Plain enclosing walls

Tsukeshoin "Table for taking writing things out of," built-in writing podium in the *tokonoma* that functions as a table

Tsukiyama Hilly landscape gardens

Tsukubai Wash basin

Tsuri-dono "Fishermen's pavilion"

Tsutsuji Azalea

Tsuzumi Hourglass shaped drum that is struck with the hand

Tympanum Recessed space bounded by an arch over a portal, door or window

Uchi "My house," to be a part of something

Uchi-kake Ancient Japanese greatcoat, also magnificent, formal women's kimono

Uchi-roji Stone washbasin

Uchiwa Round fan that does not close

Uchiwa-eban Fan pictures

Ugusoku Traditional set of three objects in the *tokonoma*: incense burner, flower vase and candle holder

Uji Ancient clans

Uji / Ujigami Tribal or territorial cults

Ukai Cormorant fishing

Ukiyo-e Pictures of the floating world, pictures of the genre of painting in the Tokugawa Period. Today equated with the Japanese woodblock print

Uramon The rear gate

Urushi Japanese lacquerwork

Usu-cha Clear green Japanese tea

Uta Song

Uta-awase Singing competition

Uta-kei "Songs-shells," poets shell game

Uta-karuta Poets card game

Utase-yū Special feature of the *o-furo*. Water pours out of bamboo pipes above head height to massage the bather's shoulders and neck

Wa Harmony, team spirit, the old word for Japan

Wabi wilted, unforthcoming, not eternal; the spontaneous grasp of the true "essence" of everyday things

Wabi and **sabi** Aesthetic ideals, closely linked to Zen Buddhism and the tea ceremony

Wa-bitsu Cupboard without feet for storing clothing. These are largely copies from the Chinese Tang dynasty (618-907)

Wadansu Chest with many drawers for keeping odds and ends in

Wagashi Traditional Japanese candy

Waka Short poem of 5 lines and 31 syllables in the arrangement: 5,7,5,7,7

Waki Supporting actor in the *nô*

Wakizashi Short sword

Wan Bay

Wanawa New Year's cord

Wanko Lacquered bowls

Warabashi Lacquered chopsticks

Waragutsu Straw boots

Waraji Straw sandals

Wasabi Japanese horseradish

Washi Japanese paper

Watanodo Wide, covered passageways leading to side rooms that turn off from one or more sides of the central *shinden* hall

Xanadu Legendary artistic place of refuge and mythical residence of the Mongolian ruler Kublai Khan (1215-1294)

Yabo Lack of taste in the choice of clothing (out-of-date, boring, vulgar)

Yadoya Another word for ryokan

Yagi Nightwear

Yagyu-shinkage-ryu One of Japan's earliest traditions of combative swordsmanship and schools for sword techniques

Yazuka Japanese mafia

Yakazu-kō Arrow-smell-detection competition game

Yama Mountain

Yamabushi Mountain priest and ascetic

Yamajiro Mountain fortresses

Yamato damashi The spirit of Japan

Yamato-e Name for paintings with purely Japanese themes, Japanese landscape painting

Yaoyorozuno kami 800 x10,000 *kami*, also "all the gods"

Yashiro The portico of the shrine

Yatate Traveling writing things, small container for pen and ink

Yedō Tokyo

Yen Japanese unit of currency

Yo The masculine style in *ike-bana*

Yogi Bedtime attire

Yōkan Candies made from red beans

Yokogi Device for altering the length of pot handles

Yoko-ōban Ōban as a horizontal print

Yome-iri-dansu Bridal chests

Yorozuro 10,000 years

Yose-mune Roof that slopes in four directions, starting from the mid-point of the ridgepole, without forming gables

Yoshiwara The extensive courtesan quarter near the Senso-ji temple in Asakusa in the northeast of Edo

Yū Hot water

Yucho-no-ma Room next to the entrance area

Yudansha Circle of the students of the way

Yugen Mysterious dimension, subtle grace, aesthetic ideal

Yūkata *Yū*, hot water, *kata*, garment. Cotton Japanese garment cut like a kimono, with blue and white stenciled patterns and worn in summer by country folk

Yukimi-shōji Windows of the *shōji* near the floor, where one sits

Yumi-hari-chochin A lantern carried on a bow

Yūtanpo Metal or china bottle for hot water

Yūto Hot water jug

Za Theater

Zabuton Cushion for sitting on the *tatami*

Zashiki Formal main living room

Zazen Zen meditation whilst seated

Zelkova Elm

Zen Sanskrit. Chinese/Japanese meditation. Buddhist school of thought, which seeks to achieve a state of oneness with the Buddha through contemplation and self-mastery

Zen Serving trays

Zeni-bako Moneybox

Zeni-dansu Money chest

Zōri Rice straw shoes with straps

List of illustrations

The editor and publishers made every effort to trace all the copyright holders for the illustrations used up until the conclusion of production. Any persons or institutions who may not have been contacted and who lay claim to rights concerning the illustrations used are asked to contact the publishers now.
All photographs
© Könemann Verlagsgesellschaft mbH, Köln/ Foto: Narimi Hatano
With the exception of:
© Gabriele Fahr-Becker, München: p.167 below, 321 above right;
© The Flower Association of Japan, Tōkyō: p.43 right;
© Hanaya, Bessho Onsen: p.89;
© Hiraki-Ukiyo-e Museum, Yokohama: p.32, 110;
© Japan-Photo-Archive/Hartmut Pohling, Düsseldorf: p.159 above, 228 below left;
© Könemann Verlagsgesellschaft mbH, Köln/ Foto: Klaus Frahm: p.8, 10, 11, 15, 27 above, 60, 65, 66, 68, 69, 70, 71, 72/73, 74, 76, 124, 125, 126, 128, 130, 131 above, 132/133, 134 below, 135, 136/137, 138, 139, 140, 141;

© Kumon Institute of Education, Osaka: p.163 left;
© Jörg Lehmann: p.257, 275;
© Nakau Collection, Japan: p.77, 107;
© Nezu Institute of Fine Arts, Tōkyō: p.2, 46/47, 48 left, 49, 108/109, 131, below, 224, 259 above;
© Collection of Nihon Mingeikan, Tōkyō: p.259 below;
© Nōgakushiryokan, Museum of Nō, Sasayama: p.31;
© Pacific Press Service, Tōkyō: p.64 below, 229 above;
© Joan Whitney Payson Gallery of Art, Westbrook College, Portland/Maine: p.111;
© Saskatoon Kendo Club: p.159 below;
© Sekai Bunka Photo, Tōkyō: p.6, 12, 13, 14 left, 20 left, 28, 51 above, 56 below, 57, 62, 87 above, 94, 95, 120, 129, 164, 171, 172, 177, 214 above, 246/247, 248, 265, 313;
from: Das Alte Japan. Spuren und Objekte der Siebold-Reisen, Exhibiton catalogue, Vienna, Munich 1997: (p.66/67) endpaper (front), (172/173) endpaper (back);
from: Makio Araki, Nihon no zōkei. Oru,

tsutsumu, Kyōto 1990: (p.18/19) p.51 below; from: Awa no Machinami Kenkyu-kai, Awa no nō-sonbutai, Tokushimo-shi 1996: Foto: Shigeo Nishida (p.10) p.29; from: Katalog zur Architektur auf Tokushima, o.J.: p.48 right; from: Kazuo Nishi/Kazuo Hozumi, What is Japanese Architecture, Kodansha International Ltd., Tōkyō/New York/London 1996: (p.76) p.67 below, (75) 75 left, (74) 75 right, (64) 160, (66) 165, (71) 207, (108) 258 below; from: Bruno Taut, Das japanische Haus und sein Leben, Gebr. Mann Verlag, Berlin 1997: (p.144) p.63, (47) 117, (278) 250; from: Tokushima no bunkazai. Kenzôbutsu, Tokushima-ken, Kenchikushi jimusho kyōkai, Tokushima-shi 1994: (p.32) p.96 right; from: We Japanese, Fujiya Hotel Ltd. (Hrsg.), Miyanoshita, Hakone 1949: (p.525) p.9, (74) 14 right, (24) 19 left, (403) 20 right, (33) 24 right, (47) 33 below, (198) 64 above, (295) 67 above, (120) 195 below, (369) 228 above, (370) 229 bellow, (17) 258 above; from: Koji Yagi, A Japanese Touch for your Home, Kodansha Internationl Ltd., Tōkyō/New York/London 1992: (p.58) p.134 above, (47) 274 right.

Index

Inset map (top left)

125° Lon.　　135°

RUSSIA

CHINA

Hokkaidō

Sea of Japan

NORTH KOREA

SOUTH KOREA

Honshu

• Tōkyō　35°

■ Ōsaka

JAPAN

Shikoku

Kyūshū

East China Sea

Pacific Ocean

TAIWAN

Okinawa

25° Lat.

500 km

Tropic of Cancer

Main map

Sea of Japan

Pacific Ocean

Honshu

Shikoku

Kyūshū

Hokkaidō

Wakkanai

Nemu

Asahikawa
▲ 2290 m

Otaru

Kushiro

■ SAPPORO

Muroran

Hakodate

Aomori

Hirosaki

Hachinohe

Akita

Morioka

Ishinomaki

Yamagata

■ Sendai

Niigata

Sado-shima

Iwaki

Jōetsu

Muikamachi

Nasu

Ryugon

Niki Club

Hōshi Onsen

Choju-kan

Mito

Maebashi

Kanazawa

Wano-sato

Fukui

Hida

Kofu

TŌKYŌ

Masu-no-ya

YOKOHAMA

Oki-shotō

Shouro-tei

Ama-no-hashidate

Hakkei-tei

Fuji-san ▲
3776 m

Oshigusa

Matsue

Bessho Onsen

Hikone

Numazu

Yagyu-no-sho

Hanaya

Dan-bayashi

Shuzenji

Kuta Sakyo-ku

NAGOYA

Ishidaya

Yatsu

■ **KŌBE**

KYŌTO

Ohashi-ya

Himeji

O-aza Akasaka

Okayama

■ **ŌSAKA**

Izu - shotō

Takamatsu

Futami-kan

Yoshino

Hinjitsu-kan

HIROSHIMA

Futami-ura

Chikurin-in

Gunpou-en

Tokushima

Tsushima

Matsuyama

Shimonoseki

KITAKYŪSHŪ

Kōchi

FUKUOKA

Sasebo

Ōita

▲ 1791 m

Geto-retto

Kumamoto

Nagasaki

Miyazaki

Tane-ga-shima

Kagoshima

Yaku-shima

125 miles/200 km

Highway

Railroad

Ryokan